The United States and International D ... American quest to internationalize the ... study reveals the origins, motivation ... the recurring contradictions and inconsiste... ... within the US overseas fight against the production, manufacture, trafficking and use of certain psychoactive substances. Drawing on extensive historical materials, David Bewley-Taylor uses the international career of America's first Drug Czar, Harry J. Anslinger, to explore how the United States successfully exploited its hegemonic superiority in 1945 to influence the philosophy of the multilateral drug control system operated by the United Nations. A re-interpretation of Anslinger's role within the US bureaucracy also illuminates the dynamics underlying Washington's frequent subordination of international anti-drug measures to security concerns during the Cold War.

More than a purely historical study, the book employs an interdisciplinary approach to understand the development, perpetuation and consequences of an Americanized multilateral drug control system. Examining the contemporary UN drug control framework, the author argues that international legislation is largely ineffective, restricts the development of appropriate drug control policies at a national level and legitimizes Washington's escalating war on drugs in Latin America.

This provocative book is the first study to provide a picture of US involvement with international drug control from its inception to the present day. Its wide-ranging scope makes it of interest not only to scholars of diplomatic history, US foreign policy and international relations, but also to anyone concerned by the universal growth of the illicit drug problem.

THE UNITED STATES AND INTERNATIONAL DRUG CONTROL, 1909–1997

DAVID R. BEWLEY-TAYLOR

continuum
LONDON • NEW YORK

Continuum
The Tower Building, 11 York Road, London SE1 7NX
370 Lexington Avenue, New York, NY 10017-6503

First published 1999 by Pinter

Paperback edition published by Continuum 2001

British Library Cataloguing-in-Publication Data
A catalogue record for this book is available from the British Library.

ISBN (hardback) 1–85567–610–9
    (paperback) 0-8264-5813-0

Library of Congress Cataloging-in-Publication Data
Bewley-Taylor, David R., 1968–
    The United States and international drug control, 1909–1997/
David R. Bewley-Taylor.
      p. cm.
    Includes bibliographical references and index.
    ISBN 1–85567–610–9 (cloth) – 0-8264-5813-0 (paper)
    1. Narcotics, Control of—United States.   2. Narcotics, Control
of—International cooperation.   I. Title.

    HV5825 .B4918   1999
    363.45'0973—dc21
                                                                98-32345
                                                                  CIP

Typeset by YHT Ltd, London
Printed and bound in Great Britain by Biddles Ltd, Guildford and King's Lynn

CONTENTS

ACKNOWLEDGEMENTS

From this project's beginnings as a doctoral thesis I have, of course, become indebted to numerous people. Sincere thanks are due to those who at different stages have read various portions of this manuscript and patiently offered me advice and encouragement. I would especially like to thank Mike Woodiwiss, Craig Phelan and Jon Roper for their assistance and support throughout the duration of this study and Alan Dobson and Jeff Newnham for their insightful comments concerning international relations theory. The usual caveat naturally applies, with any inaccuracies or mistakes within the text being my own. I am also grateful to Bev Evans, who was always willing to help solve the mysteries of word processing, Penny O'Hara for her editorial assistance and Melissa Anyiwo for her help in preparing the final draft.

I owe a great deal to the staffs of many libraries and institutions in both the United Kingdom and the United States, notably the Pattee Library at Pennsylvania State University, University Park, Pennsylvania; the Drug Enforcement Administration Library and the Washington Drug Policy Foundation in Washington, DC; the Institute for the Study of Drug Dependence in London; and the Harry S. Truman Library Institute in Independence, Missouri. I would also like to express my gratitude to all those who gave up their time to be interviewed for this project or, in a less formal fashion, were willing to discuss with me many of the issues contained within the following pages.

Special thanks are also given to the Truman Library Institute, whose research grant helped me survive my expedition to the United States in the summer of 1994, and ALCOA Manufacturing (GB) Limited, whose 1997 grant to the Border Areas Research Group of the American Studies Department at the University of Wales, Swansea, enabled me to complete the latter stages of this manuscript.

While studying away from home I have been the recipient of extraordinary hospitality and consequently I would like to thank all those who have made my often impromptu visits so pleasant, particularly Guy Escolme and Stephanie J. Smolic, erstwhile of Washington, DC, Bill Saxton in Pennsylvania, and Mark Mosher and Nick Cannon in London.

Above all else, I would finally like to thank Catherine and my family for their unswerving support of many kinds over the past few years. Their tolerance of my work-induced absenteeism has been truly remarkable.

David R. Bewley-Taylor
Gower, South Wales, 1998

ABBREVIATIONS

ADMA	American Drug Manufacturers Association
AP	Anslinger Papers, Pattee Library, Pennsylvania State University, University Park, Pennsylvania, USA
CENTO	Central Treaty Organization
CIA	Central Intelligence Agency, USA
CMO	Comprehensive Multidisciplinary Outline of Future Activities in Drug Abuse Control, United Nations
CND	Commission on Narcotic Drugs, United Nations
DEA	Drug Enforcement Administration, USA
DEAL	Drug Enforcement Administration Library, Washington, DC, USA
DND	Division of Narcotic Drugs, United Nations
DoD	US Department of Defense
DSB	Drug Supervisory Body, League of Nations and United Nations (1933–67)
ECDP	European Cities on Drug Policy
ECOSOC	Economic and Social Council, United Nations
ELP	People's Liberation Army, Colombia
FARC	Revolutionary Armed Forces of Colombia
FBI	Federal Bureau of Investigation, USA
FBN	Federal Bureau of Narcotics, USA
GA	General Assembly, United Nations
GATT	General Agreement on Tariffs and Trade
HTL	Harry Truman Library, Independence, Missouri, USA
IAL	International Antiprohibition League
INCB	International Narcotic Control Board, United Nations
INM	International Narcotic Matters, US State Department
Interpol	International Criminal Police Organization
I/TCG	Interview with Mr Thomas C. Green, UK Representative CND
KMT	Kuomintang Army
LIC	low-intensity conflict
LSD	lysergic acid diethylamide
M-19	19th April Movement, Colombia

NA	National Archives, Washington, DC, USA
NAFTA	North American Free Trade Agreement
NARD	National Association of Retail Druggists, USA
NCIS	National Criminal Intelligence Service, UK
NORML	National Organization for the Reform of Marijuana Laws, USA
NSC	National Security Council, USA
NSDD	National Security Decision Directive, US Government
OAC	Special Advisory Committee on Opium and Other Dangerous Drugs, League of Nations
ONDCP	Office of National Drug Control Policy, US State Department
OSS	Office of Strategic Services, USA
PCOB	Permanent Central Opium Board, League of Nations and United Nations (1929–67)
PRC	People's Republic of China
PRO	Public Records Office, Kew Gardens, London
UAR	United Arab Republic
UHV	Upper Huallaga Valley, Peru
UMOPAR	Rural Mobile Patrol Units, Bolivia
UNDCP	United Nations International Drug Control Programme
UNFDAC	United Nations Fund for Drug Abuse Control
UNGASS	UN General Assembly Special Session
UNICRI	UN Interregional Crime and Justice Research Institute
WCTU	Women's Christian Temperance Movement, USA
WHO	World Health Organization, United Nations

FOR CATH AND JORDAN

Of making many books there is no end; and much study
is a weariness of the flesh
Ecclesiastes 12:12

INTRODUCTION

The accepted standard of international morality in regard to altruistic virtues
appears to be that a state should indulge in them in so far as this is not
seriously incompatible with its more important interests.
Edward Hallett Carr, *The Twenty Year Crisis; 1919–1939*, 1939

The war on drugs must not in the future be sacrificed to other
foreign policy considerations.
Senate Foreign Relations Committee, 1988

The end of the Cold War brought many new challenges for American
diplomacy. The familiar contours of superpower confrontation gave way
to a plurality of diverse and complex transnational concerns. While a wide
range of interests vie for predominance, the past decade has seen the illicit
drugs trade stake its claim as a significant focus of American foreign
policy. Classified since 1986 as a threat to US national security, the issue of
illicit drugs today looks likely to go some way towards replacing what
President Ronald Reagan labelled the evil empire as an important target
for American international activism. Illegal drugs have partially filled the
vacuum created by the fall of Soviet communism, apparently providing
the collective American popular and political psyches with an external
adversary worthy of another continuous state of war. Nevertheless, the US
overseas fight against drugs is certainly not new. Since the beginning of
the twentieth century the United States has sought, with considerable
success, to internationalize the principles behind its national response to
curb illicit drug use. To be sure, Washington's contemporary transnational
actions against illicit drugs are constructed on the foundations of a
campaign pre-dating the US preoccupation with communism by almost
half a century.

Drug use and organized efforts to control such use are far older,
however. The desire of individuals to change their state of consciousness
has been present throughout human history. Indeed, the use of psychoactive substances to accomplish this process is as ancient as civilization
itself.[1] Drugs in various forms, including alcohol, tobacco, opium, cannabis, coffee and coca, have been used in different societies for many
hundreds, and in some cases thousands, of years. They have an important,

though fluid, role to play in almost all cultures. Usage transcends simple categorization, with psychoactive substances being used for medicinal, ritual and recreational purposes. Although consumption has remained ever-present in at least some form, perceptions of drugs have been constantly adjusting. Consequently, societal reactions to their use have also frequently been in a state of flux.

For centuries, many societies have placed faith in the ability of the law to control the trade, production and use of certain drugs. This has often occurred when those who create rules that govern a society have perceived the ingestion of a psychoactive substance as an abuse. In this way an individual's ability to use a drug, for whatever purpose, has been restricted. The belief among many ruling elites that drugs, as well as being a great medical good, were also damaging to the well-being of society resulted in numerous and diverse controls and sanctions. Although drugs have been widely available in entirely unregulated markets, they have over time also been subject to controls ranging from the death penalty to taxation.[2]

National responses to drugs have for many years been open to transnational influences. Some states have long since lost the ability to respond to drug use within their societies on a purely unilateral basis. A constant improvement in global communications and interaction with other cultures meant that national approaches towards drug control, like many other aspects of life, seldom remained isolated from the outside world. Indeed, the truly transnational nature of the drug phenomenon ensured that interest in the issue developed an extra-national flavour. The well-established existence of some form of international drug trade is indicative of the fact that drugs of choice often originate beyond national boundaries. Overseas influences, however, did not constitute a formalized system of international control. Situations varied greatly depending upon the individual circumstances of the countries involved, and before the twentieth century rules, or norms, governing the production, trade and use of psychoactive substances did not conform to a global pattern.

Moves were made to rectify this situation in the first decade of the twentieth century. The 1909 Shanghai International Opium Commission marked the first significant multinational meeting to be concerned with any form of drug use. The Commission made recommendations that provided the legal basis for the beginning of a homogenization of domestic drug control policies on a world-wide scale. The International Opium Commission was followed three years later by the Hague Convention, and since then, through multilateral treaties and their international obligations, members of the international community have attempted to control the growth, processing, trafficking and consumption of a category of drugs collectively known as narcotics.[3]

The process of creating an international framework, or what we can usefully call an international regime, to govern patterns of drug control has, however, encountered fundamental problems not experienced at a national level. According to Stephen Krasner's widely accepted definition, international regimes can be regarded as a set of 'implicit or explicit principles, norms, rules and decision-making procedures around which actor expectations converge in a given issue area'.[4] Any formal transnational system of control must consequently rest upon a legal framework provided by written agreements between state actors. Effective responses to issues that transcend national boundaries require collaborative action, with, as Ernst Haas suggests, international regimes providing an opportunity for a solution largely by the creation of rights and rules[5] in an international environment traditionally characterized by anarchy. Such rights and rules must be brought into being by diplomatic conferences and international agreements and overseen by some form of international machinery. The international system for drug control has been no exception, the extra-territorial dynamics of the illegal drug issue making a transnational element essential when addressing the issue of control. Like other fields of transnational co-operation, the international drug control mechanism relies upon the ability of national governments to agree upon a set of resolutions discussed by national delegates at conferences. Once this has been achieved, states must pledge their adherence to the agreed provisions by signing a convention or treaty. Legal moves must then be made to ensure that these internationally agreed measures are put into practice at the national level. This often involves the ratification of the international resolutions by a national legislature. It is crucial, then, that all the states involved in the discussions concur with the resolutions contained within the text of the international law.

The avowed aims, or norms, of the international control system are to combat drug abuse and ensure that there is an adequate supply of drugs for medical and scientific purposes. While these concepts in themselves initially appear straightforward they do nevertheless raise a number of important questions of definition. First, what constitutes drug abuse? Second, what is an internationally acceptable delineation of control? Third, what is an acceptable medical use of a drug? Since the international system can operate only if agreement exists between different states with varied socio-cultural backgrounds, the resolution of such queries can be problematic. The operation of policies, whatever their form, on a purely national footing was a relatively simple process inasmuch as they functioned within the boundaries of a single nation or society. The definitions and perceptions of terms like 'abuse' and 'control' were uniform among those who made the laws at any specific time. International collaboration, by contrast, requires agreement upon these points from diverse states with different interests. For example, interpretations of 'abuse' may vary greatly depending upon cultural heritage. In the same way, 'control' has varied connotations depending upon the concerns of different nations.

Reactions to the production, trafficking, sale and use of drugs in society have, as noted above, assumed numerous forms in different parts of the world. Nonetheless, it is possible to identify three broad headings under which to place drug control policies. The first of these headings can be termed the *libertarian approach*. Here all drugs are freely available with no formal laws or controls whatsoever. The second category can be seen as one legalistic response to drug use. In this case, laws are designed to achieve the complete *prohibition* of the production, trade, trafficking and use of certain drugs for anything other than medical and scientific purposes. Most commonly associated today with the United States, this prohibitive-based strategy includes the criminalization not only of those individuals involved in the production, trafficking and trade in drugs, but also of the user of an illicit drug, legally defined as such. Third, occupying the middle ground between the polar extremes of a complete absence of control and prohibition is what can be termed a policy of *regulation*. In a regulative system certain drug use is permitted under specified legal constraints which are reinforced by criminal sanction. Any actions outside these confines are subject to punitive measures. Here, however, the health and welfare of the drug user and wider society are important components within the strategy. The United Kingdom is a nation that traditionally pursued such regulative drug control policies. What is often called the 'medico-centric' approach was once at the core of the British response to drug use. British policies, however, like those of many states, are no longer so simple to categorize. Since the 1960s British drug policies have moved towards the prohibitive model. Changes in the characteristics of and reactions towards drug use have meant that the lines that distinguish regulative and prohibitive approaches have become blurred.

While the advent of multilateral dialogue in the first decade of the twentieth century signified an increased interest in international control of the production, trafficking, trade in and use of particular drugs, debate still existed between the nations involved concerning the type of drug control to be implemented through international law. The absence of total agreement on approach at the first discussions at the transnational level ultimately resulted in a compromise in the international legislation produced. This left the choice of domestic response predominantly to the individual governments involved. Although rules for regulating the production, manufacture and trafficking of certain proscribed drugs were agreed upon, if not always obeyed, clearly defined global patterns of concerning drug use were still unidentifiable. With the evolution of the international control system this was to change.

Today the vast majority of world states count themselves as members of what Ethan A. Nadelmann has called the 'global drug prohibition regime'.[6] States from all parts of the world, with varied social and cultural backgrounds, adhere to international legislation based upon the prohibition of certain drugs for anything other than scientific and medical purposes. As Nadelmann notes, the production, sale and even possession of narcotic drugs, hallucinogens, barbiturates, amphetamines and tranquillizers outside strictly controlled medical and scientific channels are now punished with criminal sanctions in virtually every nation.[7]

This book, then, is concerned with the American international crusade against illegal drugs and the central role played by the United States in the creation of the contemporary global drug prohibition regime. It deconstructs the history of the campaign to reveal the origins, motivations and methodologies as well as the contradictions and inconsistencies inherent within the US overseas fight against the production, manufacture, trafficking and use of certain psychoactive substances.

The book adopts a predominantly historical and evolutionary perspective. Yet, as the previous paragraphs suggest, the approach taken is not restricted solely to the realms of American foreign policy and diplomatic history. Like the illicit drug issue itself, this study also straddles boundaries. The product is best described as an interdisciplinary hybrid. It encompasses many fields and borrows from international relations theory in an effort to understand better the development, persistence and operation of a prohibitive-based international drug control system. This is not to say, however, that this book either addresses the subject matter from a rigid paradigmatic position or directly confronts the ongoing debates between realists, neo-realists, liberal pluralists and proponents of the other dominant traditions within international relations. Rather it is hoped that the arguments and empirical content of the study will contribute to the discipline by provoking interest and discussion within each of these intellectual camps.

The neo-realist update of classical realism's assertion of the primacy of the state in global politics to include the important role of hegemonic actors and co-operative inter-state relations through international organizations is certainly supported by the interpretation of the American crusade presented here. As we shall see, the realist preoccupation with national sovereignty and the protection of national interest plays an important role in both understanding the fluctuations of and highlighting the contradictions within US narcotic foreign policy. This said, alternative paradigms will also find support. The study's emphasis upon the evolution of a transnational system for drug control and, among other things, an appreciation of the role of non-state actors such as the Latin American drug cartels will be of interest to the liberal pluralist. Liberal pluralism's assumptions concerning the issue of globalization, the role of international institutions, regimes that govern many aspects of global activity and the penetration of states by external forces and pressures are all addressed within the following chapters.

Thus, in resisting the temptation to view the theoretical paradigms of international relations as hermetically sealed intellectual discourses, the study takes account of the value of competing theoretical standpoints. It uses several international relations concepts to create a thematic fabric with which to overlay the chronologically determined framework for discussion and employs a triptych of interlocking themes through which to interpret the US quest to internationalize the domestic American approach towards drug control.

The first of these is the relationship between hegemonic stability and the exportation of the prohibitive doctrine. The book charts the evolution of American narcotic foreign policy, arguing that the nation's rise to hegemony and its associated pre-eminent position within the newly formed United Nations in the mid-1940s was vital to the creation and maintenance of the current US-dominated international drug control regime.

Since the beginning of the twentieth century, the United States has been consistent in its intention to confront the issue of drug use from the prohibitionist perspective and locate the source of domestic problems beyond the boundaries of American society. The intention was to deflect blame for domestic drug problems and ultimately eliminate behaviour deemed sinful by a Protestant culture. Active within the international sphere since its calls to address the opium issue resulted in the Shanghai Commission, the United States has thus based its approach to certain drugs on the criminalization of their use for anything other than medical and scientific purposes. Nevertheless, while American endeavours before the Second World War produced a functioning transnational mechanism for regulating the production, manufacture and trafficking of illegal drugs, the creation of a universal norm dictating national responses to illicit drug use could emerge only given the influence possessed by a superpower.

The UN, as we shall see, plays a major role in sustaining and implementing the global drug prohibition regime. The UN Commission on Narcotic Drugs (CND), a functional commission of the organization's Economic and

Social Council (ECOSOC), continues to work towards the development of international legislation that builds upon the prohibitive laws put in place by the 1961 Single Convention on Narcotic Drugs. The US-instigated convention, the cornerstone of the international control system, obliges signatory nations to limit exclusively to medical and scientific purposes the production, manufacture, export, import, distribution of, trade in, use and possession of drugs;[8] eradicate all unlicensed cultivation; suppress illicit manufacture and traffic; and co-operate with each other in achieving the aims of the convention.[9] Other treaties, including the 1971 Convention on Psychotropic Substances and the 1988 Vienna Convention against Illicit Traffic in Narcotic Drugs and Psychotropic Substances, have consolidated this prohibitionist theme and extended it to include synthetic drugs. Through the rhetoric and the transnational legislation of its drug control apparatus, the organization promotes and perpetuates the American prohibitive approach to drug control, while simultaneously legitimizing unilateral skirmishes in the United States' overseas fight against drugs.

Receiving little significant international attention, and even less criticism, the UN quietly works towards the expansion of its narcotic drug control programme. By viewing illicit drug use as a 'danger to mankind',[10] the organization maintains the support of many nations, regardless of their political ideologies. Rhetoric suggests that 'no nation is immune from the devastating consequences of drug abuse'[11] and that the UN's ideals on the drug issue transcend the 'traditional concerns of the international community' and are accordingly 'concerned at the human suffering, loss of life and ... social disruption brought about by drug abuse world-wide'.[12] Projection of such an image helps to guarantee that backing for the UN policies, and thus the international drug control regime, remains widespread and robust. In March 1997, for example, 118 states were parties to the 1988 convention. As the framework for control expands it seems likely that the organization's involvement in the field will continue indefinitely. The June 1998 UN General Assembly Special Session (UNGASS) on Drugs confirmed the organization's commitment to and expansion of its ingrained policies against the 'evil' of drugs. The ongoing use of language that gives the impression of global benevolence creates an image of the UN as a well-meaning, philanthropic world organization – an organization which is intent on safeguarding the well-being of all humankind. Thus, while by their very nature international regimes are created to promote the interests of particular actors, the apparent universality of the global drug prohibition regime means that it does not openly reflect the self-interest of any individual state. By making statements claiming that the use of certain drugs for non-medical reasons is 'wrong',[13] the UN lends credibility to the notion that its control efforts are morally correct and just.

Nonetheless, problems do exist with this approach to a complex issue. By basing the entire system for control on the premise that the use of certain drugs should be limited to medical and scientific purposes, the UN has committed itself to the doctrine of prohibition. This remains the case even though alternative approaches increasingly appear less costly and more effective. The result, despite official UN and US protestations to the contrary, has been the operation of a largely ineffectual international system of control. This is reflected by a continued global growth in all areas of the illegal drugs business and the associated socio-economic problems that surround illicit drug use. The UN itself paradoxically noted in 1992 that 'the illegal use of drugs has grown at an alarming rate over the past twenty years, crossing all social, economic, political and national boundaries'.[14] Indeed, as Nadelmann comments, the emergence of a fully developed drug prohibition regime has coincided with a blossoming, in some respects unprecedented, of the activity that the regime has been created to eradicate.[15] Official estimates suggest that the annual revenue generated by the illegal drug industry is now $400 billion, or the equivalent of approximately 8 per cent of total international trade. By 2004, the global value of illicit drug funds looks set to equal the value of the world's stock of gold. Yet such statistics reveal only half of the problem. Not only has the UN-mandated regime failed to address realistically the issues of the illicit trade and drug use, but the organization's single-minded pursuit of a prohibitionist policy restricts sovereign nations in their own approach towards the development of domestic drug control laws.

Since the UN treaty system itself contains no enforcement mechanisms, its success depends upon the willingness of the signatory powers to abide by and enforce agreed laws. The UN drug control system is handicapped in the same way as are the organization's other functions inasmuch as it alone cannot use physical force to ensure that individual states, whether they have signed drug control treaties or not, adhere to international legislation. This has led Jack Donnelly to assess the norms and decision-making procedures of the UN drug control framework and conclude that it is largely a *promotional* regime. This is the case, he argues, since it encourages national implementation of international norms by such mechanisms as public information activities and the adoption of hortatory resolutions.[16] Accordingly, states are seen to retain the freedom to develop national drug control legislation. Nonetheless, the very existence of a UN-sustained international norm, which has defined a recognized standard of governmental behaviour with regard to drug use and the policies designed to address the issue, has in practice restricted such freedom. While Donnelly's categorization is useful, its assumption that the implementation of norms remains almost entirely in the hands of national actors ignores two important and interrelated elements of the global drug control regime.

First, as touched upon earlier, the centrality of moralism and the portrayal of the illicit drug issue as a universal evil within the context of the regime exert considerable pressure on nations to conform to the established norms of behaviour regarding control policies. States that flout the principles of the regime and refuse or fail to abide by the norms and rules can be labelled as deviants. They thus risk condemnation by those members of the international community that do adhere to the recognized standard of behaviour. What Robert Keohane calls 'reputational effects' of non-compliance are important because by reneging on their commitments under a regime, nations are likely to damage their reputation and forfeit potential future gains from co-operation.[17] States are willing to accept regime rules when they perceive the cost of compliance to be cheaper than non-compliance.

Second, the regime in reality plays more than merely a promotional role because the practice of linking or 'nesting' drug control with other issue areas makes cost and co-operation important concerns. Violating a particular agreement or norm of the regime can have consequences beyond the drug issue and may affect a state's ability to achieve goals elsewhere. The significance of this scenario is heightened by the inclusion of a hegemonic actor within the process. Washington's energetic support for the drug control regime ensures that states are keen to seek compliance. Deviation could prove costly when US co-operation in other international issue areas is at stake. Clearly, a fundamental condition concerning the effectiveness, in terms of acquiescence with rules and procedures, of any regime depends largely on the consensus of its participants. The persistence of the global drug prohibition regime has therefore relied upon the readiness of nations to rate the drug issue as less important than US co-operation in other fields.

Thus, as we shall see in the later chapters of the book, this dynamic has meant that nations are constrained when instigating legislation that deviates from the prohibitive norm in any significant way. Unlike many other regimes that regulate aspects of the global commons for the collective good of the international community – the regulation of the high seas, the deep seabed and the military and civilian use of space, for example – the international drug control regime greatly limits action within the sovereign state itself. While regimes that deal with atmospheric pollution influence behaviour within national boundaries, the potential universal benefits are obvious. This is not the case with the global drug prohibition regime. The constraints placed upon nations by international law have limited efforts to develop pragmatic and realistic national responses to drug use. This remains the case even though independent national responses may in practice be more suitable to a country's specific needs.

Clearly, all actors involved with the creation of regimes have a rationale for their development. As Robert Keohane notes, those responsible for the construction of regimes 'have purpose in doing so, and the rights and rules of regimes reflect visions of what sorts of behaviour should be encouraged or proscribed'.[18] Although American interest in the development and maintenance of an international system for drug control can be explained by the desire to limit the flow of illegal drugs into the United States itself, proselytization has also been a fundamental concern. The historical importance of messianic crusading in US foreign policy, combined with the perceived moral superiority of the doctrine of prohibition, ensured that drug control policy was to become a prime candidate for export. However, as the second theme of the book demonstrates, despite its morally righteous anti-drug rhetoric at both the national and the international level, Washington has frequently pursued wider foreign policy objectives that have undermined its own goals for transnational drug control – a paradox that continues to characterize contemporary US narcotic foreign policy.

The centrality of moralism in the formulation and execution of US foreign policy is a product of a historical belief in the uniqueness of the American experience and the existence of an American mission. A sense of US moral separateness, the creation of a new system unsullied by the failings of European institutions, has since the birth of the Republic produced the conviction that what is good for the United States is good for the rest of the world; the nation as a city on a hill, a beacon for democracy. A view of world affairs focused through the lens of exceptionalism has long provided a framework for American foreign policy. The legacy of America's Puritan past ensured that moral idealism remained an important theme in US dealings abroad. The emergence and popularity of the concept of Manifest Destiny in the mid-1840s also reinforced the underlying attitude regarding the nation's unique place in the world. Self-righteous presuming of the nation's innate virtue and innocence established a tradition for messianic campaigning. This has led the United States to operate abroad armed with a belief in the nation's global mission and what Stanley Hoffman has called the idea of unconscious paternalism.[19] Idealist assumptions concerning the inherently 'good' nature of humanity underpin the belief that a drive to universalize American ideals will ultimately benefit US national interest. Such a moralistic outlook, and the perception of the world as a legitimate target for reform, have therefore had a significant influence upon the shape of American narcotic diplomacy. Ernest van den Haag has lucidly argued that American foreign policy makers 'appear to share a naïve belief that American ideals and ideas can and should solve all the problems of the world and that it is their mission to actively apply these ideals abroad'.[20]

Acquisition of the Philippines after the Spanish–American war not only signalled the USA's arrival on the international stage, but also provided the catalyst for the internationalization of the evolving domestic doctrine of drug prohibition. It was felt that since the United States had now become a world power it had a moral obligation to rectify what it perceived as the immoral use of narcotics in one of its territories. It was also hoped that, in the best traditions of John Winthrop, the islands would serve as a model for other imperial nations to follow. While the USA's cyclical fluctuations between internationalism and a retreat to what has been broadly termed isolationism during the inter-war period have affected their pattern and effectiveness, American anti-drug activities abroad have consistently maintained a moral foundation. Ever since the United States developed domestic legislation worthy of emulation, international efforts for drug control have, outwardly at least, taken on the form of a moral crusade. Eleven years after the start of efforts to eliminate opium smoking in the Philippines, the United States initiated a multilateral meeting in Shanghai to discuss drug control in the Far East. It was clear by this time, however, that the moralistic impulse was not the only motivation driving US involvement in international control.

Such behaviour is interpreted by the book's third theme. Approaching US narco-diplomacy as a subset of what can be termed the American national style of foreign policy, the book argues that such contradictory policies should be viewed as the results of systemically imposed constraints. As Charles Kegley and Eugene Wittkopf comment, 'On the surface, America's daily foreign policy actions may appear erratic. But behind the ostensible inconsistencies, a pattern can be discerned.'[21] To be sure, like other aspects of American foreign policy, US narcotic diplomacy can ultimately be understood as the product of oscillation between two forces. These are, first, American moral idealism and, second, what can be termed political realism: an approach to foreign policy based on rational calculations of power and national interest.

From this perspective, as Karl Von Vorys notes, 'National interest as a standard rests on one fundamental assumption: that the nation state is for its citizens the focus of orientation' and that 'for Americans the secure existence of the United States is an altogether non-negotiable value.'[22] The acquisition of military and economic power to serve American interests and security is paramount. Such beliefs have greatly influenced the thinking of American policymakers, especially since the Second World

War. Adherents of what has come to be known as *Realpolitik* have consistently attempted to reject the moralistic reasoning behind foreign policy discussed earlier when it appears to conflict with the perceived national interest and the security of the nation. To quote Vorys once more, 'Sensitivity and concern for the needs of people throughout the world is in the best tradition of Americans. In order to help they are prepared to bear many burdens and make many sacrifices. They are driven by altruism or motivated by enlightened self-interest.' 'But', he concludes, 'in our national interest these sacrifices must stop short of sacrificing the United States for any purpose, however exalted.'[23]

While this is a real concern for the makers of US foreign policy, it does not eliminate the moralistic impulse. Political realism and moral idealism exist as continuous traditions in American diplomatic history, coexisting with one another in sometimes uncomfortable ways. Robert E. Osgood suggests that they both survive because they fulfill two needs: to stand for ideals worthy of emulation and to protect adaptively the nation from threats to its self-preservation in a hostile world.[24] To be sure, the duality they engender accounts for the willingness of the United States at times to sacrifice its cherished ideals for an expedient action, even while reaffirming its ideals and promoting their maintenance. One tradition may predominate over the other at any one single point in time, but neither has obliterated the influence of the other.[25] Thus, the American national style encompasses both moral idealism and raw self-interest, both of which play an influential role in the formulation and shape of US narco-diplomacy.

Indeed, as this book will argue, the American crusade has from its inception been underpinned by multiple motives. Despite the rhetoric and fundamental assumptions of the moralistic American approach to the foreign policy concerning narcotics, realist concerns for national interest influence the contours of drug control abroad. Since the earliest instances of US involvement in international drug control, concerns for both economic expansion and national security have accompanied, and often eclipsed, the desire for international drug prohibition. Sometimes complementing but more often conflicting with the moral goals of US international control, realist considerations limit the fulfilment of America's morally justified quest to export prohibition. Like the history of wider American foreign policy of which it is a part, the history of narcotic foreign policy can therefore be understood as the result of a dichotomy between political realism and moral idealism. Apparently contradictory international control patterns can be explained by reference to the persistent conflict between these themes. At times when the international control of drugs is seen to rate lower than other global issues concerning the US national interest, such as perceived communist aggression during the Cold War, Washington has been consistently willing to subordinate international drug control to wider foreign policy.

Using the principal themes outlined above, this work charts the American role in the evolution of the international drug prohibition regime. Chapter 1 examines the tortuous progress of American efforts to create an international drug control framework in the years before 1945 based on prohibition. American work on the international stage during this period, while significantly limited by US international influence, was closely tied to the development of domestic anti-drug legislation and greatly influenced by the endeavours of a number of individuals. Prominent among them was a great believer in the doctrine of drug prohibition, Harry Jacob Anslinger (1892–1975). As head of the US Federal Bureau of Narcotics (FBN) from its inception in 1930 until 1962 and as US representative on international control bodies from 1930 until 1970, Anslinger played a critical role in the creation of drug policy at home and abroad. His often contradictory approach to matters of drug control in many ways reflected the wider US response to the issue. As such Anslinger provides a focus for a discussion of the American Crusade in Chapters 2 through 5, complementing the systemic analysis with an exploration of US behaviour at an individual level.

Chapter 2 describes the impact of new-found US hegemony on the development of the global drug prohibition regime in the period between the end of the Second World War and 1960. Exploiting US strength within the restructured international community, Washington (through Anslinger and the American delegation) was able to use both formal and informal channels at the UN to influence the creation and maintenance of the international drug control framework. Yet, while the US was able to set the agenda for transnational drug control, it also deferred the internationalization of prohibition to larger policy priorities, a process discussed in Chapter 3.

An examination of the multiple motives underlying US drug control policy at the UN between 1950 and 1958 reveals not only the subordination of US narcotic foreign policy to a desire to contain communism, but also offers a revisionist commentary on Anslinger's position within the US government bureaucracy. Traditionally regarded as the dominant force in the field of international drug control, we will see how Anslinger exploited American anti-communist paranoia to bolster his own position, yet only achieved control over US narcotic foreign policy at the UN when it did not conflict with State Department concerns for checking the spread of communist influence.

This is a theme continued in Chapter 4, which proffers a new interpretation of the role of Anslinger in the creation of the 1961 Single Convention on Narcotic Drugs, the bedrock of the UN drug control framework.

Although disagreement between Anslinger and the State Department characterized the US response to the passage of the Single Convention, the concord remains the foundation for the global drug prohibition regime. Chapter 5 explores the legacy of the Convention and examines some contemporary consequences of the prohibitive norm around the world. These include the tacit legitimization of US unilateral overseas anti-drug actions and the increasing militarization of the fight against drugs in Latin America, a region traditionally targeted by Washington as a major source of illicit drugs entering the United States. The epilogue builds upon the discussions of the contemporary picture presented in Chapter 5 and, in the light of the arguments posited in the preceding chapters, looks to the future of the American Crusade to internationalize drug prohibition.

NOTES

1. Andrew Weil notes that 'the only people lacking a traditional intoxicant use are the Eskimos, who had the misfortune to be unable to grow anything and had to wait for white men to bring them alcohol'. Andrew Weil, *The Natural Mind: An Investigation of Drugs and Higher Consciousness* (Boston: Houghton Mifflin, 1986), p. 1.
2. Ethan A. Nadelmann, 'Global prohibition regimes: the evolution of norms in international society', *International Organization*, 44(4) (1990), 503.
3. A note on definition. In the truest sense, *narcotics* refers to the opiates: opium and its derivatives, including morphine and heroin. However, in accordance with the terminology used by the international drug control system, this study uses the term to include the coca leaf and its derivatives, and any part of the cannabis plant. The terms *cannabis* and *marijuana* (or *marihuana*) will also be used interchangeably since the name is only a matter of cultural and social variation. Synthetic, that is to say human-made, drugs are not, according to pharmacological definition, included under the heading 'narcotics'. However, although to do so is technically incorrect, the international control movement has often used the term to classify all drugs that are the focus of control efforts.
4. Stephen D. Krasner, 'Structural causes and regime consequences: regimes as intervening variables', *International Organization*, 36(2) (1982), 185.
5. Ernst B. Haas, *When Knowledge Is Power: Three Models of Change in International Organizations* (Berkeley: University of California Press, 1990), p. 2.
6. Ethan A. Nadelmann, 'Global prohibition regimes', p. 503.
7. *Ibid.*
8. S. K. Chattergee, *Legal Aspects of International Drug Control* (London: Martinus Nijhoff, 1981), p. 355.

9. House of Representatives, Annual Report for the Year 1984 of the Select Committee on Narcotics Abuse and Control (US Government Printing Office, Washington, DC, 1985), p. 9.
10. *UN Conference for the Adoption of a Single Convention on Narcotic Drugs*, Vol. II (New York: UN Publications, 1964), p. 300.
11. *The United Nations and Drug Abuse Control* (New York: United Nations International Drug Control Programme, United Nations Department of Public Information, 1992), p. i.
12. Declaration of the *International Conference on Drug Abuse and Illicit Trafficking and Comprehensive Multidisciplinary Outline on Future Activities in Drug Abuse Control* (New York: United Nations, 1988), pp. iii and 1.
13. *The United Nations and Drug Abuse Control*, p. 7.
14. *Ibid.*
15. Ethan A. Nadelmann, 'Global prohibition regimes', p. 512.
16. Jack Donnelly, 'The United Nations and the global drug control regime', in Peter H. Smith (ed.), *Drug Policy in the Americas* (Boulder: Westview Press, 1992), p. 283.
17. Robert O. Keohane, *After Hegemony: Cooperation and Discord in the World Political Economy* (Princeton: Princeton University Press, 1984), p. 94.
18. Robert O. Keohane, 'The analysis of international regimes', in Volker Rittberger (ed.), *Regime Theory and International Relations* (Oxford: Clarendon Press, 1995) p. 43.
19. Stanley Hoffman, *Primacy or World Order: American Foreign Policy since the Cold War* (New York: McGraw-Hill, 1978), p. 222.
20. Ernest van den Haag, 'The busyness of American foreign policy', *Foreign Affairs*, **63**(1) (1985), 113.
21. Charles W. Kegley, Jr, and Eugene R. Wittkopf, *American Foreign Policy: Pattern and Process*, 4th edn (New York: Macmillan Education, 1991), p. 33.
22. Karl Von Vorys, *American National Interest: Virtue and Power in Foreign Policy* (Westport, CT: Praeger, 1990), p. 19.
23. *Ibid.*
24. Robert E. Osgood, *Ideals and Self-Interest in America's Foreign Relations* (Chicago: University of Chicago Press, 1953), cited in Charles W. Kegley, Jr, and Eugene R. Wittkopf, *American Foreign Policy, Pattern and Process*, 3rd edn (New York: Macmillan Education, 1987), p. 70.
25. *Ibid.*, p. 78.

CHAPTER 1

DRUG PROHIBITION IN THE UNITED STATES AND THE EVOLUTION OF INTERNATIONAL NARCOTIC CONTROL, 1909–1945

The dominant American Tradition is that morality requires absolute condemnation without compromise to the weaknesses of the flesh.
Walter Lippmann, *The Underworld as Servant*, 1931

In the U.S., the Judeo-Christian (and especially Puritan) struggle against temptation, combined with the passion for the immediate satisfaction of 'needs,' have generated an unusually intense ambivalence about a host of pleasure-producing acts and objects, illicit drugs being but one.
Thomas Szasz, 1990

Since the first concerted effort to achieve an agreement for the multilateral control of drugs was made at the 1909 Shanghai Commission, members of the international community have moved to develop and broaden the efficiency and scope of the transnational system for control. The United States, the instigator of the commission, has been continually active within the international machinery, although fluctuation in the degree of American success, and therefore commitment, ensured that an uneven pattern of US involvement developed in the years before the Second World War.

This chapter charts the progress of American efforts for international drug control before 1945 and the emergence of the USA as a hegemonic actor. While demonstrating the symbiotic relationship that existed in the development of domestic and international legislation, it traces the fluctuating fortunes of the American quest to create international norms for the control of narcotic drugs. The section shows how, in order to export its ideas on drug prohibition, the United States had to develop comprehensive national control legislation of its own. This it achieved in 1914 with the passage of the Harrison Act. The legislation became the cornerstone for US domestic drug law and the focus of American attempts to duplicate drug prohibition abroad. The chapter also explores another main theme of the book and illustrates how, since the beginning of US involvement in the international narcotic system, the control of drugs has consistently been only one facet of a wider strategy controlled by a realist-inspired concern for national interest in the form of economic expansionism. Finally, the discussion provides a picture of the system for control constructed between 1909 and 1945. It was the machinery and the international legislative foundations laid before and during the lifetime of the League of Nations that were transferred into the institutions of the United Nations and provide the basis for the present international prohibitive regime.

THE BIRTH OF INTERNATIONAL DRUG CONTROL: THE 1909 SHANGHAI OPIUM COMMISSION

Individual states within the USA possessed drug control legislation from the late nineteenth century, with the first drug prohibition laws being passed in 1875. However, these were limited measures devised on strictly ethnic grounds. They aimed to prevent Chinese immigrant workers from importing smoking opium into San Francisco and other West Coast cities. Having outlived their usefulness on the completion of the railroads, Chinese workers in the West were regarded with suspicion and fear. They were seen as a threat not only to white labour, but also to the purity of American society at large. The Chinese immigrants' practice of opium smoking consequently made them a convenient target for legislation directed towards what was perceived to be a menacing foreign minority. Anti-Chinese sentiment was effectively reinforced by images of 'yellow fiends' debauching white women and the youth of the nation. For example, in 1881 San Francisco police reported the existence of opium dens where they discovered 'white women and Chinamen side by side under the effects of this drug – a humiliating sight to anyone with anything left of manhood'.[1] The *San Jose Mercury* also called for the practice of opium smoking to be 'rooted out' before it could 'decimate our youth, emasculate the coming generation, if not completely destroy the whole population of our coast'.[2] Early anti-drug legislation was, therefore, aimed at Chinese immigrants as much as opium itself. Despite responding to ethnocentric paranoia, anti-narcotic campaigners also became distressed by the dream-like state that opium smoking produced in Americans. 'It was', they believed, 'not at all consistent with their duties as Capitalists or Christians.'[3] Although few WASP Americans chose to smoke opium, preferring tonics or cordials that had the drug as a prime constituent, campaigners sought to extend legislation beyond merely ethnic lines.

Concern about the Chinese and their consumption of opium was not limited merely to concern about immigrants on the West Coast of the

United States. Interest in Chinese opium smoking extended well beyond American borders. Indeed, it was no coincidence that Shanghai was chosen to be the venue for the first international discussions on drug control. The opium situation in the Far East, particularly China, had been attracting increasing attention in the United States for several years. The use of opium by the domestic population of China had been widespread in the nineteenth century. Pressure from British authorities who were profiting from the opium business ensured that efforts for the control of the drug by the Chinese authorities were largely ineffective. The formation of Anglo-Oriental Society for the Suppression of the Opium Trade in 1874 signalled a growth in anti-opium sentiment in the United Kingdom. By 1905, the House of Commons had adopted a resolution that the British-dominated Indo-Chinese opium traffic was 'morally indefensible'. Nevertheless, the British efforts did not extend to support for an aggressive global campaign. American anti-narcotic campaigners, on the other hand, had different ideas. With perceptions influenced by the reports of missionaries in the Far East they felt that it was their moral duty to help the Chinese people to rid themselves of the 'opium menace'. In fact, the impact of missionaries during the early stages of the international campaign was so great that, according to Arnold Taylor, it 'might quite appropriately be referred to as a missionary movement – or better still, as missionary diplomacy'.[4]

Although the American rhetoric and ostensible motivations were replete with notions of morality and moral righteousness, the prospects of profitable economic relations with China were not forgotten. The opportunity to pursue a potentially lucrative trading policy towards China remained a central concern for Washington. It was hoped that US interest in assisting with the elimination of the opium problem in China would induce the Chinese authorities to look favourably upon American commercial endeavours. Any chance to gain access to the Chinese market and secure an advantage in the region over the Great Powers of Europe was regarded with interest and enthusiasm. Past aggressive American economic policies in China had not been particularly successful; in fact, they had to some extent antagonized the Chinese authorities. The Americans reasoned, therefore, that the Chinese government would favour US enterprise above that of other nations, particularly Great Britain, which was responsible for importing opium into China. In calling for the Shanghai Commission, the United States also hoped to ease the Chinese government's resentment at the treatment of Chinese within America. Motives for such a move, far from being humanitarian, were again based on economic foundations. Consequently, the US battle against opium in China was never independent of economic interests. Since the opium habit was seen to be largely responsible for the political, social and economic degeneration of China, its suppression was considered indispensable to the development of her commercial potential. Thus, as Kettil Bruun, Lynn Pan and Ingemar Rexed observe, the objectives of the moral crusaders coincided with, and were reinforced by, economic objectives.[5]

American interest in international narcotic control had also increased after the acquisition of the Philippines in 1898. The progressive reform movement in the United States reinforced the moral dimension of the imperialist trend and highlighted drug control as an ideal candidate for export. Wishing to set a moral example to the established colonial powers, notably France, Great Britain, the Netherlands and Portugal, the United States adopted a system of drug prohibition on the islands. The Episcopal Bishop of the Philippines, Charles H. Brent, managed to secure the interest of President Theodore Roosevelt, who ensured that the USA devoted itself to 'freeing' the colony from the perceived vice of opium smoking.[6] Roosevelt's belief in the superiority of the Anglo-Saxon race and the American duty not to shrink from strife, moral or physical, within or beyond the nation, complemented Brent's goals in the newly acquired territory. The growth of American industrial power and overseas trade, accompanied by an American-style rhetoric of *Weltpolitik* and energetic calls for the USA to fulfill its Manifest Destiny across the Pacific,[7] created an atmosphere in which the moral regeneration of the Philippines seemed the natural thing to attempt. Swept along with the consensus of the time, the US Congress passed an Act in 1905 that imposed a policy of absolute prohibition in the islands, to take effect in March 1908. Thus, the Philippines became an early expression of the American belief in the prohibition of drug use for anything other than medical and scientific purposes.

Bishop Brent's experiences in the Philippines encouraged him to broaden the focus of his efforts to combat the spread of opium use. Brent, an enthusiastic amateur diplomat and former assistant to a poor Boston parish, appreciated that the USA's interests in the region did not exist in a vacuum. He realized that they were affected by the activities of other nations in the area, particularly China. Brent therefore believed that action within the US territory needed to be complemented by international endeavours. More precisely, it was thought that the poor state of opium control in the Philippines, almost a decade after the United States had taken control of the islands, could be ameliorated by a reduction, or better still the elimination, of the opium trade in nearby China. Additionally, the USA's own domestic opium situation added impetus to efforts to control drugs beyond American borders. Although the Americans considered the situation on the islands to be a trigger for heightened involvement in international drug control, it is essential to note that by 1900 the USA itself possessed an addict population of approximately 250,000.[8] International activity, it was hoped, would help reduce the illegal flow of drugs into the United States and hence reduce domestic use. Stressing the importance he attached to the issue, and the central role he believed the United States had to play, Brent wrote to President Theodore Roosevelt in 1906. Here he insisted that it was

> almost the duty of our government, now that we have responsibility of actually handling the matter in our possessions, to promote some movement that would gather in its embrace representatives from all countries where the traffic in and use of opium is a matter of moment.[9]

The United States accordingly made moves towards this end and in 1906 started work to convene an international commission to address the opium issue.

The American representatives to the commission consisted of Bishop Brent, Charles C. Tenney (a Harvard lecturer in Chinese history and at that time the Secretary of the American Legation at Peking), and Dr Hamilton Wright. Dr Wright, a researcher into tropical and neuropathological disease and an energetic anti-narcotics campaigner, was to play a particularly important role in the development of early drug legislation both in the United States and elsewhere. Born in Cleveland, Ohio, in 1867, Wright studied medicine in Canada, Europe and the United States. Ambitious for fame and a career in diplomacy or other government service, he used his well-connected friends to advance his campaign against narcotic drugs. The historian H. Wayne Morgan has called Wright 'a major human catalyst in the drive for both domestic drug control and American participation in the international opium movement'.[10] Indeed, as will become clear, he was a major force behind the drive for the 1914 Harrison Act.

Having conducted several investigations of their own before the commission, Dr Wright and the rest of the American delegation were convinced of the wisdom of a prohibitive system. In a report Wright noted that

> Before the international commission met it had developed that the opium problem was not confined to the Far East, but that, through the misuse of morphine and other opium preparations, several of the large western countries including the United States, had become contaminated.[11]

Revelations that a domestic opium problem existed in the USA therefore served to further concentrate the American delegates' minds on a strict approach on the issue. The discovery that drug problems in the United States stretched beyond ethnic minorities increased the stakes for the

American representatives at Shanghai and well and truly 'established a material interest in the international problem beyond the Philippines'.[12] International control was no longer just an issue of moral duty and philanthropic mission.

Yet Brent and the other delegates found it difficult to accuse other nations of laxity concerning narcotics while their own country had no national legal framework to control domestic drug use. At the time of convening the Shanghai Commission, the United States had no federal laws limiting or prohibiting the importation, use, sale or manufacture of opium or coca leaves and their derivatives. Domestic legislation had to be passed before Shanghai in order to provide, as Senator Henry Cabot Lodge remarked, a 'worthy example for other nations to follow'.[13]

The widespread and easy availability of patent medicines and refreshments containing drugs such as cocaine, opium and their derivatives had already become the focus of growing concern at the turn of the century. For example, there were calls as early as 1903 to take legal action against the sale of Coca-Cola. The drink, originally advertised as a 'remarkable therapeutic agent', contained cocaine until 1905. An increased interest in the issue of drug use in the United States was also partly due to the atmosphere of the Progressive era. One strand of the general mood for reform was that governmental power could, and should, be harnessed to promote the public good. As Paul Boyer has noted, 'For the Progressives, society had the right – indeed the duty! – to intervene at *any* point where the well-being of its members was threatened.'[14] A growing belief that the excessive use of alcohol and other drugs would weaken and harm American society brought about demands for some form of legislative drug control. Such concerns, however, also crucially coincided with a growing appreciation for the need for some form of nation-wide domestic legislation to fulfill US international requirements. The Pure Food and Drug Act of 1906, which required the precise labelling of all products containing narcotic drugs and their derivatives and cannabis, was therefore arguably the first example in a series of a domestic legislative decisions influenced by international drug control concerns. Three years later, as the Shanghai meeting was in progress, another federal law was quickly passed to strengthen the American position on the international stage. This 1909 Act banned the importation into the United States of opium for smoking, putting in place legislation that would help the Americans avoid embarrassment in Shanghai. Thus, having gone some way to bring the US domestic situation into conformity with the American delegation's international goals, the United States worked at Shanghai to develop some form of international drug control.

Despite energetic calls for a full conference to consider and legislate on the issue, American-initiated plans resulted only in a commission. Requests from Great Britain and the Netherlands ensured that the resultant commission took the form only of a fact-finding forum. The conferees were careful not to make any binding arrangements about the opium trades' future throughout Eastern Asia. Any conclusions reached resulted only in recommendations. Participants had no obligation to make any commitments regarding future action.

At Shanghai nine resolutions were adopted unanimously. Among these the representatives recognized that 'the use of opium in any form otherwise than for medical purposes is held by *almost* [emphasis added] any participating country to be a matter of prohibition or for careful regulation'.[15] As the language suggests, this resolution represented a compromise between the United States and the other nations taking part, particularly Great Britain. American proposals faced considerable opposition. Despite the energetic calls for the adoption of an American stance, most nations, although moderately interested in the discussion, were unwilling to exert a great deal of effort for non-medical prohibition as called for by the United States. The principle that medical purposes constituted the only legitimate use for opium ran throughout the American resolutions. Dr Wright was later to comment that at Shanghai the US delegation 'believed in prohibition for ourselves in the use of opium except for medicinal purposes, and for the principle of prohibition for all other nations as soon as it could be accomplished'.[16] Nevertheless, Brent found it 'impossible to get general agreement that the use for other than medical purposes was evil and immoral'.[17]

Not all governments, in particular those concerned with opium as a source of revenue, most notably the British government, shared the American point of view. The British government favoured some form of regulative policy, as opposed to outright prohibition. In addition, Great Britain decided that any reference to governments assisting one another in the solution of their internal opium problems constituted 'direct interference with the internal administration of a country and was thus beyond the scope of the Commission's power'.[18] Representatives believed that any activity within the boundaries of an independent nation was the exclusive right of that country and as such did not warrant any outside interference. Such ideas concerning the control of drug manufacture inside another country were among the first manifestations of a now familiar American approach to international drug control. Indeed, Rufus King regards it as 'a novel concept', with the United States 'calling on the world to choke off at the *sources* [emphasis added] what we [the USA] wanted to keep from flowing inward across [our] boundaries'.[19] To be sure, the American insistence on flouting the sanctity of national sovereignty in the name of drug control would create tension abroad in later stages of its crusade.

During the commission's meetings at Shanghai the US delegation followed its public stance by stressing the moral angle of US opposition to the use of opium. Dr Wright's activities behind the scenes, however, clearly illustrated the multiple American motives concerning the opium situation in the Far East. In speaking with Philander C. Knox, President William Taft's Secretary of State, Wright claimed that

> our move to help China in her opium reform gave us more prestige in China than any of our recent friendly acts towards her ... the whole business may be used as oil to smooth the troubled water of our aggressive commercial policy there.[20]

Thus, although much of the delegation's hyperbole concerned their altruistic intentions, Brent, Wright and Tenney clearly pursued a pragmatic policy. This, it was hoped, would help to enhance US economic foreign policy in the region. Other nations, however, were well aware of the USA's motives and of Wright's attempt to cloak them under a simple moral message. Indeed, as David Musto notes, irritation concerning the US position, with its 'overtones of high-mindedness and superior virtue', was intensified by the expectation that while the great burden of the international control effort would be borne by other nations, the United States would be the beneficiary.[21]

On returning to the United States from Shanghai, Dr Wright realized that American drug control laws needed significant improvement. It became increasingly clear that the USA required comprehensive federal legislation if anti-narcotic campaigners were to persuade other nations to enact strict drug control laws at any future international conferences. Dr Wright's activities reflected the continued association of drug use with certain ethnic and racial groups. By this time, however, Chinese in the United States were no longer the focus of attention. The 1910 report on the International Opium Commission to the US Senate, which had been written largely by Dr Wright, mentioned a new drug of concern and the group identified with its use. It noted that 'this new vice, the cocaine vice ... has proved to be the creator of criminals and unusual forms of violence, and it has been a potent incentive in driving the humbler negroes all over the country to abnormal crimes'.[22] Exploiting many white Southerners' fears of blacks, he consequently sought to institute strict controls over cocaine. In April 1910 he wrote to the editor of the Louisville *Courier-Journal* noting that 'a strong editorial from you on the abuse of cocaine in the South would do a great deal of good [but] do not quote me or the Department of State'.[23] Despite Dr Wright's lobbying in the United States, it would be another four years before the USA possessed a wide-ranging national narcotic law. The state of the USA's domestic drug control efforts led a public health officer, Martin I. Wilbert, to comment in 1912 that 'There are few if any subjects regarding which legislation is in a more chaotic condition than the laws designed to minimize the evil drug habit.'[24]

THE UNITED STATES AT THE HAGUE CONFERENCES

Dr Wright's failure to create strict domestic drug control law did not dampen his enthusiasm to build upon the international progress made at Shanghai. Negotiations undertaken by both Dr Wright and Bishop Brent to initiate further international consideration of the drug issue resulted in a series of conferences at The Hague between 1912 and 1914. Here the American delegation followed its already familiar prohibitive approach and urged for stringent international controls on smuggling. It also expanded the scope of the conference to consider the control of the manufacture and the distribution of opium, morphine, cocaine and Indian hemp. This was to be the first move to implement the international control of the drug more usually known as cannabis or marijuana. The American delegation argued that such measures would control the increasing traffic in these drugs to China, India and other parts of the Orient. American attitudes towards the control of drug trafficking through the insistence of internal control by other nations remained the same as pronounced at Shanghai. In fact, the US delegation urged that even nations with no drug problems within their own borders would have to start policing the manufacture, export and transshipment, or they would provide bases for smuggling operations into countries that did have black markets.[25]

Although the first Hague Conference only instituted a system of licensing, record keeping and international reporting to keep track of licit production, the Americans saw it as a distinct advance for the anti-opium movement. The measures adopted essentially conventionalized some of the resolutions made at Shanghai and imposed an obligation on the parties to 'use their best endeavours' to put these principles into practice.[26] Nothing, however, was said on how the control over production and distribution of the listed drugs was to be carried out. Essentially every government was allowed to decide for itself the best method, and this permitted a certain degree of freedom for the individual nations[27] – a right that was eroded as time went by. The conditions laid down by the Hague Convention were more domestic than international in nature. Nevertheless, American observers believed that the main defect of the convention was that it did not create administrative machinery for the application of the agreed principles. Despite this deficiency, the convention did establish measures designed to deal with what was becoming recognized as a world-wide problem and shifted the focus of attention away from China to give the movement a truly international flavour. To be sure, achievements certainly fell short of the goals set by the United States, but the conference was important to the Americans because the principle of restricting the use of opium to medical and scientific purposes gained further recognition. The convention was to remain until the 1930s the only foundation on which the USA was willing to base international drug control.

Despite energetic efforts by the United States, progress in international control remained slow. The eagerness of the American delegations to conclude morally rigid legislation met with a conservative attitude from the traditional colonial powers, particularly France, Great Britain, Portugal and the Netherlands. The British, whose approach to the opium question William O. Walker III describes as reflecting 'a mixture of pragmatism, expediency and cultural disdain', in turn found the United States to be obstructionist. Walker concludes that the US representatives, 'despite wanting a more comprehensive agreement ... realized that such an accord was premature and therefore settled for what they could get'.[28] It was, after all, the British and other colonial powers who remained the dominant forces in global politics, and as such they limited any radical proposals suggested by the United States.

However, the Hague Convention proved to be one more instance when the enactment of exemplary domestic laws became necessary in order to avoid international embarrassment. The lack of federal legislation was becoming a real hindrance for American international campaigners. Even the widespread use of opium in French Indo-China was theoretically controlled by an elaborate set of government rules, while the United States still lacked federal narcotic control. At the conference, members of the international community once again asked a simple question: how could US anti-narcotic campaigners challenge other nations to tighten up their drug control laws, when the USA itself still did not possess a broad control policy? In order to fulfill commitments to international drug control and try to set an example for other nations to follow, Dr Wright and the anti-narcotic movement had to work hard to pass suitable domestic legislation.

The result of Wright's activities was the introduction by Francis Burton Harrison of New York of two bills to Congress on 8 April 1913. They were designed to 'prohibit the importation and use of opium for other than medical purposes' and 'regulate the manufacture of smoking opium within the United States'. Both, having wide congressional backing and the influential support of the Secretary of State, William Jennings Bryan, had a smooth passage through the House of Representatives and the Senate. They were consequently signed by President Woodrow Wilson to take effect on 1 March 1914.[29] While interpretation of the law initially led to confusion concerning its enforcement, what became known as the Harrison Act had by 1919 confirmed the American belief in a punitive approach to drug control.

The move towards law enforcement complemented the Progressive trend in the United States during the first decades of the century. The Harrison Act represented popular consensus against drug addiction and the drug experience. Like so many similar Progressive laws, it represented general public fear of disorder and inefficiency, and the belief that society could purify individual conduct in the name of the common good. Prominent among the Progressive laws that embodied this idea was the 1919 Volstead Act. This was passed to enforce the Eighteenth Amendment, which prohibited the manufacture, sale, transportation, import or export of intoxicating liquor. Owing to the widespread use of alcohol within the United States, the legislation received a great deal of attention. The issue of alcohol prohibition therefore effectively overshadowed narcotic drug prohibition and the Harrison Act. Despite the long-term significance of the Harrison law, the anti-narcotic movement in America had neither the depth nor the urgency of the alcohol prohibition movement.[30] Indeed, unlike in the case of the Volstead Act there had been little debate in 1914 concerning the passage of the Harrison legislation. It was not even listed in the index of the *New York Times*. Unlike alcohol prohibition, it was not seen as a question of primary national interest, but as Musto remarks, merely a 'routine slap at moral evil'.[31] A coherence of approach between the US legislature, executive and judiciary meant that the use of certain drugs was seen in basic terms: the non-medical use of narcotics was wrong; a menace both physically and morally to society.

Thus the Harrison Act, as Norman Clark has noted, left a greater legacy of enduring spiritual malignancy than the Volstead Act.[32] Despite its almost unnoticed passage onto the statute books, it established prohibition as the dominant theme in a federal strategy towards narcotic drugs. It was, he continues, 'a strange triumph of pseudoscience, racism, and mild hysteria on the part of a few people and of indifference on the part of most others'.[33] The Act set the tone for American drug legislation, and thereafter federal policy was to define drug use as a law enforcement problem. The issue thus became a matter for the police rather than the medical profession.

Having previously instigated several conferences with haphazard domestic drug control legislation that was inferior to that in many other nations, the United States could now approach the issues of international drug control from a stronger position. With the Harrison Act in place, US anti-narcotic campaigners continued in their quest to export a prohibition-ist narcotic control policy to the rest of the world.

US CO-OPERATION WITH THE LEAGUE OF NATIONS: INDEPENDENT INTERNATIONALISM

Although, as the Hague Conferences had demonstrated, there had been increasing activity towards the international control of drugs before 1914, the outbreak of the First World War brought most endeavours to an abrupt halt. After the hiatus in control efforts, however, there came a resumption of work under the auspices of the League of Nations.

While the League was predominantly a product of President Wilson's plans for the maintenance of world peace after the Great War, it was also intended to serve as an umbrella organization for the more orderly management of all world affairs: political, financial, economic, cultural and social. As Robert H. Wiebe has noted, Wilson saw the League as 'an international agency' that 'would supply coherence for the new world'. For the President it was a progressive vision for the 'bureaucratic solution to international flux'.[34] Indeed, the war clearly provided impetus for the formation of an international organization. A growing appreciation for the process of globalization and the increasingly interconnected nature of global affairs illuminated the need for some form of co-ordinated strategy towards the expanding number of issues that reached beyond national boundaries. Hence, the international control of opium and other danger-ous drugs was to be placed under the League's supervision; article 23c of the League's Covenant was directly concerned with the control of traffic in dangerous drugs.[35] At the first Assembly of the League, a Special Advisory Committee on Traffic in Opium and Other Dangerous Drugs (OAC) was created to operate the international drug control system.

During the years between the end of the First and the outbreak of the Second World War, however, the American crusade for international control became largely a question of the degree and manner of participa-tion with the League. Despite all Wilson's efforts to guarantee American involvement in the international organization, failure of the US Senate to approve the Covenant of the League in both 1919 and again in 1920 meant that for the first time the United States found itself outside the official body responsible for international opium control. Although the President argued for full American involvement with the League, political oppo-nents in Washington feared being drawn in to defend the interests of such colonial powers as Great Britain and France. With the country gripped by the 'Red scare' at home and a concern for the spread of Bolshevism abroad, many Americans were fearful that the League 'would mean an increase in contacts with the poison-infected areas of the world'.[36] The result was to be an uneasy American isolation from the organization. The USA's absence also meant that the original membership of the OAC was dominated by colonial nations. This did not mean, however, that the United States severed all ties with international drug control operating under the aegis of the League. As we shall see, although restricted by Washington's official isolationist stance towards the organization, collaboration for drug control was to increase as time passed. American involvement with international control can be seen as an important example of what Joan Hoff-Wilson has termed 'independent internationalism'[37] during a period traditionally categorized as isolationist. Indeed, by 1937 it was noted by Ursula P. Hubbard in *The Cooperation of the U.S. with the League of Nations, 1931–1936* that 'U.S. cooperation has been as complete and fully as constructive as that of many League members; indeed there has been closer alliance in this field of work than in any other'.[38]

Although the USA took a back seat in matters concerning the opium problem during the years immediately following the First World War, the entire story of world co-operation would have faded if the United States had not dominated the Paris Peace Conferences. American activity at Paris ensured the inclusion of article 295 into the Versailles Treaty, which stated that all contracting parties were deemed to have signed the Hague Convention of 1912. In order to be eligible for the benefits and privileges of the League, most of the sovereign states signed. Such a policy gave the international opium movement renewed impetus, especially in securing the co-operation of important producing and manufacturing nations. Foremost among these were the defeated countries of Germany, Austro-Hungary and Turkey. All were important producer nations that had in the past been extremely stubborn concerning narcotic drug control.

Because the United States opted not to join the League, there were early fears among campaigners that American contact with the organization's drug control machinery would end completely. As noted earlier, such fears proved to be unfounded. US–League relations, however, were any-thing but straightforward. Although Washington did keep in contact with the system through the government of the Netherlands and American diplomats in Switzerland, the State Department refused to recognize the transfer of the administration of the Hague Convention from the Nether-lands to the League of Nations. This obviously led to problems in establishing any form of co-operation between the American authorities and the League's control apparatus. Nevertheless, despite the resulting diplomatic and technical difficulties, American involvement in international control continued. Keen to remain involved with issues pertaining to international drug control, the United States pursued a delicately balanced relationship with the League. Attending meetings of the OAC in a 'consultative capacity' only, US 'observers' attempted to influence the course of the League's international drug control efforts.

Despite energetic lobbying, continuing American eagerness to make the international system for drug control increasingly rigid and in line with high moral ideals met with limited success. It became immediately apparent that the OAC and the Americans held completely different viewpoints about the non-medical use of drugs. Many members, including China, France, Great Britain, Japan, Portugal and Spain, actually operated opium monopolies in their Far Eastern possessions. In these cases opium was legally available to certain members of the population, but was subject to certain government restrictions on production, transportation and use. The imposition of taxes upon drug users also meant that the monopolies were a lucrative source of revenue. Economic interests often directly opposed any controls that the OAC might implement. Resistance from European colonial powers and drug-manufacturing countries, which Americans called the 'old opium bloc', ensured that US insistence for a dramatic and almost instantaneous tightening of international control made very little headway. In addition, the internationalization of the spirit of the Harrison Act could not be forced upon the international community. As it was, American demands that the world production of drugs should be limited to the quantity required for strictly medical and scientific purposes, and requests that national governments should limit opium production and the production of coca leaves, were met with less than enthusiastic responses from the members of the OAC.[39]

Although heavily involved in international efforts for the control of drugs since 1909, the United States had managed to make only limited progress in attaining its desired goals. Work before the creation of, and co-operation with, the League of Nations was greatly restricted by diplomatic inertia encountered from the old colonial powers.

Other nations, notably Great Britain, continued to place faith in an alternative policy towards drug control. Like the United States, Britain had passed some drug control legislation at the turn of the century. However, such policies were not based on total prohibition. Instead doctors cared for addicts, using professional judgement rather than state-imposed moral ideals. The 1926 Rolleston Report[40] had maintained that addiction was a medical, rather than a law enforcement, issue, and thus cast aside the 'sin and evil' appellations often applied by American counterparts at the time.

Because of such different approaches to drug control, Britain and other nations regarded US efforts at strict global enforcement of prohibitionist policies as not only misguided but also an infringement of national sovereignty. Throughout the operation of the League, member countries considered the issue of national sovereignty to be central to any effective working of such an organization. The failure of American delegations to achieve prescribed aims and, as will be shown, their consequent withdrawal from discussions at various stages of international deliberations illustrates the US frustration with the nature of extranational narcotic control politics. The awkward relationship that the Americans had with the League hampered the progress that the US proponents of strict drug control had achieved in influencing the rest of the world. Although some headway had been achieved since initial involvement on the drug scene, the United States still lacked the necessary international influence to shape global control strategies. The USA had succeeded in instigating international conferences and forcing other nations to address an issue that had previously been felt to be of little real consequence and limited to the Far East. Nevertheless, progress was slow and greatly limited by the American position on the world stage. The colonial powers and European drug-manufacturing nations still dominated the international scene.

Despite setbacks, the United States nevertheless remained active within the international drug control arena, and the development of international legislation continued. The decade that elapsed since the Hague Conference in 1912 had revealed many shortcomings in the existing system, and moves were subsequently made to tighten control.

THE WALK-OUT IN SWITZERLAND: US AND INTERNATIONAL CONTROL DURING THE 1920s

The conferences of 1924–5 attempted to improve on the Hague agreements for the control of opium in the Far East and use the League's machinery to establish a broader system of quantitative limitation on licit drug production and manufacture. Whereas the Hague treaty had focused on domestic obligations, the emphasis in Geneva was transnational control. The conferences also began a process of improvement in the relations between the United States and the League, although they were also to provide further examples of the immaturity of the American delegates in their dealings with the organization.

The chief US representative at Geneva was Republican Representative Stephen G. Porter of Pittsburgh, chairman of the House Committee on Foreign Affairs. Porter was a figure who played an important role in the development of drug control in both the United States and the international arena. Nonetheless, from his first contact with the League he showed little real understanding of its function and status. In a complete misinterpretation of the organization's role he initially claimed that the United States should deal with the League on an equal footing, although he was finally persuaded that such an approach was unwise. In adopting what was felt to be a morally superior stance, Porter and the American delegates sought to secure major concessions from the other nations present at Geneva. The United States illustrated its broad intentions for drug control by proposing that the conference consider the limitation of coca leaves and the elimination of opium smoking in the Far East. Porter, who believed that 'heroin addicts spring from sin and crime',[41] also proposed the prohibition of the manufacture of heroin. Having introduced domestic legislation for this purpose in March 1924, Porter was deter- mined to obtain a world-wide ban of the drug. This would, he believed, eliminate any surplus available for misuse. However, such an uncompro- mising approach ultimately proved to be damaging to the American goal of strict prohibitive international control. Having lobbied for a rigid US stance on the issue, Porter ensured that the American delegation was bound by instructions from the US Congress. More precisely, the resulting congressional resolution stated that 'the representatives of the U.S. shall sign no agreement which does not fulfill the conditions necessary for the suppression of the habit forming narcotics drug traffic'.[42] It comes as little surprise to learn that the USA withdrew from the proceedings after an unsuccessful attempt to persuade the conference to completely outlaw all drug production for anything other than medical and scientific purposes. Clearly stating the American stance, the departing US delegation noted that 'it must be recognized that the use of opium products for other than medical and scientific purposes is an abuse and not legitimate'.[43] Display- ing the general US feeling of anger and frustration, Porter, dispirited with the whole international system at Geneva, asserted that 'if when I get back to America anybody says League of Nations to me he ought to say it conveniently near a hospital!'[44] Brent, displaying similar feelings but in a manner more in keeping with his clerical position, concluded that the limited efforts at Geneva were to be 'deplored' because 'Christ and his religion are brought under reproach and put to open shame'.[45] Conflict was inevitable. The League's drug control machinery operated in the slow fashion typical of any large organization while the American delegation preferred to adopt a strategy dominated by the desire for immediate results.

Although the United States justified the pursuit of a rigid prohibitive line in terms of moral superiority, motivations stretched well beyond the realm of drug control. Adhering to the ideals ostensibly displayed by the US delegation in Geneva, Bishop Brent claimed that 'we are laying our whole case before the Conference without reserve or ulterior motive'.[46] Such rhetoric, however, conveniently ignored the American intention to use any agreement to improve trade relations with China. For that purpose the USA followed a familiar realist-inspired economic tactic – an approach that had also been adopted at Shanghai in 1909. By the mid-1920s pharmaceutical concerns in Europe and the United States were producing large quantities of heroin, morphine and cocaine. Consequently, according to William B. McAllister, in the absence of serious attempts at national control by governments, much of this output found its way into illicit channels and was smuggled to Asia. By demonstrating its willingness to try to halt the illicit drug trade to the East, Washington hoped to promote investments in China. Therefore, stimuli behind US involvement with the League's drug control apparatus were never far from concerns for economic expansionism.[47]

While the United States distanced itself from the proceedings at Geneva and refused to sign the treaty, the results received some grudging approval from Washington. Whatever faults the US delegation saw in the convention, it became clear that the drug control debate had gained further international recognition. Indeed, in closing the conference the Danish President proclaimed that 'the drugs question has now entered upon a new period. It is now caught up in the day-to-day machinery of the League of Nations. It cannot escape.'[48] In addition, the convention extended the national control of narcotics, as provided by the 1912 agreement, to the supervision of international traffic by means of a system of certificates authorizing the import and export of drugs.

Geneva is also significant because it saw the question of cannabis raised again on the international agenda. At the insistence of the Egyptian delegate, El Guindy, the second conference considered the issue of cannabis control. Encouraged by the drug's inclusion within the terms of the convention, Porter was pleased to see the League move to provide concrete provisions for the control of a drug that the United States was beginning to view as dangerous. A subcommittee, made up of doctors, professors and persons with experience in public health and the pharmaceutical service, was drawn from sixteen nations, including the USA, to study the drug.[49] All but three members – Great Britain, the Netherlands and India – reported in favour of its complete prohibition. Cannabis's incorporation within the Geneva legislation therefore went ahead despite concerns from the British delegate to the OAC, Malcolm Delevinge, that not enough research had been completed into the effects of the drug. Indian objections that there were social and religious uses of the drug were also overruled. The resultant clauses in the convention encouraged contracting parties to impose internal, import and export controls over cannabis and all its preparations. Evidence provided by the United States in the 1930s, which claimed that the use of cannabis led to the development of criminality, would also encourage other nations to place faith in a prohibitive policy.

The United States also supported the formation of the Permanent Central Opium Board (PCOB), the idea for which came from an old American proposal. The board comprised eight experts, who to avoid government influence were supposed to act in their personal capacities. Although this was the case in theory, the board's chairman, the American Herbert May, stayed in constant contact with the US State Department for his entire tenure. May's participation with the activities of the board indicated a gradual increase in US co-operation with the League's drug control apparatus, albeit at what was officially a non-governmental level. May had been a successful executive in the pharmaceutical trade, and having retired at the early age of 45 became active in the Foreign Policy Association, particularly its Opium Research Committee.[50] After becoming chairman of the PCOB he was to remain a prominent figure in the field of international drug control until the mid-1940s and, as we shall see, played an important role in the design of the United Nations drug control machinery. May's task at the PCOB was to implement the collection of statistics on drug trade and use the board as a lobbying group, applying pressure on countries to sign, ratify and effectively implement the Geneva Convention. The US government regarded the PCOB as completely independent of the League. This stance justified its involvement with the League's control machinery without compromising any ideas of isolationism or aligning itself with the OAC, a body that it perceived to be dominated by the colonial and drug-manufacturing countries.

Even so, hopes for effective collaboration ended in disillusionment. America still regarded the interests of the other controlling nations as suspect and influenced by financial gain and economic benefits that could be achieved from the manufacture and trade in drugs. A young American writer, Ellen LaMotte, wrote in the *Nation* magazine, 'The whole Orient is anxious to put down opium' – although some European nations, she continued, particularly Great Britain, were equally keen to keep it up.[51] Disillusioned American observers in Geneva began to call the meetings of the Opium Advisory Committee the 'smugglers' reunion', reflecting the perceived interests of the so-called old 'opium bloc'. In fact, so intense was American feeling against the League's international drug control system that the United States attempted to undermine it during the 1920s. American policymakers made advances encouraging Latin American governments to refuse to sign the Geneva Opium Convention. The scheme failed only because the convention already had the necessary number of ratifications.

It is therefore fair to conclude that American influence was at its lowest ebb during this period. The American dissatisfaction and consequent withdrawal from the 1924 Geneva Conference merely highlighted the confrontational relationship that existed between the US delegation and the OAC. The United States, having founded the world international anti-narcotic movement, now saw it apparently taken over by the League of Nations and controlled by the very nations that, as William O. Walker III has noted, the USA sought to shame or force into a narcotic policy that it regarded as morally acceptable.[52] The tenacity of American endeavour, however, ensured that by the mid-1920s the main themes of the American approach to international control had become evident – themes that, as we shall see, persist today. As Arnold H. Taylor's study *American Diplomacy and the Narcotics Traffic, 1900–1939* demonstrates, three fundamental tenets were clearly identifiable. First, the United States regarded the use of opium and other narcotic substances for other than medical or scientific purposes as a moral and social evil. Second, as a corollary, the United States concluded that the only legitimate transactions in these drugs, from production to consumption, were those designed to meet medical and scientific needs. Third, Washington maintained that the basic solution to the drug problem lay in limiting the production of raw materials to the quantities necessary to fill the world's legitimate requirements.[53]

Clearly, American ideas of high morality and production limitation had not considered the fact that in demanding the acceptance of their pro-gramme the Americans were asking other countries to make considerable sacrifices. These included financial losses, the loss of independence in jurisdiction and even national sovereignty. By the late 1920s, the USA's single-minded pursuit of control at source had effectively blinded the policymakers. Washington's supply-driven strategy overlooked the eco-nomic and cultural obstacles that producer states had to overcome in order to carry out any anti-drug convention effectively.

Indeed, failed attempts to involve Latin American nations in transna-tional anti-drug activities were due partly to US cultural misunderstanding and political arrogance within the hemisphere. The disregard given to calls for wider support of the US programme at the fifth Pan-American Conference in Chile in 1923 demonstrated the lack of succour in the region. Latin American nations did not respond well to US encouragement, particularly given Washington's morally superior atti-tude and self-declared right of intervention. The aspirations of President William H. Taft for the future of the region in 1912 still seemed to sum up the sentiment of most Washington policymakers. Taft's comment that

'The day is not too far distant' when 'by virtue of our superior race' the whole hemisphere 'will be ours . . . . It already is ours morally' appeared as pertinent to the United States in the 1920s as it had in the previous decade. Moreover, the aggressive nature of US economic, political and military policies that rested upon the continuing legacy of the Monroe Doctrine ensured that resentment and anger characterized Latin American attitudes towards the North.

Thus, despite American national confidence and a continuing sense of destiny in the Western Hemisphere, it was becoming clear that in order to make further headway Washington had to adjust its uncompromising attitude towards the League's control apparatus. Drug-producing nations in Latin America remained largely unimpressed with direct US efforts for control. In the absence of either sufficient political leverage or philosophical empathy with the doctrine of prohibition, independent action proved fruitless. Although the Americans pursued a policy of heavy financial investment in the region, nations stubbornly resisted US influence where they could. Latin American countries were unenthusiastic about the concept of Pan-Americanism for fear of domination by the North. As the reaction at the Pan-American Conference in Santiago had shown, they did not respond well to either bilateral or unilateral US efforts for international drug control. Instead, Latin American nations saw membership of the League of Nations as the preferred option for the conduct of most of their extra-national relations. This reality forced American diplomats to appreciate that the best bet for success lay with a multilateral approach.

HARRY J. ANSLINGER AND IMPROVED US–LEAGUE RELATIONS

The 1930s consequently saw the Americans modify their attitudes towards the League. Increased involvement with the international movement would, it was hoped, allow more influence abroad. Official non-recognition of the League had isolated the United States, with Porter's morally determined inflexibility contributing to the partial failure of American efforts for control. It was no coincidence that the adoption of a more pragmatic approach towards the League came soon after Porter's death late in 1930. This change in approach was to result in the limitation of opium manufacture to medical and scientific needs, a long-time goal of US delegations. Accordingly, Washington's decision in the late 1920s to abandon unilateral efforts at control and make an effort to work with the OAC indicated a tactical, rather than a strategic, alteration of international policy.

The American position on the international stage was also affected by events within the United States. Despite moves in the late 1920s and early 1930s to repeal the Eighteenth Amendment and abandon alcohol prohibition, influential sections of US society remained opposed to the non-medical use of narcotic drugs. While the public did not agree with liquor prohibition, there was little doubt that narcotic drugs should remain outlawed. Although by the early 1930s most Americans claimed to be in favour of temperance, this was a term that was seldom used concerning opiates and cocaine. During the years leading to the passage of the Harrison Act prominent newspapers, physicians, pharmacists and congressional representatives had broadcast the belief that opiates and cocaine 'predisposed habitués toward insanity and crime'.[54]

These perceptions were strengthened by the propaganda of anti-narcotic campaigners like Richmond P. Hobson. Lay groups founded by Hobson in the 1920s and 1930s, such as the International Narcotics Defence Association, the World Conference on Narcotic Education and the World Narcotic Defence Association, popularized the belief that narcotics prompted crime. Using newspapers, the radio and even school textbooks, Hobson, a hero of the Spanish–American war, successfully transmitted his anti-drug message across America. His use of a quasi-medical approach to heighten anti-drug sentiment can be seen in a 1924 issue of *The Saturday Evening Post*. In this he wrote

> The entire brain is immediately affected when narcotics are taken into the system. The upper cerebral regions, whose more delicate tissues, apparently the most recently developed and containing the shrine of the spirit, all those attributes of man which raise him above the level of the beast, are at first tremendously stimulated and then – quite soon – destroyed.[55]

Hobson, however, did more than perpetuate theories concerning drug use and crime. He also blamed foreign nations for the United States' domestic drug problem. Like many individuals and newspapers in the 1920s[56] he viewed North America as surrounded by other, dangerous continents. According to Hobson, 'South America sent in cocaine; Europe contributed drugs like heroin and morphine; Asia was the source of crude opium and smoking opium and Africa produced hashish.'[57] In believing this he compounded the view that domestic drug use was not an American problem. Hobson also exploited the xenophobic paranoia surrounding drug use in the United States, stating that 'Like the invasions and plagues of history, the scourge of the narcotic drug addiction came out of Asia.'[58] By the adoption of such an approach, the issue could be attributed conveniently to non-American elements. Hence, foreigners and minority racial groups in the United States continued to be seen as both the source of drugs from abroad and the culprits of drug use inside the nation.

While important for his popularization of such ideas, Hobson was destined to play only a peripheral role in the US drug control issue. Things could have been different had he been the successful candidate to head a new drug control agency. The man who beat him for the position was to be a central figure in both the domestic and international quest for prohibition. That man was Harry J. Anslinger. Although Anslinger began his career as chief of the national narcotic control body in an environment where drug prohibition was already well established, he strove to make the patterns of law enforcement more efficient.

Since 1914, the Narcotics Division had enforced drug control laws within the Prohibition Unit of the Treasury Department. The creation of an independent Narcotics Bureau in 1930, however, provided the means to ensure that US narcotic laws were effectively implemented by a government agency solely concerned with narcotic drugs. Appointed to head the newly created Federal Bureau of Narcotics (FBN), Anslinger was commissioner for 32 years and 'remained steadfast in his belief that enforcement and a punitive approach to narcotics ... were necessary to eradicate the problem of drug addiction'.[59] As the extraordinary length of tenure suggests, Anslinger possessed a great ability for bureaucratic survival. His biographer John McWilliams notes that Anslinger 'had a knack of making himself seem indispensable and a preservationist instinct'.[60] As we shall see, although he was an ardent proponent of prohibition, his awareness for self-preservation determined many of the judgements he made concerning drug control.

At the helm of the FBN, Anslinger not only endeavoured energetically to enforce the legislation already in place, but also sought to create more prohibitive narcotic control laws. With a background in alcohol control with the Treasury Department, the commissioner never doubted the doctrine of prohibition. Even in its twilight years, Anslinger was convinced that the Volstead Act could be made to work. He believed that progress could be made through the strengthening and better co-ordination of the enforcement agencies. Stiff fines and prison sentences, combined with the inclusion of the navy in efforts to halt smuggling, would in Anslinger's opinion make the Volstead Act work.[61] For Anslinger there was only one solution to illegal drugs use. 'Get rid of users and pushers, period.' Addicts were, he believed, 'criminals first, and addicts afterwards'.[62] With Anslinger leading the anti-narcotics campaign, the United States continued to place faith in the belief that harsher fines and longer prison sentences could control individual behaviour with regard to drug use.

Some opposition to this approach did exist. But views that opposed those held by the FBN were actively countered, or simply subsumed by the bureau's propaganda. In this way the bureau aimed to eliminate any suggestions that prohibition was ineffective. In countering reports that criticized the FBN's policies, Anslinger used tactics that the author and drug policy specialist Arnold Trebach has described as 'unethical, immoral, and sometimes, apparently, even criminal'.[63] Attempts to silence Professor Alfred Lindesmith of the University of Indiana in 1939 involved false claims that the academic was dealing with a 'criminal organization'. The organization transpired to be the research and reform group the World Narcotics Research Foundation. The foundation, although critical of the FBN, was far from criminal in its designs. Lindesmith merely opposed the FBN's prohibitive approach to drug control, favouring maintenance and treatment over law enforcement. Consequently, as Trebach has noted, such attacks on freedom of speech and press against Lindesmith and other critics of the bureau were common despite the protections of the First Amendment and the federal civil rights statutes making it a crime to interfere with those rights.[64] Another notable opponent of the FBN's punitive approach to drugs was August Vollmer. As the foremost police reformer of the day, Vollmer argued for a regulatory rather than a punitive approach to drug use. He concluded in his 1936 book *The Police in the Modern Society* that drug addiction was first and last a medical problem. 'Like prostitution, and like liquor,' he wrote, 'drug use was not a police problem; it never has been and never can be solved by policemen.'[65] Nonetheless, in a nation where prohibition was unquestionably the dominant narcotic drug control paradigm, Vollmer's ideas received little significant attention.

The commissioner's concerns, however, did not lie solely within the borders of the United States. Anslinger realized that difficulties in detecting and preventing the unlawful importation of drugs into the USA posed a major problem for domestic narcotic law enforcement. He reasoned that illegal importation from foreign overproduction created an abundant supply of illicit drugs in the United States, and maintained low prices for addicts. In 1929 the League called for a new international conference to consider how manufactured drugs might be better controlled, and the resulting 1931 conference for limiting the manufacture and regulating the distribution of narcotic drugs was to be Anslinger's introduction to multinational narcotic drug control. As a member of the American delegation in Geneva, Anslinger worked hard to ensure that the United States played an influential role in the formulation of the convention.

An adjustment in the US approach to involve greater co-operation with the League's control machinery heralded the beginning of a new era in

American relations with the world drug control community. Nonetheless, US participation in the 1931 conference was initially in doubt. In what turned out to be one of his last contributions to the US effort for international control, Representative Stephen Porter tried to prevent any American involvement with the proceedings in Geneva. He believed that American participation would imply that the United States had shifted its stance from demanding a limit on raw production to what he regarded as the secondary issue of manufacturing. This position was not acceptable to the State Department, which, as noted, desired increased involvement with the League's control efforts. Consequently, Porter was finally persuaded to abandon his rigid stance. As discussed earlier, Porter's insistence that the United States would co-operate with the League only on its own terms had led to the walk-out in Geneva. The State Department was careful to avoid a repetition of this situation and when naming the American delegation in 1931 did not include any congressional representatives in the group.

Anslinger, however, appeared to be an ideal member of the US delegation. His participation in two conferences to suppress the illegal trade in liquor, held in London and Paris in 1926 and 1927 respectively, had convinced him that effective prohibition of illicit substances required international co-operation. Driven by his past diplomatic experience, he approached the conference with the belief that prohibition would be the only effective policy to adopt. The combination of a more practical American stance and a change in personnel at the State Department[66] helped ensure that the United States would have more success in 1931 than it had at the earlier conferences.

Because of the United States' modified stance in the international arena, the US delegation finally agreed on a convention that was to be more palatable to other nations. This renewed and more realistic approach produced agreement in Geneva in 1931, and the American notion that drug abuse within the USA could be curbed by production restrictions throughout the rest of the world became irreversibly established in international law. The 1931 Convention for Limiting the Manufacture and Regulating the Distribution of Narcotic Drugs was to become one of the cornerstones of the international control system. Its basic principle was the limitation of three dangerous drugs, morphine, diacetylmorphine (heroin) and cocaine, strictly to amounts required for medical and scientific purposes, in addition to the restriction of the quantity of these drugs available to each country. Consequently, the convention finally succeeded in formalizing American-initiated ideas concerning manufacturing quotas. The 1931 decision was also important because it required signatories, and requested non-signatories, to anticipate drug needs and furnish the

League with information concerning the quantities required for the coming year; theoretically avoiding surplus production world-wide. After American insistence the Convention also created the Drug Supervisory Body (DSB) to administer the system. Yet, as S. K. Chattergee notes, 'the greater part of the responsibility' for control 'was given to the High Contracting Parties, and hence it was intended that the medical and scientific requirements for drugs for a country should be determined by the government concerned'.[67] The League, therefore, still lacked control over national drug control frameworks.

Nevertheless, the United States regarded the 1931 legislation as a significant advance in the anti-drug campaign. It was of particular significance because it gave Washington a legal basis for co-operation with the League on the narcotic issue. The United States gradually increased involvement with the PCOB and the DSB, ensuring influence in the formulation and the functioning of the international drug control system. As Arnold Taylor comments, the USA grew to believe that it was 'on the operation of these two Boards, supplementing and co-ordinating the efforts of the individual nations, that the entire fabric of international control ultimately rests'.[68] The creation of both the DSB and the estimates system bore marks of US initiative, indicating the extent of increasing US influence upon the international system. And by the 1930s American policymakers had realized that the move away from unilateralism could only help to serve their policy. Officials were hoping that their tactical switch would enable them to achieve US goals more effectively, without abandoning their traditional aim of control at source.

The 1930s, then, saw the United States greatly improve its position *vis-à-vis* international control. Having achieved a working relationship with the League of Nations, American delegations again played a role in the formulation of international drug control legislation. Despite persisting fears from some quarters of the American press and public that the European 'opium bloc' was still attempting to undermine international control,[69] American ideas concerning the medical and scientific use of drugs were becoming more widely accepted. Nevertheless, the United States remained sceptical of some aspects of the League's approach to international control. This was particularly true of the provisions contained within the Convention for the Suppression of the Illicit Traffic in Dangerous Drugs in 1936. The legislation, which stemmed from an initiative by the International Police Commission, aimed to make trafficking offences punishable in the penal systems of the contracting parties. Although the United States attended what turned out to be the last international meeting before the Second World War, it chose not to sign the treaty, arguing that the legislation failed in its aim of strengthening the international system. According to Stephen Fuller of the State Department's Narcotic Division, the convention was also seen to have been 'inadequate in so far as cannabis is concerned'.[70] Failure of the Americans to gain rigid terms for the suppression of illicit traffic demonstrated the nature of the US relationship with the League in the last few years before the outbreak of war in Europe. Although on working terms with the League's drug control apparatus, American influence undoubtedly remained limited. The colonial nations remained dominant.

While the United States continued to operate predominantly through the League, American domestic concern for cannabis use within the USA's own borders was to provide a trigger for a rare example of successful unilateral action against a source nation. More significantly, the incident foreshadowed the US use of economic leverage to achieve desired goals in the field of drug control, albeit at this stage at a regional level. Worried by the rising levels of drug addiction in the United States, Washington looked south towards Mexico, a country identified as a major source of illicit marijuana, with particular concern owing to its extensive land border with the USA. Marijuana had long been associated in the south-west with 'indolent Mexican labourers who were perceived by most Americans as criminal types',[71] and an increasing concern regarding the drug's illegal use across the United States provoked an initially reluctant FBN to address the issue. Anslinger had doubts about FBN involvement with the control of a drug that grew so readily in many parts of the nation. He feared at first that failure to control the drug would harm the reputation of the FBN. But soon realizing that he could harness growing public concern and safeguard the Bureau's position in Washington during the uncertain years of the Depression, Anslinger played a central role in ensuring a safe passage through Congress of a harsh anti-marijuana law. Such a reversal in policy concerning the drug was by no means remarkable for the commissioner. Anslinger used his powers of persuasion with the press, politicians and community groups to rally support for legislation to outlaw marijuana. In July 1937, for example, he co-authored with Courtney Riley Cooper an article entitled 'Marijuana assassin of youth' published in the *American Magazine*. This and other sensationalist pieces with which the commissioner was involved portrayed marijuana as the cause of sex crimes, murder and other amoral and depraved forms of behaviour. Yet throughout his long career he failed to maintain a constant line on the effects of the drug. In the course of appropriation hearings in December 1936 Anslinger had stated that marijuana was 'as hellish as heroin', despite the fact that the previous year he had claimed that it was not even addictive. During passage of the anti-marijuana act into law, Anslinger again asserted that use of the drug did not lead to the use of opiates, particularly heroin. His rejection of the so-called 'stepping-stone theory' was, however, to be regularly contradicted over the next 33 years.

Although Anslinger's opinions on the addictive properties of the drug vacillated, there was little doubt concerning the stringency of the new legislation. The 1937 Marijuana Tax Act banned the marijuana plant and imposed an occupational tax on importers, sellers, dealers and anyone handling cannabis. Violations were punishable by a $2000 fine, five years' imprisonment or both. However, as McWilliams notes, the provisions of the Act were not designed to raise revenue, or even regulate the use of marijuana. 'Their purpose was to provide the legal mechanisms to enforce the prohibition of all use of marijuana.' Thus the Act failed to distinguish between marijuana, a non-addictive substance, and opiates like heroin and morphine. Marijuana had become permanently categorized with other drugs that possessed entirely different properties.[72]

Having established legislative measures against marijuana in the United States, Anslinger and his colleagues became fearful that moves towards liberal drug policies in Mexico not only were morally misguided but would also increase illegal traffic northwards. The perceived lax attitude towards control of the drug displayed by Leopoldo Salazar, the chief of the Alcohol and Narcotic Service of the Mexican Public Health Department, provoked the United States to employ aggressive unilateral tactics. The subsequent application of pressure on the Mexican government resulted in Salazar's dismissal and a move in Mexico towards US-style drug control polices.

President Franklin D. Roosevelt's Good Neighbor Policy improved the strained relations with countries to the south. By removing the US political and military policies that had deeply angered Latin American nations, Roosevelt went some way towards dissipating the resentment that had long characterized North–South relations. Yet the new atmosphere of co-operation also allowed the United States to increase its economic influence. Thus, while Washington's revamped regional policy strove ostensibly to distance the USA from its traditional image as the 'Colossus of the North', the Salazar incident brought the Roosevelt administration's interpretation of the reciprocal nature of the policy into question. To be sure, the Mexican authorities resented American interference. Nevertheless, as long as US companies maintained *de facto* control over Mexican oil, Washington possessed sufficient diplomatic advantage to influence Mexican policies on drug control. Indeed, according to the historian Clayton Koppes, a combination of military, economic and diplomatic levers in Latin America demonstrated that the Good Neighbor Policy was little more than US hemispheric hegemony pursued by other means.[73] As will be discussed later, a well-ingrained sense of paternalistic mission towards the region, disrespect for national sovereignty and Mexico's proximity to the United States ensured that narco-diplomatic relations between Washington and Mexico City would remain tense.

American success in Mexico in the late 1930s proved to be an exception during a period marked by limited multilateral progress. Impending war in Europe did little to help the League in its work for international drug control. Seen by the United States as a positive, though limited, step forward, much of the work undertaken to compile reliable statistics on the production of and transactions in narcotic drugs was to be impaired by the political climate of the late 1930s. As the Second World War loomed, military issues became the central diplomatic focus of the European nations. Consequently, concerns for international drug control lost their place on the foreign policy agendas of many governments. Without the serious involvement of these important countries, and with the rest of the world cautiously watching the unfolding events in Europe, the effectiveness of the international control system waned. The outbreak of war in 1939, however, was to strengthen the American position within the international drug control movement.

THE AMERICAN CRUSADE AND THE SECOND WORLD WAR: A NEW ERA DAWNS

As the conflict spread across Europe, operation of the League's drug control machinery in Geneva became understandably difficult. Seeing an opportunity to further enhance the US role, the Americans made efforts to exploit the USA's geographically isolated position and invite the Permanent Central Opium Board (PCOB) and the Drug Supervisory Board (DSB) to leave war-torn Europe and set up in Washington, DC.[74] Herbert May, then president of the Drug Supervisory Body, claimed that he had 'persuaded the State Department to allow [him] to operate from Washington', and there being no League of Nations funds available to set up the office, two American foundations donated the necessary money.[75] Both bodies consequently established their headquarters in Washington in 1941.[76] The process of relocating to the United States can be seen as an indication of the USA's renewed and increasing role in the international drug control movement.[77] The League's reliance upon US funds to keep the two bodies functioning also provided a graphic illustration of just how central such a role was during this period.

The new location served Anslinger and the US movement well. From Anslinger's perspective it meant that the control of the machinery became more open to direct American pressure. The commissioner believed that an FBN-influenced American public opinion and press would now play a central role in the operation of the bodies in Washington. Despite differences in opinion within the international movement, it was generally agreed that Washington provided it with a lifeline.[78]

By the end of the 1930s the United States consequently regarded the drug control apparatus and legislation developed by the League as a definite advance in the crusade for international drug prohibition. Hence despite the USA's official isolationist stance, the twenty years since 1919 had seen a notable increase in American involvement with the organization's activities for international control. However, as its refusal to sign the 1936 Convention indicated, Washington remained dissatisfied with the stringency of many of the League's control measures. Although the United States made a significant contribution to the international movement, European domination of the OAC had effectively prevented the passage of legislation based entirely on American prohibitive ideals. While desiring some form of international regulation, these nations were not prepared to relinquish national control over drug legislation, or lose the revenue produced by colonial opium monopolies.

War in Europe changed this traditional relationship. Despite much domestic opposition, Roosevelt ensured that after the outbreak of war the European nations fighting the fascist coalition received American financial and political backing. Carefully coaxing the American populace to discard the isolationist mindset and embrace an internationalist spirit, the President ensured that assistance also stretched to military supplies after 1940. For our purposes it is important here to note that an increasing reliance, particularly by Britain and France, upon US support in the war altered the power balance within the remnants of the League and its drug control apparatus. The nation's rising prominence on the world stage meant that the United States possessed more leverage in the field of international drug control. No longer a hostage to the now weakening power of the colonial nations within the League, Anslinger and the State Department's Narcotic Division exploited the USA's changing role. As we shall see, both the relocation of the League's control bodies to Washington and an elevation of status within the international community ensured that in the last few years of the League's life the United States would secure more favourable terms for control.

Washington's actions concerning Allied opium monopolies provides a symbolic example of growing American ascendancy and the crucial change in the balance of power occurring within the international control movement during this period. After American entry into the war in both the European and the Pacific theatres late in 1941, the Allies became increasingly reliant upon Washington in the war effort. This permitted the

American anti-narcotic bureaucracy at the State Department and the FBN to extend control policies abroad. By exerting pressure on the Allied powers that maintained opium monopolies, the United States successfully urged nations to begin to phase them out and replace them with American-style prohibition regimes.

At Anslinger's request in January 1943,

> representatives of Great Britain, Canada, Australia and New Zealand, the Netherlands and China were summoned to the U.S. Treasury Department to discuss what was going to happen when some island or territory where they had formerly permitted opium smoking came to be recaptured.

Consequently, when the US occupying forces took control of much of the Far East, US attitudes towards drug control were widely imposed.[79] The United States, now with considerable influence over its allies during the Second World War and over Japan after the war, insisted on exporting its anti-maintenance policy to Asia. Any arrangements that permitted addicts continued legal access to drugs were abolished. Since the United States was the dominant power in the wartime coalition, and subsequently among the victorious Western nations in 1945, countries that came under American scrutiny with regard to drug control, whether they were recaptured former Allied territories or conquered Axis powers, were soon to follow US directives. The Allied zones of liberated Germany consequently followed an American approach to drug control. After V-J Day American dominance was to result in the MacArthur regime introducing a Japanese Harrison Act.[80]

Such a strategy neatly dovetailed with Anslinger's accusations made against Japan during the war. Claiming that 'Japan's war started a decade before the opening gun was fired at Pearl Harbor', the commissioner charged Japan with attempting to undermine American strength by exporting narcotic drugs. The offensive, he claimed, had used narcotic drugs as weapons.[81] 'A drug sullen nation', he continued, is 'an easy conquest and cannot offer adequate resistance to attack.'[82] Thus, by exploiting anti-Japanese sentiments in the United States, Anslinger ensured that he and the FBN continued to remain prominent. He also succeeded in promoting and perpetuating the concept that many of the USA's drug problems were the result of foreign conspiracies.

The commissioner and his supporters were naturally delighted by the abolition of Allied opium monopolies. Congratulatory correspondence received by Anslinger revealed the continuing centrality of a sense of morality and mission among many of those concerned with drug control. The commissioner, praised for his efforts to 'rid the world' of illegitimate narcotics[83] and congratulated for his services to humanity, was also seen as an inspiration for man's duty to his fellow man.

Anslinger, however, remained sceptical about the former European colonial powers' commitment to phase out their opium monopolies and believed that continued US political pressure was necessary in order to ensure that countries such as France and Great Britain would comply with what were essentially US demands. Even in the declining years of the League of Nations, American distrust of the old 'opium bloc' powers remained real. This distrust was also to become apparent during discussion of the transfer of the League's powers to the United Nations, which took place in San Francisco in 1945. Nevertheless, the traditional patterns of power in the international drug control movement were clearly beginning to change. Subsequently, members of the old 'opium bloc' were gradually being forced to move towards the American prohibitive model. Indeed, in 1946 the Permanent Central Opium Board congratulated the Americans on their actions in Asia,[84] which marked a dramatic departure from the traditional attitude of indifference that the Americans had become accustomed to in the previous years of the League's control efforts.

A critique of the League's endeavours reveals that the organization certainly succeeded in providing foundations upon which later efforts for international drug control could be built. Yet, while the legislation reflected the US preference for a supply-side approach to drug control, the results produced by League machinery still fell short of ambitious US expectations. This was the consequence of a number of interrelated factors. First, as noted earlier, for most of the League's lifetime the United States lacked sufficient international influence to dictate its drug control policies and therefore export the idea of prohibiting all non-medical and non-scientific drug use. Second, although delimiting rules for the international control of the production, manufacture, distribution and use of licit drugs (in 1925 and 1931), and making efforts to eliminate the trafficking of illicit drugs (in 1936), the League, as Alan Block notes, 'had no real, lasting power to discipline unreasonable nations'.[85] This was a product of the third factor to be considered: a general absence of faith in a collective system. European nations were unwilling to surrender national sovereignty over domestic drug control or relinquish profitable opium monopolies in their colonies until the League was effectively dead. To quote S. K. Chattergee, there was 'a pronounced lack of community interest'.[86]

The combination of the three factors was to result in international legislation that did not impinge upon national sovereign rights in any significant way. The League's drug control system, like the UN's today, relied upon voluntary adherence. However, in the absence of an international norm concerning drug use and a hegemonic actor capable of encouraging adherence to policies to control it, national drug legislation remained largely the province of individual governments. No concerted multinational desire for drug prohibition existed, and League-imposed constraints were therefore limited. A global drug prohibition regime to govern domestic control policies simply did not exist at this time. With this thought in mind, Bertil Renborg (former member of the League Secretariat) noted in 1947 that 'One of the most important steps to be taken … is to prohibit or do away with all non-medical consumption of narcotic drugs.'[87] And although this was a daunting task, it was one that the United States was to continue to work for under the auspices of the UN.

CONCLUSION

The years between the United States' first transnational endeavours and the end of the Second World War clearly witnessed a huge transformation in the fortunes of American international efforts for drug control. American international influence before 1945 had not provided US delegations with sufficient sway to fulfill ambitious expectations, but some progress had certainly been made. A framework for international control was put into place and American ideas were becoming more accepted by the other nations involved with transnational drug control. Having instigated the international movement, and then lost faith in its abilities, the United States in the 1930s and early 1940s saw an increase in participation and influence. Although the USA had yet to gain complete leadership of the international drug control movement, consistent themes within the American approach can be identified.

First, the United States continually addressed the issue from what was believed to be the moral high ground, although in reality the rhetoric of moral righteousness was often also a cover for more practical economic and political concerns. A realist concern for national interest through acquisition and maintenance of economic power accompanied the moralist impulse. Multiple motives, therefore, remained constant in the US approach to international drug control.

Secondly, the American initiation of multinational control efforts accelerated the need for US federal domestic legislation. The resultant laws often reached the statute books with the help of racist hysteria and pseudo-scientific analyses of the effects of drug use, yet they permitted American delegations to work for international control with an increased sense of legalistic, as well as moral, superiority. With what was felt to be exemplary legislation in place, delegations worked to encourage other nations to follow US-style drug control policies. In true messianic fashion, US anti-narcotic campaigners hoped that the rest of the world would emulate American prohibitive-oriented legislation. The exportation of the belief that all non-medical and non-scientific drug use should be outlawed thus became a central tenet of US international efforts.

Finally, the United States consistently put its faith in a policy that held control at source to be the most effective way to halt drug use within its own borders. Consequently, the source of the drug problem had already been placed outside American societal boundaries. The practice of drug use for anything other than medical and scientific purposes was conveniently blamed on foreigners or particular racial groups. The paranoia that this imagery induced also assisted reformers to secure support for strict anti-drug legislation. As Musto notes, 'Projection of blame on foreign nations for domestic evils harmonized with the ascription of drug use to ethnic minorities. Both the external cause and the internal locus could be dismissed as un-American.'[88] To be sure, strategies that focus upon halting the supply of drugs to the United States, rather than the demand created by American society, remain dominant.

The scope for US progress in control before 1939 had undoubtedly been limited by the United States' position within the international community. The relatively weak status of the United States on the world stage limited the proselytizing efforts of American anti-narcotic campaigners. The absence of hegemonic status deprived the USA of the leverage necessary to influence drug policies on a global scale. This changed irreversibly as the Second World War altered beyond recognition the established balance of world power. The outbreak of war in Europe ensured that both the geographical and the political focus of the international control movement became firmly established in the United States. Harry Anslinger once remarked that 'the world belongs to the strong. It always has done and always will.'[89] Indeed, it was only after the global balance of power in the post-war world had been restructured in favour of the United States that the USA was transformed, from being simply one player in the League's system, into the driving force behind international narcotic drug control.

NOTES

1. Steven B. Duke and Albert C. Gross, *America's Longest War: Rethinking Our Tragic Crusade against Drugs* (New York: G.P. Putman's Sons, 1993), p. 83.
2. Michael Woodiwiss, *Crime, Crusades and Corruption: Prohibitions in the United States 1900–1987* (London: Pinter, 1988), p. 3.

3. Norman H. Clark, *Deliver Us from Evil: An Interpretation of American Prohibition* (New York: Norton, 1976), p. 222.
4. Arnold H. Taylor, *American Diplomacy and the Narcotics Traffic, 1900–1939* (Durham, NC: Duke University Press, 1969), p. 29.
5. Kettil Bruun, Lynn Pan and Ingemar Rexed, *The Gentlemen's Club: International Control of Drugs and Alcohol* (Chicago: University of Chicago Press, 1975), p. 9.
6. William O. Walker III, 'An analytical overview', in Raphael F. Perl (ed.), *Drugs and Foreign Policy: A Critical Review* (Boulder: Westview Press, 1994), p. 10.
7. Paul Kennedy, *The Rise and Fall of the Great Powers: Economic Change and Military Conflict from 1500 to 2000* (London: Fontana, 1989), p. 317.
8. David F. Musto, *The American Disease: Origins of Narcotic Control* (Oxford: Oxford University Press, 1987), p. 5.
9. W. W. Willoughby, *Opium as an International Problem: The Geneva Conferences* (Baltimore: Johns Hopkins University Press, 1925), p. 21.
10. H. Wayne Morgan, *Drugs in America: A Social History, 1800–1980* (Syracuse, NY: Syracuse University Press, 1981), p. 98.
11. W. W. Willoughby, *Opium as an International Problem*, p. 22.
12. Arnold H. Taylor, *American Diplomacy*, p. 59.
13. *Ibid.*, p. 60.
14. Paul Boyer, 'Battling the saloon and brothel: the great coercive crusades', in Allen F. Davis and Harold D. Woodman (eds), *Conflict and Consensus in Modern History* (D. C. Heath, 1992), p. 264.
15. Herbert L. May, 'The international control of drugs', *International Conciliation*, 441 (1948), 320.
16. David F. Musto, *American Disease*, p. 293.
17. *Ibid.*, p. 36.
18. Arnold H. Taylor, *American Diplomacy*, p. 69.
19. Rufus King, *The Drug Hang-Up, America's Fifty-Year Folly* (Springfield, IL: Charles C. Thomas, 1974), p. 209.
20. David F. Musto, *American Disease*, p. 39.
21. David Musto, 'The global phenomenon: lessons from history and future challenges', in Raphael F. Perl (ed.), *Drugs and Foreign Policy: A Critical Review* (Boulder: Westview Press, 1994), p. 3.
22. John Helmer, *Drugs and Minority Oppression* (Seabury Press, 1975), p. 12.
23. David F. Musto, *American Disease*, p. 283.
24. H. Wayne Morgan, *Drugs in America*, p. 102.
25. Rufus King, *The Drug Hang Up*, p. 209.
26. Herbert L. May, 'The international control of drugs', p. 321.
27. S. K. Chattergee, *Legal Aspects of International Drug Control* (London: Martinus Nijhoff, 1981), p. 142.
28. William O. Walker III, 'An analytical overview', pp. 10–11.
29. The stated intention of the Act was 'to provide for the registration of, with collectors of internal revenue, and to impose a special tax upon all persons who produce, import, manufacture, compound, deal in, dispense, sell, distribute, or give away opium or coca leaves, their salts, derivatives, or

preparations, and for other purposes'. Arnold S. Trebach, *The Heroin Solution* (New Haven, CT: Yale University Press, 1982), p. 118.

30. Norman H. Clark, *Deliver Us from Evil*, p. 222.
31. David F. Musto, *American Disease*, p. 65.
32. Norman H. Clark, *Deliver Us from Evil*, p. 222.
33. *Ibid.*, p. 223.
34. Robert H. Weibe, *The Search for Order 1877–1920* (New York: Hill and Wang, 1967), p. 273.
35. Article 23c stated that 'in accordance with the provisions of international conventions existing or hereafter to be created, the members of the League will entrust the League with the general supervision over the execution of agreements with regard to ... the traffic in opium and other dangerous drugs'. Herbert L. May, *op. cit.*, p. 323.
36. Lloyd C. Gardner, *Safe for Democracy* (New York: Oxford University Press, 1984), pp. 258–60.
37. Joan Hoff-Wilson, *American Business and Foreign Policy, 1920–1933* (Lexington, KY: University of Kentucky Press, 1971), pp. xiv–xvii, 26, 241.
38. Ursula P. Hubbard, *The Cooperation of the U.S. with the League of Nations, 1931–1936* (New York: Carnegie Endowment for International Peace, 1937), p. 372.
39. It has been argued that during the early years of the fight against opium colonial powers were indifferent to, or frankly welcomed, drug use among potentially dangerous elements of the populations they controlled.
40. The Rolleston Report came out on the side of drug addiction as a sickness, not a crime, and stated that indefinite prolonged administration of morphine and heroin would be permitted for those 'in whom a complete withdrawal ... produces serious symptoms that cannot be treated satisfactorily under ordinary conditions of private practice' and for those who 'are capable of leading a fairly normal and useful life so long as they take a certain quantity, usually small, of their drug of addiction, but not otherwise'. Rolleston Report, Ministry of Health, Departmental Committee on Morphine and Heroin Addiction (London: HMSO, 1926), p. 18.
41. David H. Musto, *American Disease*, p. 201.
42. R. L. Buell, *The International Opium Conference* (Boston: World Peace Foundation, 1925), p. 100.
43. S. K. Chattergee, *Legal Aspects*, p. 125.
44. *New York Times*, 3 June 1923, cited in William O. Walker III, Bernath Lecture: 'Drug control and the issue of culture in American foreign relations', *Diplomatic History*, **12** (Fall 1988), 375.
45. W. W. Willoughby, *Opium as an International Problem*, p. 447.
46. *Ibid.*, p. 147.
47. See William B. McAllister, 'Conflicts of interest in the international drug control system', in William O. Walker III (ed.), *Drug Control Policy: Essays in Historical and Comparative Perspective* (University Park: Pennsylvania State University Press, 1992), p. 146.
48. J. M. Scott, *The White Poppy: The History of Opium* (London: Heinemann, 1969), p. 146.

49. The nations also included Belgium, Brazil, Canada, the Dominican Republic, Egypt, France, Germany, Greece, Italy, Japan, Poland, Spain and Switzerland.

50. The Committee was established in 1922 for the purpose of following and reporting on the development of the international control over opium, coca leaves and their derivatives.

51. Brian Inglis, *The Forbidden Game: A Social History of Drugs* (London: Hodder and Stoughton, 1975), pp. 160–1.

52. Ronald Hamowy (ed.), *Dealing with Drugs: The Consequences of Government Control* (Lexington: University of Kentucky Press, 1987), pp. 60–1.

53. Arnold H. Taylor, *American Diplomacy*, p. 330.

54. David F. Musto, *American Disease*, p. 65.

55. Edward J. Epstein, *Agency of Fear: Opiates and Political Power in America* (London: Verso, 1977), p. 27.

56. For example, the *New York Times* proclaimed on 9 November 1924 that 'The United States is assailed by opium from Asia as a base, by cocaine with South America as a base, and by heroin and synthetic drugs with Europe as a base.' H. Wayne Morgan, *Drugs in America*, p. 124.

57. David F. Musto, *American Disease*, p. 248.

58. Edward J. Epstein, *Agency of Fear*, pp. 23–31.

59. John C. McWilliams, 'Unsung partner against crime: Harry J. Anslinger and the FBN, 1930–1962', *Pennsylvania Magazine of History and Biography*, 2 (April 1988), p. 210.

60. John C. McWilliams, *The Protectors: Harry J. Anslinger and the Federal Bureau of Narcotics, 1930–1962* (Newark: University of Delaware Press, 1990), p. 86.

61. Letter from Anslinger to Prize Committee on the Eighteenth Amendment, Anslinger Papers (hereafter cited as AP), Pattee Library Labor Archives, Penn State University, Pennsylvania, Box 3: File 12.

62. *New York Times*, 18 November 1975.

63. Arnold S. Trebach, *The Heroin Solution*, p. 164.

64. *Ibid.*, p. 165.

65. Edwin M. Schur, *Narcotic Addiction in Britain and America: The Impact of Public Policy* (London: Tavistock, 1962), p. 67.

66. US moves towards greater co-operation with the League's OAC were enhanced by a change in staff, and hence perspective, at the Department of State. The new chief narcotics officer, Stuart J. Fuller, who rejoined the State Department in 1930, worked effectively with Anslinger. According to Walker, by the time of Fuller's death in 1941 'the two men had succeeded in bringing the world drug control movement under the influence of the United States'. See William O. Walker III, 'An analytical overview', pp. 13–14.

67. S. K. Chattergee, *Legal Aspects*, p. 152.

68. Arnold H. Taylor, *American Diplomacy*, p. 264.

69. Although the State Department saw the 1931 Convention as an advance, it was criticized by the Hearst press. The American delegation's use of quieter diplomacy was attacked in derogatory headlines such as 'Britain leading America by the nose'. Anslinger also received correspondence from the late

Dr Hamilton Wright's wife warning him of the dangers of dealing with European nations. Letter from Mrs Elizabeth Washburn Wright to Anslinger, 23 June 1931, AP Box 3: File 4–9.

70. See Ursula P. Hubbard, *Cooperation of the U.S.*, p. 370.
71. John C. McWilliams, *Protectors*, p. 48.
72. *Ibid.*, p. 77.
73. Clayton Koppes, 'The GNP and the nationalization of Mexican oil: a reinterpretation', *Journal of American History*, **79** (1982), 80–1.
74. For an example of American concern regarding the continued functioning of the PCOB and the DSB during the Second World War see 'Opium discussed before the Advisory Committee; excerpts of remarks, May 20 1939, in Twenty-Fourth Session of Opium Advisory Committee', by Stuart J. Fuller (American Representative), *The Union Signal* (3 February 1940). AP Box 12: File 20.
75. *Bulletin on Narcotics*, **15**(2) (1963), 5. Cited in Bruun, Pan and Rexed, *Gentleman's Club*, pp. 138–9.
76. Letter from Sharman to Anslinger, 1 March 1941, AP Box 2: File 21.
77. The US desire for a swift relocation can be seen in Anslinger's correspondence. For example, see letter from Sharman to Anslinger, 1 March, 1941, AP Box 2: File 21; and letter from Anslinger to Sharman, 4 March, 1941, AP Box 2: File 21.
78. Malcolm Delevinge, the chief representative of the United Kingdom and one of the principal architects of the whole League control system, acknowledged this fact in 1946. In a letter to Anslinger he wrote, 'At a moment when big changes may be impending in regard to the international control of narcotic drugs, I feel that I should like you to know how greatly your help and cooperation during the difficult years of the war, when the offices of the SB [i.e. DSB] and Central Board had to take shelter in Washington, have been appreciated by me and those who have worked with me.' Letter from Delevinge to Anslinger, 28 January 1946, AP Box 2: File 18.
79. Rufus King, *The Drug Hang-Up*, p. 215, and William O. Walker III, *Drug Control in the Americas* (Albuquerque: University of New Mexico Press), pp. 176–7.
80. Rufus King, *The Drug Hang-Up*, pp. 215–6.
81. The Commissioner claimed that 'We in the Treasury had been in a war against Japanese narcotics policy and practices for more than ten years.' Harry Anslinger, 'An account of the Eastern narcotics situation', p. 15, Opium in China File, Harry J. Anslinger Papers, Harry S. Truman Library (hereafter cited as HTL), Independence, Missouri.
82. Radio interview, WFBR Baltimore, 28 February 1947, AP Box 1.
83. Letter from M. J. Hartung to Anslinger, 14 January 1944, AP Box 2: File 19.
84. Rufus King, *The Drug Hang-Up*, p. 210.
85. Alan A. Block, 'European drug traffic and traffickers between the wars: the policy of suppression and its consequences', *Journal of Social History*, **23** (1989–90), 331.
86. S. K. Chattergee, *Legal Aspects*, p. 201.

87. Bertil A. Renborg, *International Drug Control: A Study of International Administration by and through the League of Nations* (Washington, DC: Carnegie Endowment for International Peace, 1947), p. 227.
88. David F. Musto, *American Disease*, p. 248.
89. Letter from Anslinger to Reginald Wright Kaufman, editor of the *Bangor Daily News*, 19 March 1945, AP Box 3: File 22.

CHAPTER 2

THE EXPORTATION OF DRUG PROHIBITION:

US hegemony and the UN drug control system, 1945–1960

The limits of action in the drug field are, like in many other fields, set by the lines of political relationships prevailing in the world at large.
Kettil Bruun, Lynn Pan and Ingemar Rexed, *The Gentlemen's Club*, 1975

The United Nations has always been an absurd name for the peculiar body located on the East River of New York City, which would only be open to more ridicule if it referred to itself as the United Peoples or United Races of the World. Its proper title ought to be, not the United Governments of the Globe, because that is equally a temptation to satire, but the United States. However, this august name has already been annexed. And so, in many ways, has the institution. In both cases by Washington D.C.
Christopher Hitchens, 'Made in America', in *UN Blues: 50 Years of the United Nations*, 1995

As we have seen, the 1930s witnessed the United States gradually regain the leadership of the international drug control movement. This restructuring process was first accelerated, and then completed, by the dislocations created by the Second World War. By 1945 the United States occupied a new-found position of prominence within the international community as a whole. Its economic, military and political strength ensured that the nation played a crucial role in the functioning of the post-war world. 'No matter what the yardstick of measurement or indicator of power and influence,' Robert Gregg notes, 'the U.S. was pre-eminent, and by a wide margin.'[1] Indeed, the United States' pre-eminence inevitably encompassed virtually every realm of modern life. The issue of drug control, although apparently not high on the post-war agenda for reconstruction, was consequently an area that was to be greatly affected by the shift in the balance of power away from the established European foci to the United States.

The central role that the nation played in the creation of the United Nations Organization ensured that the wider transition in the global power balance was mirrored in the sphere of international drug control.

Although other states were important in the foundation of the UN, the Charter was very much the handiwork of the United States. Consequently, to quote Gregg again, 'The Charter was perceived as a reasonably accurate reflection of U.S. interests and values and the UN was widely viewed within the U.S. as an important tool for the exercise of the leadership that was expected of the world's pre-eminent power.'[2] In viewing the UN in this way, the United States set about developing the international system in line with American views on drug control, achieving success impossible before the acquisition of superpower influence. The United States, having initiated the movement at the turn of the century, had by 1945 established itself as the dominant force in international drug control. American prominence in the organization ensured that US delegations to the Commission on Narcotic Drugs (CND) had a considerable impact upon the creation and implementation of international drug control legislation.

This chapter examines US dominance within the UN drug control framework. It traces American efforts to construct an international control system and develop a global regime designed to reflect its morally determined visions concerning the ingestion of certain psychoactive substances. The chapter views the internationalization of the doctrine of prohibition as an important, but hitherto largely ignored, facet of the US quest to determine the contours of the new global order and impose self-determined rules upon the international system and sovereign nations within it. It is widely acknowledged that the close of the Second World War saw the United States exploit its new-found hegemony to create multilateral regimes in the fields of trade and money. Both the Bretton Woods monetary system and the open world trade regime centred on the General Agreement on Tariffs and Trade (GATT) amply demonstrate this fact. While these regimes enjoy significant attention, the global drug control regime, a product of the same international political environment, remains largely ignored. This chapter goes some way to rectify this shortfall, and in so doing, it highlights the creation of a world-wide prohibition regime that significantly affects both national and international responses to drug control around the globe. Harry Anslinger, as the chief US representative to the Commission for many years, features prominently in the study and will provide a focus for the examination of examples of US ascendancy.

THE CREATION OF THE UNITED NATIONS DRUG CONTROL MACHINERY

Just as the League of Nations had emerged from the First World War, so the United Nations was a product of the Second World War. As the conflict had spread, it had become clear among the officials of the US-dominated Allied powers that a new, major international organization would be needed to maintain peace and security in the post-war world. The basic statement of intentions with regard to such an organization had initially been made by the United States and the United Kingdom in August 1941, in the Atlantic Charter. However, the main principles of the UN were to be formulated at the Dumbarton Oaks Conference, held in Washington, DC, between August and October 1944.

Approval of the idea for the new organization by China, the USSR, the UK and the USA set the scene for the 1945 San Francisco Conference on International Organizations where agreement was made on the UN Charter, the constitution of the new organization. As with the League, the UN not only was to be concerned with the issues of peace and security but also made provision for social and economic issues. As a result the Charter established the Economic and Social Council (ECOSOC) as one of the six principal organs of the organization, article 68 directing the Council to set up 'commissions in economic and social fields and for the provision of human rights and such other commissions as may be required for the performance of its functions'.[3] ECOSOC's work regarding drug control, services hitherto provided by the League, were taken over by a section of the UN secretariat, the international civil service that administers the UN system. This was designated the Division of Narcotic Drugs (DND); it was the body responsible for the preparatory work for conferences on international drug control and providing the Secretary-General with material relevant to these conferences. Acting under the provisions of article 68, in the course of its first session in February 1946 ECOSOC established the Commission on Narcotic Drugs as a functional commission to replace the League's Opium Advisory Committee (OAC). The PCOB (Permanent Central Opium Board) and the DSB (Drug Supervisory Body), the specialized agencies concerned with narcotics control that had operated during the League of Nations period, were to function under the CND. In essence, the League's drug control framework was to be transferred to the UN. However, before the CND had an opportunity to meet, a solution had to be found to the legal problems encountered concerning the transfer of powers and functions relating to narcotic drugs formerly exercised by the League of Nations.

During its first session, on 12 February 1946, the UN's General Assembly adopted a resolution on the report of the League's commission on the transfer of certain functions, activities and assets of the League. It was noted how under various international agreements and treaties the League exercised functions that it would be desirable for the UN to inherit after the dissolution of the former organization. Some of these instruments were of a technical and non-political character, and, according to the ideals of the organization, included international narcotic control. It was consequently decided by the General Assembly to examine which of the organs of the UN, or which specialized agencies, should in the future exercise the functions in question. The Assembly charged ECOSOC with this task, directing that

> pending the adoption of the measures decided upon as a result of its examination, the Council should on or before the dissolution of the League assume and continue provisionally the work hitherto done by ... the Opium section and the secretary of the Permanent Central Opium Board and the Supervisory Body [DSB].[4]

Although the CND itself did not have sufficient time to submit proposals for the transfer of power and functions of international narcotic control from the League to the UN, the Norwegian Secretary-General, Trygve Lie, prepared a preliminary document on the issue. As a result, on 3 October the draft protocol amending the instruments on narcotic drugs was approved by the Council and passed to the General Assembly, where it was approved unanimously on 19 November 1946.

The Protocol was signed at Lake Success, on 11 December 1946, and made amendments to each of the existing international instruments that were to come into force when the majority of parties to each of the instruments became parties to the Protocol. Accordingly, pending entry into force of the Lake Success legislation, the PCOB and the DSB were to continue functioning, with the Secretary-General of the UN taking over the role of the Secretary-General of the League of Nations in connection with international instruments on narcotic drugs.

Lake Success, which created a precedent in the transfer of powers and functions exercised by the League in various technical fields, received the necessary number of assessions so that ECOSOC was able to proceed with the appointments to the PCOB at its sixth session in February 1948. By this date all the amendments contained in the Protocol were in force and the UN became the legal successor of the League of Nations in respect of the international control of narcotic drugs.

The end of the Second World War clearly signalled the beginning of a new epoch in international relations. The position of the United States within the structure of this revamped geopolitical environment naturally had a great impact upon the expectations of Washington, DC, on the US role within the organization of the UN. The enormity of the upheaval was not lost on American military planners, who before the end of the war noted in a policy paper that the successful termination of the war ... will find a world profoundly changed in respect of relative national military strengths, a change more comparable indeed with that occasioned by the fall of Rome than with any other change occurring during the succeeding fifteen hundred years .... After the defeat of Japan, the United States and the Soviet Union will be the only military powers of the first magnitude.[5]

Indeed, in moving away from the pre-war Eurocentric world system it appeared, as Paul Kennedy comments, as if 'only the United States and the USSR counted ... and of the two, the American "superpower" was vastly superior'.[6] American prominence in the post-war world clouded Washington's perceptions of not merely the American role in the new organization, but the role of the UN itself. Hegemony was construed to mean that the UN would be a relatively pliant instrument of US policy. It was a simple syllogism: the United States was the hegemonic power with the primary responsibility for a stable world order; the UN was a major US-approved vehicle for achieving such a stable world order; ergo, the UN would respond to US leadership in the creation and maintenance of such a stable world order.[7] Gregg notes that such logic was badly flawed, and consequently US expectations were to be shattered early and often in the years after 1945.[8] Nevertheless, having acknowledged this, the United States' influence, both official and unofficial, within the organization naturally led Washington to perceive the UN as a malleable instrument for the implementation of American policies. The United States' moral, political, financial and psychological authority, openly regarded as evidence of the nation's dominance, was also complemented by a more sinister side of American diplomacy. According to Shirley Hazzard, Byron Price, the UN's Assistant Secretary-General for Administrative and Financial Services, was a secret agent of the US government. As a result, 'Price devised and controlled the UN's administrative policies throughout the organization's formative years'.[9] The fact that Secretary-General Lie, despite disobeying specific provisions of the UN Charter, also permitted the United States to force political screening into the personnel selection process in 1949[10] must have helped perpetuate the view that the organization was merely an adjunct of the State Department. Such feelings were surely also heightened when Lie granted the US Federal Bureau of Investigations (FBI) permission to set up an interrogation office on the third floor and install fingerprinting equipment in the basement of the UN building. Indeed, as will be shown later in this chapter, Anslinger also achieved some success in influencing the selection of personnel within the organization's drug control framework. The ability of the United States to secretly influence the operation of the organization enhanced the image in Washington of the UN as a 'pliant instrument of US policy'.

Such initial preconceptions were to play an important role in the manner in which the United States approached the issue of international drug control. American drug control activists, being susceptible to the ideological consensus of the period, saw the UN drug control framework as a vehicle for the exportation of what was perceived to be exemplary moral prohibitive control legislation. To quote Gregg, as 'principal architect' of the organization, the United States 'quite predictably sought institutions that would reflect U.S. preferences .... The UN, which had been tailored to U.S. specifications, would evolve under U.S. guidance, in directions largely compatible with U.S. interests and values.'[11] Consequently, American efforts for the international control of drugs through the UN became one facet of a larger global policy of reconstructing the post-war world in the image of the United States. President Truman's address at a Jefferson Day dinner in Washington, DC, on 5 April 1947 encapsulated the spirit of American mission and duty. Truman announced that 'The burden of our responsibility today is greater, even considering the size and resources of our expanded nation, than it was in the time of Jefferson and Monroe.' Interpretations of the President's message varied between groups and interests, but to be sure, such a mood encouraged progress in the American crusade. Anslinger and the American delegations were therefore to view the UN as a platform from which to launch prohibitive ideology into the refashioned post-war global atmosphere. Having attempted to proselytize nations of the world since 1909, the dominance of the United States within the UN ultimately provided promising opportunities for the exportation of US-style drug control strategies. It was at the CND, the heart of the UN's control apparatus, that the Americans sought to shape the international control legislation of the post-war world.

THE CND: ITS FUNCTIONS AND DYNAMICS

The Commission on Narcotic Drugs was established to provide machinery to implement the international conventions relating to narcotic drugs, and to provide for continuous review of the progress towards international control of such drugs. The original criteria for selecting members of the CND was that there should be adequate representation of those countries which either produced or manufactured drugs, or which were the victims of illicit traffic. Members were appointed for a three-year period and were eligible for reappointment. ECOSOC consequently requested the governments of Canada, China, Egypt, France, India, Iran, Mexico, the Netherlands, Peru, Poland, Turkey, the USSR, the UK, the USA and

Yugoslavia each to designate one representative to make up the first commission.

Being an advisory organ to ECOSOC, the commission had the task of applying and supervising the application of the various international treaties, and was at the same time created to be the policy-formulating body on all questions relating to the control of narcotic drugs. It was also therefore responsible for making the preliminary studies and drafts for new international agreements. In addition, the CND was a governmental commission. 'In this capacity', claimed Herbert May in 1948, 'it affords a meeting place for many of the officials who are directly responsible for the control of narcotic drugs in their national administrations. Their regular collaboration in this Commission can be of enormous service in co-ordinating the policies of the various governments in this field.'[12] This point is in itself valid enough. However, May neglected to mention the enormous potential for intergovernmental pressurization. This factor was to become a crucial part of the US approach to drug control policy at the UN. The operational dynamics of the CND were naturally to reflect the balance of power in the international community. American post-war power was a crucial factor in the development of UN narcotic control legislation.

Power in basic terms can be defined as the capacity to produce intended results. In this case we are concerned with the ability of the United States to impose its ideas on drug control upon other members of the inter-national community. As noted above, 1945 saw the USA stand alone as the world's strongest nation. In the post-war world the USA occupied the position of military dominance. This was, therefore, to be central to any role that the United States played in the restructured global system. American military power also helped shape the US position within the newly formed United Nations. However, other factors were also impor-tant within the organization. Power as a factor in international relations should not be thought of solely in terms of military strength; it also includes economic, political and psychological elements.[13] Johan Galtung, in his discussion of international organizations, claims that power can be classified into three categories. There exists 'ideological' power, chan-nelled by culture and the international transmission of ideas; 'renumerative' power, exercised by the promise of rewards through trade and economic concessions; and finally 'punitive' power, exercised by, at the extreme, the threat of military force. It is possible to argue that in the drug control field, power is exerted by both the threat of sanctions and by the promise of rewards.[14] Accordingly, despite the UN's commitment to the use of rational and deliberate procedures, states do attempt to coerce one another. In accordance with such principles the United States has exploited its position of strength and has been able to apply pressure on other nations. Through the pursuit of a strategy that William O. Walker III has called 'derivative control',[15] the United States has successfully linked issues not necessarily related to drugs with narcotic matters at the UN. As discussed in the Introduction, by linking or nesting the acquiescence of other nations in the CND to economic aid and political support, the United States has been able to dominate the CND decision-making process and play a central role in the instigation and design of many pieces of international narcotic legislation. Indeed, as Bruun, Pan and Rexed observe, when a 'superpower' exhibits this degree of involvement, there is unlikely to be much resistance or unresponsiveness on the part of the countries appealed to for support, unless such support is contrary to the national interests. Generally speaking, co-operation with the United States in drug control matters does not conflict in any significant way with the interests of other Western countries, and it is therefore readily provided.[16] Although Bruun, Pan and Rexed restrict such observations to Western nations, US influence has of course also been brought to bear upon non-Western nations. The pursuit of US-oriented policies in many such countries, for example in the countries of Latin America, does in this case often conflict with national interests. Nevertheless, as will be discussed later, US economic, political and military strength has ensured adherence to, and support for, American-favoured drug control policies.

The United States was to use its economic and political might in the early post-war world, and hence the UN, to press other nations to follow a largely prohibitive policy to international drug control at the UN. Nations have not been willing to damage political and economic relations with the United States for the sake of drug control. Issues concerning drug use have never occupied such a position of ascendancy on the political agenda. As Paul Kennedy notes, 'the United States was the only country which became richer – in fact, much richer – rather than poorer because of the war'.[17] This fact alone provided massive leverage in dealing with the rest of the international community. With regard to drug control and law enforcement this point can be well illustrated by quoting the recollections of FBN agent Charles Siragusa. When discussing his operations abroad, the ex-Office of Strategic Services (OSS) agent recalled that

> The police overseas almost always worked willingly with us. It was their superiors in the government who were sometimes unhappy that we had entered their countries. Most of the time, though, I found that a casual mention of the possibility of shutting off our foreign aid programs, dropped in the proper quarters, brought grudging permission for our operations almost immediately.[18]

The United States in 1945, therefore, approached the issue of transnational control from a position of great strength. Expectations for the UN, which with the benefit of hindsight can be labelled idealistic and unrealistic, instilled hope in the American international narcotic control movement. The CND was seen as a vehicle for the internationalization of the US prohibitive strategy on drug control. And the American position in the UN seemed to provide the opportunities to dominate the international movement as had never been possible before.

Thus, the United States approached the new organization's drug control mechanism with lofty expectations. American hopes ran high, with the US drug control community believing that the work started at the turn of the century could be completed under the auspices of the UN. However, although traditional UN literature gives the impression that the transfer of power from the League of Nations was relatively smooth, both Anslinger and the Canadian representative to the OAC, Colonel Sharman, were uneasy at the prospect of the resurrection of a European-dominated organization. Having established the focus of the control apparatus in the United States during the war, both Anslinger and Sharman were reluctant to see it return to Europe, in terms of both geography and political focus.[19]

Despite Anslinger's private misgivings concerning the extent of European influence, the United States officially showed a keen interest in the continuation of the control of drugs through international organization.[20] It became evident that Washington was enthusiastic to place drug control on the agenda. During hearings before the influential Committee on Foreign Relations of the US Senate in July 1945, Senator Arthur H. Vandenberg and Dr Leo Pasvolsky, an American UN planner, discussed the future of international control. In assessing the progress being made in San Francisco, they concluded that it was an area well worth US support and encouragement. In closing the discussion on drug control the Senator demonstrated the importance placed upon the issue. Because it was 'a matter of considerable importance', and the 'U.S. delegation was unanimous in its desire to have the present work continued', he requested that additional paragraphs from a report to the US President be printed in the record of the meeting.

Following the official line in Washington, Anslinger himself also apparently put his anxieties to one side and demonstrated his hopes for the new organization. An FBN publication stated in 1946 that

> the success of the OAC of the former League of Nations in international control of narcotic drugs stands out as one of the most important achievements of the former League. There is every hope that even greater success will be attained by the CND.[21]

Despite forthright American rhetoric concerning support of and involvement in the inception of the UN's drug control apparatus, the US government was soon to demonstrate its inexperience in dealing with the complexities of the system. The American role in the creation and design of the UN control framework was undeniably crucial, yet confusion existed concerning the kind of structure to be adopted. This was perhaps a manifestation of the USA's long-term aloofness from the functioning of the League's control machinery. The Department of State's efforts to formulate an effective programme ran into problems at a very early stage. Mrs Howell Moorehead of the Opium Research Committee of the Foreign Policy Association, experienced the disarray evident in the approach of the State Department to the issue.[22] In a letter to a friend, she noted that 'when the U.S. delegation went to San Francisco we were still dissatisfied with the State Department's grasp of the narcotics problem'. Consequently, despite the Department's enthusiasm for the development of a new era in international control, it was not adequately equipped to deal with the matter. In fact, it was only Herbert May's timely intervention that prevented the American delegation offering a 'resolution so badly drafted that it might have forbidden all export of opium for manufacture of drugs for medical needs'.[23]

Conflicts within the approaches adopted by the State Department and those who had been active in the field of drug control revealed a legacy of the years of limited governmental contact with the international control movement. Yet despite confusion within the State Department's strategy towards the issue, efforts of the Opium Research Committee and the veteran international activist Herbert May ensured that the commission was born a creature of the United States. As Walker notes, the State Department clarified its approach to narcotic control, and Anslinger and George A. Morlock of its narcotics division made moves to ensure that the CND would be guided by an American agenda.[24] Having dominated the structural development of the CND, the United States was also poised to control its operation after 1945.

As we have already seen, Anslinger had been extremely influential within the international control system during the war years, and this influence was to increase yet further after the close of hostilities, with the commissioner taking on a prominent role within the CND. Anslinger was appointed as the US representative to the CND by President Truman and confirmed by the Attorney General on 1 July 1946.

When we consider the legacy of personnel and issues that the CND inherited from the League, it is no surprise to discover that Anslinger and the US authorities wasted little time in working to Americanize the drug control policies of the defeated Axis powers. The US government was quick to act to ensure that a rigid drug control strategy was implemented in Germany. Anslinger was requested by the State Department to 'urge the Governments of France, the Union of Soviet Socialist Republics, the United Kingdom ... to organize and establish through their Allied Control Authority, an effective centralized narcotics administration for all Germany'.[25]

Although the war was over, the United States also persisted with its charges against the alleged activities of Japan. The Americans continued to claim that the Japanese had been using narcotics as a weapon of war. In addition to exploiting anti-Japanese sentiments in the United States, Anslinger and the State Department made efforts to impose a prohibitive drug policy on the defeated nation. At a meeting in 1946 between George A. Morlock of the State Department's narcotic section and Dr Szeming Sze, the Chinese representative to the CND, the United States claimed to have 'considerable information regarding Japanese activities in Manchuria and North China during the War'. The Chinese, supporting the US position, displayed their concern. Dr Sze stated that 'China was worried about what would happen in Japan after the withdrawal of the American forces.' He 'wondered whether ... prohibition could not be written into the future peace treaty with Japan'. Although the State Department saw no 'urgency in the matter',[26] American hegemony in the East after victory in Japan ensured that Anslinger's wishes became a reality. Consequently, as noted earlier, the MacArthur military regime built a Japanese Harrison Act into the nation's post-war political system.

The internationalization of the US attitude towards Japan's alleged use of narcotic drugs as a weapon of war can be seen in the CND's adoption of resolution E/CN.7/W.28 submitted by Anslinger in 1948. The resolution sought to charge Japan with crimes against humankind, and the US representative gave details of the 'factory for the manufacture of narcotic drugs built by the Japanese authorities in Mankeden during the Japanese occupation of Manchuria'. This factory, according to the opinion of an 'expert' consulted by Anslinger, had an annual capacity of 50,000 kg of heroin. Although such claims and figures lacked solid corroboratory evidence from sources other than the United States, members of the CND appeared to follow the American line. The commission, therefore, having 'been profoundly shocked by the fact that the Japanese occupation authorities in Northeastern China utilized narcotic drugs during the recent war for the purpose of undermining the resistance and impairing the physical and mental well-being of the Chinese people', considered such action to be a 'most hideous crime against mankind'.[27] Thus it appears as if Anslinger and the United States dominated the commission sufficiently to dictate official resolutions such as the one targeted at Japan. This in effect meant that American views on alleged Japanese use of narcotics for military purposes became the official stance of the UN on the issue. Similar practices were to be repeated many times in Anslinger's long career at the CND.

ANSLINGER AND US PROMINENCE IN THE CND

The US delegation to the CND displayed its powerful position from the very beginning of the commission's life. Indeed, Anslinger played a crucial role in determining the location and timing of the CND's first meeting in 1946. Concerned that the meeting should be held in New York, the commissioner ensured that the UN secretariat understood that the US government would prefer the session to be conducted in the United States.[28] American pressure ensured that the first meeting was indeed held in New York in November and December. Although the first few sessions of the CND were primarily concerned with procedural issues, most notably the transfer of powers from the League's drug control framework to the UN, it soon became clear that Anslinger was the dominant force in the commission. His long experience in the field of drug control, combined with his position as the representative of the pre-eminent nation in the UN, ensured that he played an influential role.

Since his appointment as head of the FBN in 1930, Anslinger had been determined to curb the illicit narcotic traffic. Consequently, he ensured that the US delegation used the CND as a forum for targeting those nations he perceived to be the culprits of such traffic. This was particularly the case with regards to Mexico. The US relationship with the Mexican government concerning the issue of drug control had always been pressing. As noted earlier, Mexico's extensive land border with the United States, and position as a major producer of the illicit drugs entering the USA, ensured that US officials kept a close eye on their southern neighbour. The two countries had been engaged in bilateral narcotic diplomacy since at least the mid-1930s, albeit with the USA taking the lead. As a result the CND provided the US government with a convenient international arena within which it could continue to pressurize the Mexican authorities to adhere to strict US drug control measures. Anslinger recounted such a scenario in a less than serious manner in 1948. In a letter to Sharman, he described a photograph containing the Mexican ambassador to the United States and some central members of the pro-US drug control community, including Colonel Sharman and Herbert May. Anslinger wrote that

> The Mexican Ambassador appears full of contrition, on the defensive, and quite ready to say 'Colonel, we will do everything that you suggest.' Herbert

May appears to be saying (although I can't see behind those thick-shell rimmed glasses) 'You had better damn well do it.'[29]

Indeed, American pressure placed upon the Mexican authorities did produce results, with the Mexican representative to the CND reporting in 1948 that his government 'had increased penalties, eradicated poppies on six hundred and sixty three plantations, arrested 2,284 persons and requested the help of neighbouring countries in this work'. In demonstrating the apparent Mexican resolve he concluded that the 'Army, Police and Air Corps had been used' in the fight against the drug problem.[30] Such efforts were naturally welcomed by Anslinger, who congratulated him 'on the good results which he reports' and 'the extensive campaign which has been conducted in Mexico'.[31] American pressurization resulted in the development of a system for drug control closer to that of the United States than anywhere else in the hemisphere. However, having consistently made efforts to accommodate US desires for strict control during the eight years since 1948, the Mexican authorities were also keen to gain reciprocal American support in the CND. Accordingly, the Permanent Mexican Representative to the UN, Luciano Joublanc Rivas, wrote to Henry Cabot Lodge, Jr, in 1956 noting that

> The government of Mexico have lent full cooperation to the work being done by the Commission on Narcotic Drugs and considers that the participation of their representatives in the Commission has always been constructive and in accordance with the Mexican Government's desire to implement the high objectives sought by the United Nations in the field of control of narcotic drugs. My delegation earnestly hopes that the delegation of the USA will be in a position to grant its favourable vote to the candidacy of Mexico for reelection and will be deeply obliged ... [32]

Such a relationship between the delegations of the United States and Mexico was by no means unique. However, it illustrates the methods adopted within the UN control system. A great deal of bargaining went on between various national delegations, and it was the United States that usually operated from the strongest position. This can also be seen in Anslinger's efforts to encourage nations to sign the 1948 protocol.

One of the most significant issues to concern the CND during 1948 was the international control of synthetic drugs. The production of such drugs had been on the increase since the Second World War for a number of reasons. First, during the war nations did not have the access to raw materials and therefore developed synthetics to avoid low stocks. Second, it was thought that drugs with the benefits of morphine, but without the addictive qualities, could be found. Finally, as the UN admits, 'it is impossible to put limits on scientific research'.[33] As a result, the CND moved to create a protocol to control synthetic drugs that were outside the scope of the earlier international treaties. The issue was one of great interest to Anslinger, who was keen to limit the availability of drugs that could be open to abuse. Aware of the political muscle held by the United States within the drug control system, Mr Leon Steinig, the American director of the Division of Narcotic Drugs, requested that Anslinger 'communicate with the Latin American countries and urge them to sign the Protocol to control synthetic narcotics at the forthcoming meeting of the GA [General Assembly] in Paris'.[34] The protocol was signed in Paris in November 1948, the speed of its passage into international law no doubt having a great deal to do with US interest.

The early years of the commission certainly appeared to have functioned to Anslinger's satisfaction. The United States dominated the proceedings, keenly supported by the Canadian representative, Colonel Sharman. Aware of Sharman's efforts as chairman of the first two CND sessions, Anslinger noted, 'You accomplished a magnificent job. I actually dread to see you leaving the Chair because of the able and efficient way in which you have started the Commission on its journey.' Referring to the work that the two men felt was needed to strengthen the transnational control system, Anslinger continued, 'I hope in the light of impending international events, our journey will not be a short one.'[35] The commissioner clearly believed that there was a lot of work to be done in order to create an international system that was in line with US prohibitive ideals. The USA's position within the UN greatly assisted the American quest for global prohibition and Anslinger's stable position within the US drug control bureaucracy made his own work far easier. Support from Washington ensured that the commissioner did not have to concern himself with bureaucratic challenges to his authority. This point was illustrated in 1948 when support from influential sections of the US government safeguarded Anslinger's FBN, and hence his own position, from potential restructuring.

Howell Moorehead, of the Foreign Policy Association's Opium Research Committee, articulated the views held by much of the drug control community in the United States. She explained that the current structure of the US drug control system was efficient, owing to the flexibility it displayed in approaching the issue of drug control. Illustrating Anslinger's continuing flair for bureaucratic survival, Moorehead notes that

> the reality of this flexibility in administration is due to the work of H. J. Anslinger, Commissioner of Narcotics (Treasury) . . . . He is one of those rare

government officials who know how to use the machinery of Government effectively, not to be hampered by it. He gets willing cooperation from other departments, rather than arousing resistance due to bruised prestige.[36]

Anslinger's appreciation for the workings of government meant that he did his utmost to remain indispensable, without alienating other parts of the US bureaucracy. He thus safeguarded the longevity of the FBN and hence his own position within it, and consequently at the UN. By protecting his post within the United States Anslinger was able to use his position in the FBN to utmost effect at the CND.

Support for Anslinger as the head of the FBN is further illustrated by an incident in 1952. According to the established convention on the election of a new President of the USA, Anslinger was required to resign from all his federal and international positions. Consequently, the election of Dwight D. Eisenhower as President threatened to compromise Anslinger's position. However, as appears to have been the norm during most of Anslinger's career, support for his re-election was tenacious and wide ranging. Accordingly, the State Department, with which Anslinger was later to have a considerable number of disagreements, actively sought his reappointment to the CND. George Morlock, of the State Department's Narcotics Division, informed Anslinger that he had been asked to assure him that 'the Department of State is doing everything that it can to have you appointed by the new President as US representative on the CND ... the Department has already written a letter recommending and urging your appointment'.[37]

In addition to State Department support, the commissioner was to receive a great deal of support from the core of what McWilliams has called 'Anslinger's Army',[38] the pharmaceutical industry. Letters to George Humphrey, Eisenhower's choice for Secretary of the Treasury, illustrate the strength of feeling existent favouring Anslinger continuing his work at both the FBN and the UN. The National Association of Retail Druggists (NARD), one of the largest trade associations in the United States, echoed the belief held by many other pharmaceutical organizations. In comparing Anslinger and the head of the more glamorous Federal Bureau of Investigation (FBI), NARD stated that

Mr. Anslinger is just as successful in his work as J. Edgar Hoover is in his. He has enforced the narcotic laws very energetically and under his administration the traffic in narcotic drugs have [sic] decreased greatly ... . The druggists of the country feel that Mr. Anslinger has been very fair to them. He has been an outstanding administrator, and they hope that he will be maintained in his present position.

The Association believed that it did 'not know of any individual in the US better informed insofar as narcotics are concerned'. As a result, he had been 'a delegate to internation [sic] conference after conference and has served with distinction'.[39] Other letters of support reiterated the respect that people had for the commissioner.[40] Such solid support ensured that Anslinger remained at the helm of the FBN during five presidential administrations, and remained the US representative at the CND until he retired in 1970. Having secured his position on the CND, Anslinger was thus able to forget about challenges to his authority, and concentrate upon what King has called America's quest to proselytize the world.[41]

With such support from within the United States, Anslinger found himself in a powerful position at the commission. As the leader of the CND's most dominant delegation, the commissioner resolved to play an important role in setting the agenda for international drug control efforts. As noted earlier, Anslinger and the American delegations were active in the first meetings of the CND. Although the organizational structure of the League of Nations had been transferred to the UN, many familiar faces inevitably remained present. According to Mr T. Hutson, the United Kingdom's representative to the third session of the CND in May 1948, the 'membership of the Commission represented a rich blend' of 'old hands like Anslinger' and 'Sharman ... who had very close relations with the USA delegate'.[42] In fact, as Bertil Renborg has noted and the examination of the commissioner's correspondence illustrates, Colonel 'Sharman was one of Anslinger's staunchest supporters ... he and Anslinger saw eye to eye on most problems and collaborated very closely both in and outside the [Advisory Opium] Committee and later the Commission [CND].'[43]

Because the United States had become more prominent during the final years of the League, the transfer of its drug control functions to the UN naturally resulted in the existence of a familiar personnel line-up. Thus, according to reports from the United Kingdom's delegate, there was a 'distinct tendency for the meetings to be dominated by the old hands, especially Sharman and Anslinger'. Hutson elaborated by noting that 'not only are they old hands, but they represent the two countries par excellence that look to international cooperation to mitigate drug consumption in their own countries'.[44] In a fascinating and remarkably far-sighted analysis of the international drug situation, Hutson reported that

the world drug problem has two fundamental aspects. Consumption of drugs, in an indigenous manner, by indigenous peoples (opium smoking in the near and far East and coca leaf chewing in South America); and consumption of drugs, chiefly alkaloids, by elements of the populations of civilized states but [in 1948], chiefly the USA, and a lesser degree Canada. It is this which has tended to make the USA the world task master in the field of narcotics.

He continued by saying that perhaps if it had not been *'for the white drug problem in the USA ...* [Hutson's emphasis] [the] suppression of the raw material and their indigenous consumption in a relatively harmless form would not have carried on as far as it has'.[45]

As this report shows, the British were well aware of the driving forces behind the international system. Hutson recognized the continuing American belief that through international regulations and continuing efforts for control at source the United States' own domestic narcotic drug problem could be solved. Although Hutson displayed a typically colonial view of the differences between 'civilized' and pre-industrialized non-Western societies, he did recognize at a very early stage an alarming phenomenon. The British delegate clearly appreciated the fact that the continuation of the American strategy had critical implications for the indigenous drug use of other nations – particularly countries which had value systems and cultural frames of references very different from those of the industrialized world, most notably the United States. He thus anticipates an intrusive impact of UN international drug control legislation: the imposition upon some nations of prohibitive policies that aim to outlaw the use of drugs that have been used indigenously for many years, sometimes centuries. This aspect of the US approach to international drug control was to become more significant as time went on.

Just as Hutson was critical of the US attitudes towards drug control, the British were themselves not above reproach in the eyes of Anslinger and Sharman. In response to the British practice of prescribing drugs to addicts rather than making them criminals, as in the United States and Canada, Sharman expressed his doubts on the effectiveness of what came to be known as the 'British system'. Thus, the Canadians and Americans continued to approach the drug issue in different ways from the British. This was an area that became a great point of contention between both governments for many years. The US delegation was convinced that, compared to other approaches, its prohibitive stance on drug use was not only morally sound, but also extremely effective.

Assured that the development of a strict international system was responsible for the reduction of drug addiction in the United States, Anslinger used the CND as a forum for preaching the prohibitive gospel. Only one year after the establishment of the UN control apparatus he proudly 'attributed to the development and efficiency of the international control system the fact that addiction in the United States among men examined for military service declined from 1 per 1500 in World War I to 1 per 10,000 in World

War II'. This is a considerable reduction, if the commissioner's figures are to be believed, although, of course, it is difficult to attribute categorically such a decline to the international system for drug control. As ever, Sharman agreed with this view, and stated that the figures for Canada were similar. Anslinger's belief that prohibition would solve all the problems surrounding the use of narcotic drugs gave him encouragement to pursue the internationalization of such a doctrine.

In 1948 the emerging patterns of domination and direction were becoming apparent within the UN. The United States, especially Anslinger, largely dominated the meetings of the CND and hence to a large extent controlled the formulation of policies for control. The American rise to prominence in the UN effectively meant that US delegations could continue their quest for the principles laid down during and before involvement with the League of Nations. The United States, however, was now in a position whereby it could achieve more concrete progress. Through American pressure and policies of linkage the USA was able to instigate and play a dominant role in the development of UN legislation.

During the operation of the CND the commissioner often appeared to have what essentially amounted to a free hand in the running of things. This can be seen in his support for the election of Monsieur C. Vaille, the French representative to the CND and the PCOB, to the DSB. Anslinger's support for Vaille provoked an unfavourable response from the UK representative to the CND. Although the move violated ECOSOC regulations that disallowed the appointment of an individual to the DSB while still a member of the PCOB, Anslinger managed to get support for Vaille's appointment.[46] The issue demonstrated the US prominence, while a telegram from Geneva to Britain's Foreign Office illustrating Anslinger's influence in the commission described how other representatives viewed the decision. The telegram stated that the Brazilian representative to the CND, Mr Garcia, supported Vaille's appointment to the DSB 'in a speech believed to have been written for him by Anslinger'.[47] The commissioner thus not only ignored ECOSOC regulations in order to further his influence through the appointment of delegates favourable to his position on drug control, but also had considerable influence over particular delegates.

In this case it is not surprising to note that the Brazilian representative appears to have yielded to pressure from Anslinger. It was noted earlier how economically insecure nations, especially in Latin America, often became the target of US pressure. In an interview for this study, Tom Green, the UK representative to the CND from 1957 to 1964, recalled how the United States exerted a great deal of influence over Latin American nations. The US delegation operated what was in essence a 'carrot and stick' policy and made no secret of the fact that they were actively pressurizing nations to follow the American line in the CND. According to Green, the use of economic aid was the favoured weapon and Anslinger is said to have often used his 'army of FBN agents', who appeared to have followed him everywhere, to persuade delegates to vote with the USA on drug control resolutions. Although the most notable use of such tactics was on the South and Latin American nations, Anslinger also put pressure upon the opium-producing nations of Turkey and Afghanistan.[48] It is therefore likely that a possible threat to withdraw foreign aid was sufficient to ensure that Brazil remained securely in the American corner. Consequently, Brazil was forcibly encouraged to concede to American-formulated prohibitive attitudes towards drug use, despite a dramatic difference in cultural heritage and history of use and control of psychoactive substances. Brazil, however, did not stand alone as a Latin American nation exposed to such US tactics. The political leaders of nations under US influence were encouraged to change the legal boundaries within which their populations had to live, not because of a democratically agreed consensus, but for other, usually economic, policy reasons. Thus national paradigms of drug control have clearly been influenced by external factors. A prime example of such a phenomenon can be seen with the UN's response to coca in the Andes, and we will return to this later in the chapter.

Although Anslinger remained one of the dominant figures in the CND, he did little to convince other delegates of his professional competence in running the proceedings. Always determined to ensure that the commission adhered to all American requests, Anslinger frequently allowed his enthusiasm to confuse the operation of the body. At the 1957 session of the CND, Tom Green informed the UK Home Office that 'I should not be a bit surprised if we get in a bit of a jam, particularly in view of the incompetence of the Chairman'[49] – the chairman on this occasion being Harry Anslinger. At the same session the discussions concerning the establishment of a UN laboratory to determine the origins of illegal drugs ran into difficulties – again, according to Green, owing to Anslinger's mismanagement.[50] Always keen to fight for the attainment of American drug control objectives, Anslinger frequently permitted his personal goals to hinder the operation of the commission. Despite being in the chair, the commissioner's blinkered approach often resulted in confusion at the CND meetings. This was the case in 1957 when the commission came together to discuss the proposed Single Convention on Narcotic Drugs. The UK delegation reported that

A proposal by Canada that the Commission should first consider the important points of principle received considerable support at the outset, but was eventually defeated, largely because the Chairman Anslinger, who was opposed to the suggestion, continually confused his position as Chairman and as US Representative.[51]

Anslinger's desire to accomplish his goals at the UN led him to adopt many different, sometimes underhand, strategies. His obsession with the prohibition of drugs often led him to pay scant regard to the rights of individuals and, while he was at the UN, of sovereign nations. Anslinger's passionate determination to fulfil his mission to internationalize prohibition and safeguard the interests of the United States meant that he would use almost any means necessary. In addition to working towards this goal at the official CND sessions, Anslinger also endeavoured to influence the operation of the UN's drug control framework through other important channels. These were the informal relationships that existed between individuals 'behind the scenes' at the United Nations.

ANSLINGER BEHIND THE SCENES: US INFORMAL ACTIVITIES AT THE UN

Although, as Bruun, Pan and Rexed observe, the primary source of influence within the international system is nations rather than people, they also recognize that 'influence is wielded by states through individuals'. As a result, 'a policy never emerges without having gone though the process which is carried on by individuals. Thus attempts at locating the sources of power must take account of persons also.'[52] These ideas have also been discussed by John Hadwen and Johan Kaufman, who note that 'The UN operates far more through personal relations and informal discussion than by formal exchanges and public debate.' They conclude, therefore, that 'The UN visitor ... hears, except in cases of major conflict, the public explanation of what has been argued in private.'[53]

Anslinger, a prominent figure in the CND, by virtue of both his position as the chief representative of the United States and his forceful character, naturally used such informal methods to influence the operation of the control apparatus, particularly the selection of personnel to work in the UN's drug control system. It is clear that Anslinger's ultimate aim was to create an efficient pro-US system. Although, as will be shown, Anslinger had some informal influence upon the decisions made in the other bodies within the drug control framework, it was the members of the CND who were the primary recipients of his informal activities.

As a direct successor of the League's Opium Advisory Committee, and under the Protocol of December 1946, all the functions formerly exercised by that body became the CND's responsibility. This produced a large degree of overlap in attitudes and personnel from the final days of the League. However, although the relationships between the national delegates on the CND may have resembled those of the League's OAC, the CND itself was to develop into an exclusive body as the years passed. This process was to have an enormous impact upon the informal decision-making procedures evident within the structure of the UN's drug control framework.

According to Bruun, Pann and Rexed, the original fifteen member nations of the Commission constitute a 'gentlemen's club'. This evolved with the continual renewal of contact between the same countries attending the yearly sessions.[54] A result of this has been to create an informal environment in which decisions are made exclusively and beyond the scrutiny of those nations that are not members of this select club. However, the authors of *The Gentlemen's Club* also recognize the existence of a club made up of persons. This, they claim, meets *prior* to the sessions of the CND to 'settle, in advance, some of the issues which are expected to crop up at the coming session'.[55] Since Anslinger was active on the international scene from 1933 until at least the mid-1960s,[56] it comes as little surprise that he featured prominently within this informal group. The fact that such a group exists is not unusual within an international organization. Indeed, as has been noted, most UN decisions are settled by informal negotiating processes outside the formal meetings. Informal negotiation often allows more flexibility because in private negotiating there is less need for face saving. Additionally, discussions away from formal circles permit personal relationships to play an important role. It has been noted that in the General Assembly of the UN 'personal contacts and friendships may at crucial moments count heavily in securing access to negotiations, if not as direct bargaining assets'.[57] The same can be argued for the situation encountered by members of the commission. Tom Green has substantiated this point. Green recalled how representatives on the commission frequently voted along the same lines as their friends. This often occurred for the simple reason that the resolutions were too complicated to be fully understood within the limited time available. The result was that delegates often voted for resolutions in the same manner as their closer colleagues.

However, although such informal discussion may provide opportunities for constructive negotiation away from the restrictive scrutiny of the 'outside world', it does present an alarming side. Such discussion can also allow dominant forces within the negotiating environment to play an extremely active and persuasive role. Away from public scrutiny, stronger nations are able to pressurize other countries into adopting a favourable stance on particular issues. This was to be the case with Anslinger and the US delegation at the CND. Anslinger's experience in the field of drug control and his forceful personality ensured that he became a leading figure at the Commission. These factors, combined with his position as representative of the UN's most prominent nation, permitted him to exert considerable pressure upon other national representatives. Consequently, through activities in informal channels, the United States has been able to complement activities in the formal sphere and apply pressure on countries to adhere to treaties or to enforce drug laws.

Since the creation of the CND in 1946, US centrality within the UN as a whole enabled US representatives to maintain good relations with the upper echelons of the organization. As noted earlier, close American relations with the first Secretary-General, the Norwegian Trygve Lie, provided the United States with an influential role within an organization that was supposed to favour no individual nation. US representatives consequently occupied an advantageous position in relation to other national delegations. Lie, the Secretary-General from 1946 to 1952, had been suggested and backed for the position by the American chief delegate to the Preparatory Commission of the UN, Adlai E. Stevenson. Ever conscious of his powerful backers, Lie was to become desperate to obtain US approval, particularly as he realized that without American support he would not gain re-election in 1951. During his tenure American–UN personal relationships generally appeared to mirror the relationship between Lie and the US government. The situation, as we shall see in the next chapter, was to change with later Secretaries–General. However, Lie's subservience to the US government permitted American delegations a great deal of freedom in action within the organization. Within the narcotic control framework, Anslinger was to maintain close and informal relations with the Assistant Secretary-General, the Chinese ex-Vice Minister of Foreign Affairs and one of the commissioner's old friends, Dr Victor Hoo Chi-tsai. Anslinger and Hoo had maintained close relations since working for narcotic control in the East before the outbreak of the Second World War. The Assistant Secretary-General occupied an influential role within the UN, and his friendly relationship with Anslinger was indicative of US ascendancy in the informal as well as the formal realm of the organization.[58] The commissioner's prominence and good relations with influential members of the UN permitted him a great deal of influence away from the formal channels of procedure. Having been presented with a dominant role within the CND, the commissioner worked to ensure that the rest of the control apparatus was staffed by individuals sympathetic to his own views on drug control. This was a process he pursued almost entirely away from the formal setting of the CND meetings. Anslinger's quest for a rigidly prohibitive UN framework for control reveals his important position within the system, and demonstrates the extent and impact of informal activities in the creation of the UN's control bodies.

Constantly concerned with the operation of a prohibitive-based international control system, Anslinger often worked to have what he felt to be suitable personnel appointed to important positions. This concern for staff selection was also heightened by what he saw as a breakdown in the UN drug control framework, particularly the Division on Narcotic Drugs, the section of the UN secretariat responsible for assisting ECOSOC with drug control matters. Noting as early as 1951 that the Division 'had disintegrated to the point of zero', the commissioner worked to select personnel who could maintain the effective functioning of the control apparatus. Evidence of unrest among the staff working in the drug control bodies also encouraged Anslinger to use his personal influence in an attempt to improve the situation. The DND, according to one staff member, was 'shot to pieces'.[59] This led the commissioner to believe that something needed to be done, and in the late 1950s Anslinger became actively involved with activities aimed at ensuring the election of suitable candidates to the Permanent Central Opium Board (PCOB) and the Drug Supervisory Body (DSB). Anslinger strove to place within these drug control bodies individuals who were either malleable or in agreement with US ideas on control. The result was to safeguard his own interests and strengthen the prohibitive outlook of the UN's control apparatus.

Such covert efforts can be seen in the summer of 1957, with correspondence between Sharman, himself a member of the PCOB and the DSB, and the commissioner, illustrating the 'behind the scenes' activities conducted in connection with appointments to both these bodies. To recap, the PCOB's role was to receive and compile statistics on narcotic drugs. It also had the power to embargo shipments to or from countries suspected of being centres of illicit trade. The DSB examined the estimates of national narcotic drug requirements and had the right to question, revise or establish estimates under certain conditions. They both, therefore, played a central role in the UN's control apparatus. Both the Colonel and Anslinger showed concern regarding the possible appointments of inexperienced individuals to the Supervisory Body. They consequently urged the American Herbert May, already a member of the PCOB, to stand for the position. This would, they claimed, have been beneficial for a number of reasons. First, it would have meant that an extremely experienced man, with ideas in line with those of the United States and Canada, would have worked with the DSB. It also seems to have fitted in with a separate scheme concerning the possibility of Anslinger's future appointment to the DSB. Sharman told Anslinger that 'Herbert has told me more than once that he is only too willing to retire as soon as you are willing and able to stand for the vacancy on the board that would thus be created and I think that an excellent program.'[60]

Such a suggestion may have only been speculative, yet it is illustrative of the way in which the established members of the control community seem to have regarded the system as their exclusive domain – a place where they could interchange their positions without hindrance from the rest of the organization. However, further discussions concerning the appointment of May must be seen in context to the so-called 'Personal Union' introduced by the Secretary-General in 1957. This concerned the proposed amalgamation of the DSB and the PCOB. The independent existence of the two bodies had been a historical accident, and as a consequence the functions of the DSB and the PCOB were closely related. Their combination was therefore intended to increase the efficiency of the control framework by reducing the duplication of tasks. The joining of the two bodies was provided for in the Single Convention on Narcotic Drugs, then still in the drafting stage. Although Anslinger opposed the Union, his plans concerning the appointment of May to the DSB were affected by the possibility of its implementation.

The CND, the body responsible for electing one of the four members of DSB, the other members being elected by the PCOB and World Health Organization, provided Anslinger with a solid platform from which to influence the selection process. He concurred with Sharman's ideas concerning the election of pro-US individuals to the DSB. However, although he agreed that May would have been a fine selection, Anslinger was keen to have his first choice appointed to the DSB. This was the long-serving French representative Monsieur Vaille. As already stated, Vaille was ultimately appointed to the DSB. This demonstrated both US dominance, and Anslinger's willingness and ability to ignore resolutions made by the ECOSOC. However, Anslinger's support for Vaille also illuminates the commissioner's informal activities, and his tendency to follow different policies from those favoured by the US State Department.

Anslinger's choice of the French delegate, who followed the traditional French policy on strict domestic controls, was ideal. Vaille had often supported Anslinger's prohibitive stance at CND sessions, favouring particularly strict control for cannabis and encouraging the 'forceful application' of control measures by governments.[61] Although France did not show complete support for prohibitive controls in any of its colonies or possessions, it favoured strict controls at home. The commissioner no doubt felt that Vaille would have been a trusted ally at the Drug Supervisory Body. Anslinger consequently wrote to the Colonel:

Your suggestion about Herbert representing the Commission on the Supervisory Body is a good one and will be followed in the event the Commission
rejects the personal union resolution of the Secretary-General. About half of
the Commission is in favor of Vaille to represent the Commission on the
Body and we are working to that end. If we have to pass on that the May
selection will be ideal.[62]

However, putting great faith in the power of the US delegation, Anslinger
believed that the Personal Union would be defeated in any event, thus
affecting the selection process to be adopted.

While monitoring the situation the State Department acknowledged
that Anslinger did not consider the Personal Union to be necessary.
Additionally, and regardless of Department wishes, it noted that he was
not keen to have Herbert May elected to the DSB, preferring Vaille instead.
A Department memorandum of a conversation with Anslinger noted that
he had 'expressed doubts about the advisability of Mr. May serving on
both bodies because of the strain it would mean for one of his advanced
years'. (By 1958 May was 81 years old.) Yet as the Department noted, 'Mr.
Anslinger had recommended Mr. May for re-election to the PCOB in
1957.'[63]

Thus, despite the State Department's clear desire to have Herbert May,
an American 'insider', appointed to the DSB, Anslinger used his personal
influence to push for Vaille's election. Anslinger resisted the calls of the
State Department to dictate his actions at the UN and essentially pursued
his own agenda on the issue. Hence we can see that the significance of
informal negotiation is not restricted to confrontations between nations.
As the Vaille case illustrates, activities beyond the formal negotiating
circles of the CND sometimes produced different approaches between
national governments and their own UN delegations. In this case,
Anslinger's actions met with Sharman's approval, and he noted in May
1958 that

I was particularly glad that the Commission rejected the attempted outside
dictation and appointed Vaille to the SB [Drug Supervisory Body], even if it
involved the rejection of our old friend Herbert. I am sure that he realizes
that it was the principle involved (anti-dictation) rather than anything
personal.[64]

It is therefore clear that neither Anslinger nor Sharman liked external
influences upsetting their plans. However, in this instance Anslinger,
much to the dissatisfaction of the State Department, prevailed. This point
was not lost on the British delegation, who observed at the fifteenth
session of the CND that

the State Department – but not … Anslinger – are upset by the Narcotic
Commission's decision to appoint Vaille (Fr) to the Drug Supervisory Body,
both because it was at the expense of May (US), and because it is a clear
violation of ECOSOC Resolution 667 H(XXIV).[65]

Anslinger's actions consequently demonstrate that as an individual he
held a significant degree of informal personal influence beyond the realm
of the official CND circles and the State Department. Although usually
safeguarding his own interests by conforming to State Department directives, the Vaille case illustrates the commissioner's willingness to follow
alternative policies on some occasions. This difference in opinion between
the US's chief representative to the CND and the US State Department was
not dramatic. However, it provides an insight into Anslinger's potential to
hold different opinions and pursue alternative paths to those favoured by
the State Department. Another, far more significant example of this
behaviour will be examined when Anslinger's attitude towards the Single
Convention on Narcotic Drugs is discussed in a later chapter.

Anslinger's behaviour concerning Vaille's appointment to the DSB
clearly supports Bruun, Pan and Rexed's claims concerning the existence
of a 'gentlemen's club' within the UN's narcotic control framework.
Anslinger, playing a leading role within such a group, was actively
involved in ensuring that individuals selected for important positions
viewed drug control policy from a pro-US perspective. The existence of
such a group is likely in any organization where individuals work
together over a period of years. Anslinger, with twenty-five years of
experience within the field of narcotic control, was bound to be a dominant figure within such an informal environment. Consequently, given
that Anslinger received solid support from other 'old hands' like Sharman
and May, it comes as little surprise to discover American dominance. Such
prominence was also used in influencing the selection of personnel for the
PCOB. In 1958 Anslinger, Sharman and Vaille used 'considerable muscle'
to affect the composition of the Board.[66]

In addition to his friendships with other national representatives, particularly Colonel Sharman, Anslinger also maintained close informal
relationships with members of the secretariat. A particularly important
example of such a relationship can be seen between Anslinger and the
American international civil servant Adolf Lande. Lande played a central
role in the development of the UN's international narcotic control legislation. In fact, he was primarily responsible for drafting all the drug treaties
enacted between 1946 and 1971, including the 1961 Single Convention.
According to the extensive correspondence between Anslinger and Lande,
the commissioner introduced Lande to the field of international drug

control.[67] It is also interesting to note that when Lande left the employ of the UN he represented the American Pharmaceutical Manufacturers Association at the 1971 Vienna Conference among other gatherings. Anslinger subsequently possessed an influential ally in the secretariat and his friendship with Lande was significant because of the central role the international civil servant played in the development of transnational drug law.

An examination of Lande's correspondence to Anslinger reveals the extent of the supposedly neutral civil servant's pro-American stance on international drug control. Although, as noted earlier, the US-influenced UN Charter sought to prevent staff from favouring their own national governments, it becomes clear that Lande did function in a partisan fashion. In doing so, he was consistently to support the US approach towards prohibitive drug control. Lande's pro-American, or more accurately pro-Anslinger, stance was particularly evident during the early 1960s; a period when the representatives of many non-Western, and frequently former colonized nations became more active within all areas of the UN's work.

Decolonization had been one of the United States' post-war aims and the decline of the European colonial nations after 1945 ensured that many fledgling states made their debut onto the international stage in the years that followed. This inevitably included their involvement with the UN. Rosemary Righter comments that it was natural that newly established governments 'should seek to use the UN organization' while they suffered 'institutional fragility' and 'diplomatic inexperience'.[68] However, the pace of increase in UN membership, particularly the involvement of independent African and Asian nations, was unexpected. As Righter notes, Brian Urquhart, a long-serving UN under-secretary, recalled that in 1945 most nations assumed that decolonization 'would take a hundred years'. In reality the process was far quicker. This fact was reflected in a rapid expansion in the organization's membership from 51 to 159 within four decades.[69] One significant product of such an increase in representation at the UN of what have been labelled Third World countries was a growth in their influence within the organization. The process, however, led Lande to worry that the UN drug control apparatus was being staffed increasingly by non-Westerners. He felt this lowered the standards maintained by the Western personnel, who, he believed, appreciated the importance of strict international control. In his opinion the result would undermine the years of work done by Anslinger and the US delegation.[70] Lande's fears regarding the increase in non-Western appointments became particularly evident when the UN adopted a policy of so-called geographic distribution during the early 1960s. This procedure aimed to increase the representation of the growing number of smaller non-Western nations of the UN in all areas of the organization's work. This involved all functional agencies, including those concerned with drug control. The result, in the eyes of many of the established, primarily Western, members of the organization, was that it lowered professional standards. This was a view shared by Lande. He felt that the UN narcotic drug control apparatus was being used as a 'dumping ground' for national representatives who were 'only interested in their salaries' and who did not 'have the necessary knowledge and experience to make a useful contribution' to drug control.[71]

Lande's attitude towards the involvement of non-Westerners in the drug control framework also displayed his racial prejudice and lack of understanding for cultural differences in the perception of drug use. For example, when in 1962 it looked likely that a Pakistani was to be appointed to head the DND, Lande noted that the man, Mr Mir Khan, was unsuited for the position. He claimed this was because Khan did not see drug abuse in the same terms as the Western, or more precisely American representatives, of the UN. Accordingly, he noted that Khan had

> no knowledge of narcotics control and his home country Pakistan where opium eating is still tolerated does not seem to me to be the best place for acquiring an appropriate understanding of our problems. In this part of the world they often look upon narcotics consumption as we regard alcoholic drinks.[72]

Clearly then Lande, a man who played a central role in developing UN control legislation, had little respect for cultural differences. The fact that different drugs had different places in cultures of varying backgrounds was ignored in preference for the dominant Western perception of drug abuse. Lande's culturally biased attitudes also became evident in his belief that opposition to the American prohibitive stance on cannabis represented 'the low intellectual level' and 'violent anti-Americanism' of the Africans who worked in the DND.[73] Again Lande's stance was in direct conflict with the provisions of the UN Charter. This states in article 1 paragraph 3 that one of the organization's aims was 'To achieve international cooperation in solving international problems of an economic, social, cultural or humanitarian character, and in promoting and encouraging respect for human rights and for fundamental freedoms for all without distinction as to race.' Lande, much like Hamilton Wright and other international campaigners, including Anslinger, continued to associate drug use with non-Western, particularly non-American, peoples.

Lande, like Anslinger, possessed a keen awareness for bureaucratic survival. When serving as a staff member of the DND, he argued convincingly for a single secretariat. However, when after the passage of the

Single Convention he was appointed secretary of the International Narcotic Control Board (INCB), his arguments were equally convincing in the other direction. The close and informal nature of the working relationship nurtured by the two men illustrated Anslinger's prominent position within the drug control machinery. His endeavours to control personnel selection, and help Lande in his career, provide further evidence of the influence of both Anslinger and the United States in the UN drug control system.

In the early 1960s Anslinger once again became involved with attempts to 'stack' the PCOB with pro-US personnel. Answering Lande's request that he use the United States' authority to assist in his own appointment to the board's secretariat, Anslinger made moves to use his considerable influence within informal circles. Lande, keen to become the Secretary of the PCOB, asked Anslinger to make an 'intervention' to ensure that the contract of Swiss international civil servant Mr L. Atzenwiler as the Secretary of the PCOB 'should not be prolonged'. Lande was concerned because Atzenwiler 'had been able to induce the Swiss to intervene on his behalf'. This was a serious consideration because, as Lande remarked, 'Switzerland having bought United Nations bonds is not a negligible influence in United Nations affairs.' It is interesting to note that, according to Lande, not only the United States benefited from financial involvement with the UN. However, Lande continued to inform Anslinger that Swiss support for Atzenwiler could be countered and 'offset by a similar approach ... by the local U.S. delegation'. The civil servant's comments also revealed interesting aspects of Anslinger's own position with regard to the rest of the US delegation. Lande commented that, 'I am a little afraid that the U.S. delegation will perhaps not approach' the pertinent individuals as mentioned, 'but will limit itself to contacting the Bureau of Personnel in New York which might not be equally effective. Do you think you could do something about this?'[74] The remarks suggest that Lande saw Anslinger's influence as being independent of that of the US delegation as a whole. Although in this particular case Atzenwiler continued to hold the position as Secretary to the PCOB for one more year, Lande still had faith in the influence of the US delegation. Writing to Anslinger in August 1962, Lande noted that although he had lost out to the Swiss civil servant in this instance, 'an intervention of the U.S. delegation on my behalf will be very helpful for the future and I am most grateful to you for the initiative you took in this connexion'.[75] Lande's efforts were eventually to result in his appointment as Secretary of the PCOB – an appointment no doubt aided by Anslinger's lobbying.

ANSLINGER'S T-MEN AT THE UN

Anslinger did not restrict his lobbying tactics to the UN control apparatus in Geneva. With few inhibitions about sending his FBN agents, who were often called Treasury T-men, abroad on investigations, Anslinger readily used men from the bureau to collect information for his own use at the CND. They, like the commissioner, often refused to allow matters of etiquette or diplomatic tact to get in the way of their 'fact'-finding missions.

An example of such a 'fact'-finding expedition which seems to exemplify the entire American approach towards other nations' drug control systems can be found when looking at the so-called 'Special Mission' of Federal Bureau of Narcotics agent Wayland 'L' Speer. Speer's position in the FBN as one of Anslinger's top agents was to result in his becoming second in command in the bureau after Anslinger's retirement in 1962. As a favourite operative he was to engage in many activities concerning the UN's narcotic control efforts. In January 1954 Speer made a trip to the Far East with the chief purpose of collecting information for the use of the US representative at the CND, that is to say his boss Harry Anslinger.[76] His destination was the Portuguese possession of Macau, an island identified by the UN as a source of illicit opium. A letter to the British consulate in Macau from a British political adviser in Hong Kong describes the results of Speer's investigations:

> He visited Macau at the end of February and called upon the Governor … and various officers of the police, to all of whom he made the most direct and indiscreet enquiries as to the political 'rackets' … the size and origin of the personal fortunes of the more senior residents of Macau and narcotic and strategic smuggling. Spear [sic] then commenced to discuss the details of Macau's strategic trade with the mainland, but was in each case ejected from the various offices he visited at about this stage of the conversation. I rather gather he also endeavoured to bribe the Head of the Special Branch after some three to four minutes of introduction …. The upshot of this visit has been a very firm note of protest from the Government to the US Consul-General in Hong Kong, so David McKillip, the assistant Consul-General tells me; and my Portuguese contacts inform me that the Portuguese propose also to deliver another note on the subject in Washington.[77]

Speer's lack of discretion and understanding of political etiquette clearly did nothing to help his mission. This comes as no great surprise since, according to the recollections of the UK representative Tom Green, Speer was at the best of times 'indiscreet and blunt'. In addition to this, his apparently blinkered approach towards achieving his aim of providing dramatic evidence of drug smuggling and production in the Far East for Anslinger led to further encounters with diplomatic officials. The correspondence between the British diplomats continues by stating that

> Spear's [sic] opening remarks to the police were, I gather, along the lines that he had already had considerable success in uncovering various forms of vice and embargo beating in Hong Kong, and was hoping to 'keep up his record in Macau'. He was instructed to leave Macau on the second day of his visit by order of the Governor.

Speer's behaviour in Macau led the political adviser to Hong Kong to note that Speer's antics reminded him of 'Admiral Lamb's [recent] comments that the Americans appear determined to solve the Eastern problem by all means short of diplomacy'.[78]

THE UNITED STATES, THE UN, CANNABIS AND COCA

American diplomatic efforts in the UN drug control sphere were in reality making considerable headway, albeit in a heavy-handed fashion. Through the exploitation of a dominant position in the CND, Anslinger and the US delegation not only achieved a large degree of influence at the procedural level, but, as a direct result, played a formative role in the creation of international control legislation. Consequently, many of the deeply entrenched beliefs that the United States held concerning the control of psychoactive substances became firmly established in the body of UN-designed international law. During the course of the CND's operation, a number of key issues remained prominent. Among these were the topics of cannabis and coca, and this provides a good example of American attitudes towards the use of drugs in other societies.

The UN's approach to the control of cannabis directly followed that adopted by the League of Nations' OAC, as discussed earlier. The CND automatically inherited an approach to controlling the drug that was dominated by the policy of prohibition. Commissioner Anslinger's practice of sensationalization and misinformation helped ensure that no other policies were considered. For instance, at the first session of the CND he claimed to have concrete examples that proved the relationship between the use of cannabis and crime. Consequently, although the Commission admitted that in some areas of the world, particularly the India–Pakistan subcontinent, the drug was widely used as a medicine, moves were made to outlaw the cultivation of cannabis globally.

The World Health Organization (WHO) also echoed American beliefs on the drug's addictive properties. The WHO's Expert Committee on

Drugs Liable to Produce Addiction, which was obligated under the UN's drug control treaties to act in an advisory capacity to the CND, concluded that cannabis use definitely came under 'the terms of its definition of addiction'.[79] Although debate on the properties of marijuana continued, the UN refused to deviate from its prohibitive policy. For example, at the request of the CND the Expert Committee prepared a study on the subject in 1953. It came to the predictable conclusion that cannabis was dangerous 'from every point of view, whether physical, mental, social or criminological'.[80] Ignoring some opinion in the United States which argued that cannabis did not pose any real danger, most notably the La Guardia Report of 1944, the UN moved to outlaw cannabis completely. With the influential WHO staunchly supporting a pro-American stance, the CND was bound to pursue a policy of prohibition. The rationale behind the WHO's rigid position on the drug becomes clear when it is discovered that the German Pablo Osvaldo Wolff was the Secretary to the Expert Committee. Wolff, described by Rufus King as the 'American protégé',[81] had a very close working relationship with Anslinger and fully endorsed the commissioner's ideas linking cannabis with crime and insanity. In fact their impressions of the deleterious effects of the drug were so similar that in 1949 Anslinger had written the foreword to one of Wolff's publications on cannabis. His role in determining the Expert Committee's interpretation of particular drugs' addictive properties resulted in a committee that was essentially subservient to American interests. With WHO backing, 1954 and 1955 saw the CND adopt a rigidly prohibitionist line towards cannabis. The Expert Committee ordained that the use of cannabis was no longer justified for any legitimate purpose. Having dropped the drug entirely from the US pharmacopoeia, the United States became the main force in the drive for a global ban on all cannabis use. Despite Anslinger's statements in 1937 claiming that marijuana did not lead to the use of other drugs, the USA fully endorsed the CND's view that there was a 'danger that cannabis abuse is very likely to be a forerunner of addiction to more dangerous addicting drugs'.[82] In a blatant move to protect the CND from attack for its policies on the drug, the Commission also 'emphasized that any publicity to the contrary was misleading and dangerous'.[83]

Following a strictly prohibitionist approach to the drug, the USA pushed for and was eventually successful in securing the inclusion of cannabis in the Single Convention of 1961. American domination of the UN control apparatus was consequently to ensure that the organization pursued a US-oriented policy of control for cannabis. Despite a long history of use, a time scale of thousands of years for many nations, and the culturally ingrained place of cannabis in many countries around the world, the CND adopted prohibition.

However, cannabis was not the only drug with a special place in non-Western societies to suffer such a fate. The official attitude taken by the CND towards the practice of coca chewing was that it was a drug 'abuse' and as such should be eradicated. From a reading of official UN literature it appears as if the UN took such an approach to the issue in response to the request of Peru, Peru being an Andean nation where the practice was widespread and deeply ingrained within the fabric of the population's cultural heritage. Indeed, as records of the 1947 CND session observe,

> At the request of the Government of Peru for a survey of the effects of the chewing of the coca leaf by a large part of the population in many states in South America, the Commission recommended to the Economic and Social Council that a commission of inquiry should be sent to Peru and such others of the countries concerned as may give their approval, and that the inquiry should include the possibilities of limiting the production and regulating the distribution of coca leaves.[84]

The results of the survey were expected to have a great impact upon the practice. Those involved with the CND and other groups keenly awaited its conclusions. The editor of the *Encyclopedia Americana* expected the results to be 'tremendous', believing that 'the report of the Commission would have a great effect on Peru, Bolivia, Argentina, Chile and Colombia'.[85]

However, when one looks into the reality of the situation it becomes evident that there are considerable problems with the traditional interpretation of the UN approach. Research had been conducted by some sections of the Peruvian academic community which strove to prove that coca chewing was a harmful practice. Work pioneered by Dr Carlos Gutiérrez-Noriega attempted to prove that coca-chewers were usually 'alienated' and 'antisocial', as well as being inferior in intelligence, initiative and adaptability, and more likely to suffer from 'behavioural abnormalities'. These experts then proceeded to invite the UN to conduct a full international inquiry into the coca 'problem'. In this way they hoped, as Anthony Henman puts it, to secure 'research money and finally bring enough political pressure to bear on their unfortunate countryman to achieve their ultimate aim, which was " ... to free a people from the slavery of an addictive drug" '.[86] It appears that the Peruvian authorities were not motivated entirely by the desire to improve the lives of the population. Despite attacking an ancient and commonplace activity, the prospect of UN funding and a means for the nation's elite to control the populace obviously provided ample reason to request a UN investigatory commission.

Additionally, the UN Commission of Inquiry on the Coca Leaf was itself far from objective from the outset. Its head, the American Howard B. Fonda, vice-president of Burroughs Wellcome and a director of the American Pharmaceutical Manufacturers Association, could not claim to be an impartial observer. As a keen supporter of Commissioner Anslinger, Fonda clearly set out to develop US beliefs on the drug and simultaneously defend the interests of the pharmaceutical industry in the United States. In fact as early as 1949, following the recognizable US approach towards drug use and non-American races, Fonda stated openly that the use of coca was harmful and a possible cause of 'racial degeneration' among the Indians. The findings of the commission, he was confident, would definitely confirm his assumptions.

However predetermined the results of the commission appeared to be, few individuals or nations opposed its objectives. Anslinger's ally Dr Wolff, representing the WHO, confirmed the UN's stance on the coca-chewing issue in 1952 by stating that in the view of the WHO, the practice definitely did lead to addiction.[87] Henman argues that one reason for this lack of opposition may have been that the 'particular period under consideration – the Second World War and its sequel – constituted a veritable high-water mark in the ascendancy of the U.S. in Latin America and the flowering of *yanqui* expansionism in its classic phase'.[88]

The commission considered the 'problem' in two ways, and claimed that both aspects were closely linked,

> since the Indians chew the coca on account of its cocaine content, and since as long as there is a large production of coca leaf for chewing purposes, it is inevitable that some of it be used for the extraction of illicit cocaine.[89]

On the basis of the preconceptions of the commission, many people in the Andes region were to be pressurized into outlawing a traditional practice because it provided the potential to supply a Westernized drug habit. As the UN saw it, as long as there was chewing, there could be no effective control of production and clandestine manufacture of cocaine, a drug which was largely in use beyond the borders of the Andean region.

As a result of the coca leaf commission's work and active support and lobbying from the United States, the ninth session of the CND in 1954 saw all countries at the meeting agree that 'coca leaf chewing constitutes a form of drug addiction and is harmful'. The CND proposed to ECOSOC a resolution

> recommending that governments concerned limit gradually and as quickly as practical the cultivation and export of the coca leaf to medical, scientific and other legitimate purposes ... [and] continue their efforts to abolish

progressively the importation of coca leaf for chewing and adopt or continue
to carry out appropriate programmes of health education.[90]

Despite such an apparent success in the US quest for the world prohibition of drugs for anything other than medical and scientific purposes,
Anslinger was not completely satisfied. In connection with the issue's
inclusion within a draft of the proposed Single Convention, CND records
note that 'Referring to the majority recommendation that the chewing of
coca leaf should be suppressed gradually over a period of 15 years, he
[Anslinger] recalled that a similar decision had been taken in regard to
opium smoking, with generally unsatisfactory results.'[91] The commissioner was not content to permit the nations involved with the
suppression of coca to approach the issue in a gradualist manner. This
would, in his opinion, produce a situation whereby drug use would never
be totally eradicated. Anslinger compared the coca leaf situation with that
of opium smoking in India. He believed that 'the Peruvian Government
might make the same undertaking as those that India had accepted for
opium, i.e. to fix a definite date after which the chewing of the coca leaf
would be prohibited'. Although he did agree 'that certain countries might
find it hard to eradicate an ingrained habit, the suppression of which was
conditioned in economic and social progress',[92] it is clear that Anslinger
was determined to use his position to outlaw coca chewing in South
America as quickly as possible. Any obstacles that appeared to obstruct
this goal were forcibly opposed. This was indeed the case when there had
been some disagreement concerning the commission's approach to the
coca issue. Anslinger

> recalled that the CND had hitherto accepted WHO's definition of drug
> addiction, i.e. drugs that produced addiction and those which caused the
> formation of a habit. One of the characteristics of addiction producing drugs
> was that they were detrimental to the individuals and to society. Now that
> was precisely the case with the coca leaf. [Anslinger] did not understand
> how the Commission could dismiss the question and hold that it did not
> come within its terms of reference.[93]

Despite such differences in opinion at the CND, once the official anti-
coca strategy had been adopted the UN proceeded to take measures to
implement the commission's recommendations. At UN-sponsored
regional meetings in Rio de Janeiro and Lima, in 1961 and 1962 respectively, 'The Commission considered that discussion of the problem could,
therefore, be abandoned since unanimous conclusions had been reached,
and that the time had come for action.'[94] Even at this stage in the battle
against coca chewing, some fifteen years since its birth, Anslinger and his

colleagues remained acutely aware of the existence of opposition to the US-style prohibitive stance on the issue. Anslinger was informed that the Lima conference 'may be considered to have been successful. It recommended unanimously that coca leaf chewing, being a harmful habit, should be abolished.' However, he was reminded that 'As you know there are strong forces in this part of the world who still expound the view that coca leaf chewing is good for the Indians.'[95] By the early 1960s, and despite sporadic opposition, the UN had adopted irreversibly the policy to outlaw coca leaf chewing. The highly Americanized 1947 commission into the issue had provided the foundations upon which prohibitive measures could be taken. The question of coca was ultimately included in the final draft of the 1961 convention, with article 49 stating that coca leaf chewing must be abolished within twenty-five years of the convention's coming into force. Its inclusion, though ludicrously unrealistic and too gradualist for Anslinger's pleasure, was a demonstration of the extent of US influence within the CND's approach to culturally ingrained drug use.

THE US BATTLE AGAINST THE 'EVIL' OF OPIUM

As an example of the prominence of US ideas on the control of drugs, coca was not to stand alone. The United States' dominance in the wartime Allied coalition had ensured that the process to eradicate opium smoking quickened after 1945. Although the 1912 international conference at The Hague had made the abolition of the practice a treaty obligation, progress before the Second World War remained slow. No agreement was reached on a definite date for the prohibition of opium smoking. Having successfully eliminated opium monopolies in both Allied and captured territories, the United States consequently pushed eagerly for the outright prohibition of opium smoking world-wide. In 1946 Anslinger enunciated the US position to Secretary of State James F. Byrnes: 'The Government of the United States has on every appropriate occasion endeavoured very earnestly to induce other Governments to accept the doctrine that the use of opium should be restricted to medicinal and scientific purposes.' In circumstances similar to that of coca, the commissioner conceded that some nations were experiencing difficulty in the suppression of the practice. He continued, 'A number of governments have signified their acceptance of this principle, but unfortunately some countries have not found it possible owing to special circumstances, to eliminate completely the use of opium smoking and eating.'[96] Although acknowledging that in many nations the practice of opium smoking was culturally ingrained, and thus difficult to eradicate, Anslinger continued to push forcefully for a policy of prohibition. He also again 'recalled how it had always been the U.S. policy to combat the abuse of narcotic drugs, and to limit their use to strictly medicinal and scientific requirements'.[97] At the 1948 CND session Anslinger was critical of the pace of change in some regions, noting 'the slow progress of the French in suppressing the use of smoking opium in Indochina' and urging that 'the opium smoking territories forbid imports of opium for non-medical purposes'. Such pressure resulted in a resolution for ECOSOC from the Commission which invited 'all countries in which opium smoking has been at any time prevalent to adopt the policy of suppression', and further requested 'such Governments forthwith to prohibit the import of raw opium into their territories except for medical and scientific purposes'.[98] As a result of such efforts, in 1953 the CND made further forceful recommendations to ECOSOC to suppress the practice. In 1959 Thailand became one of the last countries where opium smoking was commonplace to join the list of nations that had prohibited the custom. Consequently, according to UN literature, 'the practice became illegal throughout the world with minor exceptions'.[99]

The question of opium control was one that occupied a great deal of the CND's time. The issue was complex owing to the drug's medical value, it being the natural source of morphine and codeine. Although in 1946 some parts of the world still consumed opium for non-medical purposes, its production was largely for the extraction of morphine. However, fears existed that the overproduction of the drug would supply illicit markets, and thus constitute a source of drug addiction. Anslinger, adhering to the established US policy of urging the prohibition of the drug for anything other than scientific and medical purposes, worked hard to control the production of opium. He used the forum of the CND to warn nations against producing raw opium in quantities that exceeded the world's medical and scientific needs. Demonstrating his strict prohibitionist beliefs, Anslinger countered claims that a multiple-approach strategy could reduce opium use and noted that 'Education could not replace the adoption of legislative measures. The best remedy against drug addiction would obviously be to reduce the production of opium to the quantities required to cover medicinal needs.'[100] Although opium had a clearly defined medical use, Anslinger still believed that its production could be completely eliminated. He was convinced that synthetic drugs could be used to replace opium as a source of medicinal products and strove to convince the international community that poppy cultivation should be eradicated. 'In his view, complete elimination of all opium production, supplemented by rigid enforcement and controls over licensed manufacturers of synthetic narcotics, would result in a tremendous reduction in drug addiction.'[101]

This belief, however, did not gain widespread support. Particular opposition came from nations where opium was used widely. For example, the Indian representative, Mr Mendia, noted that

> Indians considered edible opium not only a tonic but a panacea. Moreover the consumption of it, whatever might be its actual medical value, was so moderate that it in no way induced the drug habit as did the use of drugs in Europe or America.[102]

Mendia thus made an important point, for which Anslinger clearly had no appreciation; that is to say, the difference between the intensity of drug use in different societies. Although Anslinger wanted the complete eradication of raw opium, he continued to make efforts for the interim control of the drug's production. Commenting on the progress made towards opium control in 1950, he noted that 'Efforts had been made over the past 40 years to limit the production of opium and work must not be abandoned when at last it was beginning to bear fruit.'[103] Indeed, Anslinger was not forced to wait long for the UN to adopt an opium control policy that he found satisfactory.

The commissioner remained convinced that strict regulations on all aspects of drug control would reduce the incidence of drug addiction. This included all stages of the opium cycle: the production of opium and the trafficking, sale and use of heroin. Indeed, in claiming that the United States' continuing pursuit of strict narcotic legislation was the only effective approach to the drug issue, Anslinger used the CND to praise America's draconian laws of control. In a statement concerning addiction among teenagers in the United States, Anslinger followed his recognizable though contradictory tack. He pronounced that 'Addicts first used marijuana, but after they had become inured to the drug and it was no longer powerful enough, they had started to use heroin regularly.' He then informed the commission that 'The joint action of the Federal and State authorities was the imposition of severe penalties for traffickers supplying drugs to minors – in some cases the law provided for the death penalty – and achieved excellent results.' Insinuating that the other members of the CND were not approaching the drug issue with the same enthusiasm as America, Anslinger finally

> stressed the fact that the U.S. had had the courage to admit the problem and to face it squarely and energetically. It would be good if some countries where drug addiction existed among minors but was wilfully ignored by the authorities, were to follow that example.[104]

Although Anslinger was unable to coerce other nations into adopting laws which were as harsh as those in the United States, American efforts at the

UN did succeed in securing legislation that followed another US tactic targeted at reducing opiate addiction. This was the US goal of controlling the production of opium at source.

THE 1953 OPIUM PROTOCOL

The year 1953 saw the completion of a protocol to limit the production of opium, an American aim since the early years of US involvement in the international control movement. The scheme was originally instigated by the French as an alternative to an oppressively strict American international monopoly plan. However, Anslinger and the American delegation had ensured that the protocol made great strides towards the all-important goal of limiting opium production at source.

The Protocol for Limiting and Regulating the Cultivation of the Poppy Plant, the Production of, International and Wholesale Trade in and Use of Opium was based on the central provision that the 'production of opium would be limited with a view to equating the amounts harvested to the amounts needed for medical and scientific purposes'.[105] It restricted the number of states permitted to produce opium for export to seven: Bulgaria, Greece, India, Iran, Turkey, the USSR and Yugoslavia. The condition required for protocol to come into force was that it be ratified by at least three of these nations. The protocol empowered the PCOB to employ certain supervisory and enforcement measures, such as requests for information, proposals for remedial measures, local inquiries, and sometimes the imposition of an embargo on the importation or exportation of opium, or both.

Although the protocol was heralded as a major advance for the international control system, S. K. Chattergee argues that it was of limited scope in that it concerned itself only with combating the illicit traffic in opium. Limitation of use to medical and scientific purposes was, Chattergee claims, a 'loose undertaking', since a precise determination of the medical and scientific needs of a country was fraught with difficulties.[106]

The Americans, however, saw the protocol as a huge step forward in their battle against illicit opium production. On 27 June 1953 Anslinger reported that '34 countries represented at the UN opium conference in New York today ... signed a Protocol under which annual production of opium is reduced [to] the medical needs of the world'.[107] According to the commissioner the United States would 'be one of the chief beneficiaries of the agreement because overproduction of opium feeds the illicit traffic into the US'. He continued stressing the traditional American supply side strategy, claiming that

US delegates to international narcotic conferences for the past forty years have been working toward the acceptance of an agreement to limit opium production.... This is a new departure and marks the most important single step in the fight against drug addiction. For the first time the solution gets at the crux of the narcotic problem, and limits the source of the evil of the cultivation of the opium poppy.[108]

Although the American aim of limitation of the use of narcotic drugs to medical and scientific needs had been incorporated in the Hague Convention of 1912, no working machinery had been provided by that convention for carrying out its prohibitionist intentions. As a result, Anslinger reiterated the traditional American stance regarding the issue of opium production, stating that

while many provisions of this first international opium convention have stood the test of time and have served as the basis for far reaching restrictive legislation, including enactment of the Federal Harrison Narcotic Act in the United States, it became evident that it did not go far enough. Some sort of international watchdog was essential to keep the recalcitrant nations in line .... The Protocol signed today will help close these gaps.[109]

The protocol was also deemed to have been an advance for the American prohibitionist cause in that there was no exception 'for the use of smoking opium', which was as a result 'outlawed except for a very few areas in Pakistan and India'. Not missing the opportunity to chastise the former colonial powers, the US representative went on to highlight the fact that, according to American perceptions of the situation, the past treaties relating to opium had served as protection for countries like Great Britain, France, the Netherlands, Portugal and Japan, which had maintained smoking monopolies in the Far East. Continuing on this theme, Anslinger stated that the protocol recognized the abolition of these monopolies, which was accomplished through the representations of the US government during the Second World War. Despite the fact that several countries had large commercial interests at stake, the commissioner noted that the US government received co-operation in this 'diplomatic, economic' and, significantly, 'moral reform'.[110] Anslinger's mention of moral reform illustrated his continuing belief that the American prohibitive approach to drug control remained morally superior to other policies. He naturally declined to refer to the pressure that had been applied in order to encourage other nations to adopt such terms. As a final cautionary note, Anslinger also stated that 'In countries like Communist China, Burma, Thailand and Mexico, where opium is grown illegally those Governments must take firm measures to cope with this illegal production'.[111]

Although it awaited ratification until 1963, the passage of the protocol was symbolic of US prominence within the UN control framework. Taking much credit for the protocol, Anslinger informed his friend Judge William T. McCarthy that

> As the Chief US delegate at this Conference I have to carry the ball. It has been a very tough period for me, and although I feel the need for a rest I have to stick to my duty and try to have our Government the first country to ratify this important treaty.[112]

The commissioner's work did not go unnoticed within the US government. Richard S. Wheeler, Acting Chief of the State Department's Division of International Conferences, wrote to Anslinger, 'On behalf of the Department may I express appreciation for the able leadership you have given the United States Delegation and for the contribution you and your colleagues have made to this important international project.'[113]

With the acceptance of the protocol by the UN, the United States succeeded in internationalizing a central tenet of its drug control strategy for opium: control at source. Although the USA had to wait for another ten years before the protocol came into force upon ratification by a sufficient number of adherents, the protocol was dramatically indicative of the heightened support that the international community gave to schemes that followed American principles of control. Great progress had clearly been made and Anslinger demonstrated his satisfaction with the course taken by the international movement. In the introduction to a book he co-authored in 1953 he wrote that

> It is a little known and too seldom mentioned fact that there is one important field of international diplomacy in which the US Government has for several decades met with amazing and continuing success. There have been few more dramatic or more forceful efforts at international collaboration than those in the field of the control of narcotic drugs.[114]

Indeed, while the 1950s saw the exportation of US political and military doctrines, the internationalization of drug prohibition went largely unnoticed.

Greatly encouraged by the developments in the international control system, after 1953 Anslinger continued to use the CND as a platform to encourage the export of US prohibitive ideals. Always enthusiastic in his praise for the US system at the UN, Anslinger was keen to answer the queries of the French delegate, Vaille, concerning the reported decrease in the cases of addiction in the USA, at the CND's twelfth session in 1957. The US representative replied that 'the reasons lay in the severe penalties imposed by the courts in accordance with Federal and State legislation'.[115]

Citing Pennsylvania and Louisiana as two examples, he went on to claim that 'a relaxation in the severity of penalties and of lowering the minimum prison sentence, was immediately reflected in the statistics by an increase in the number of drug addicts'.[116] Reflecting the US establishment's satisfaction with the 1951 Boggs Act, and the even harsher 1956 Narcotics Control Act, the CND became a place where American delegates espoused the virtues of strict mandatory sentencing for drug offences. The Acts raised fines and lengths of imprisonment, particularly in relation to marijuana, and introduced a maximum sentence of death on the recommendation of a jury to anyone who sold or gave heroin to a person under 18 years old. They were, according to David Musto, 'the high point of federal punitive actions against narcotics'.[117] As such these laws were regarded by successive US delegations as the benchmark for all national drug control strategies.

Regardless of national preferences for the formulation of drug law, the United States continued to use its strength within the UN drug control apparatus to force other countries to follow a prohibitive policy. Some delegations were in a position to resist such US pressure. Tom Green noted that

> It must, however, be remembered that some amendments and changes in emphasis might be necessary when adapting to one country what had been found useful in another .... It would also be less easy to pass measures imposing very heavy mandatory penalties in a country like the UK, where drug addiction and illicit traffic were not serious problems, than the US.[118]

Many nations with culturally ingrained ideas on drug control that differed from those in the United States were less able to resist. As the case of UN coca policies demonstrated, the economically weaker countries of the world were not in a position to withstand predominantly US pressure. This facet of the Americanization of transnational drug control will be discussed in more depth in a later chapter. Without facing serious opposition, the United States continued to make attempts to influence the direction taken by the UN's international drug control system. With the success of the 1953 Opium Protocol, Anslinger and US delegations sought to further develop an international system within which all drug use was prohibited except for scientific and medical purposes.

CONCLUSION

The hegemonic status possessed by the United States in the early post-war era led to its intimate involvement with the creation and functioning of the

UN. Harry Anslinger, as the USA's chief delegate to the CND, was able to exploit US influence and work, through both formal and informal channels, towards the development of international legislation and the subsequent creation of a prohibitive regime for the control of drugs. The exploitation of economic and political power and the practice of linking the issue of drug control to other, usually economic, foreign policy issues permitted the US representative to pressurize nations into supporting American-instigated transnational drug control laws. Although not always entirely successful in the quest for the export of US-style legislation to the rest of the world, American efforts at the CND went a long way to ensuring that UN laws followed a traditional US prohibitive ideal.

Pursuing the doctrine that drug use should be limited to medical and scientific purposes only, American activity at the UN between 1945 and 1960 moved a considerable way towards the creation of a rigid international control framework. The period was consequently a crucial stage in the development of a global prohibitionist norm; a process by which reactions and attitudes to drug use and control become standardized. The 1953 protocol also succeeded in making the long-time US goal of the control of opium at source a reality. Having founded the international control movement in 1909 and temporarily lost its direction during the years of the League of Nations, the United States successfully took up the helm at the CND in 1946. As Anslinger's annual reports to a long line of US Secretaries of State noted, 'The United States was able to maintain leadership and substantial support throughout' the CND's sessions.[119] Yet, in spite of such leadership, the diplomatic atmosphere of the Cold War often caused the USA to subordinate international drug control to the pursuit of a foreign policy dictated by anti-communism. It is this process that will be the focus of the next chapter.

NOTES

1. Robert W. Gregg, *About Face?: The United States and the United Nations* (Boulder: Lynne Rienner, 1993), p. 5.
2. *Ibid.*
3. Evan Luard, *A History of the United Nations*: Vol. 1, *The Years of Western Dominance, 1944–1955* (New York: Macmillan, 1982), p. 11.
4. *Ibid.*, p. 346.
5. Paul Kennedy, *The Rise and Fall of the Great Powers: Economic Change and Military Conflict from 1500 to 2000* (London: Fontana, 1988), p. 460.
6. *Ibid.*
7. Robert W. Gregg, *About Face?*, pp. 6–7.
8. *Ibid.*

9. Shirley Hazzard, *Countenance of Truth: The United Nations and the Waldheim Case* (London: Chatto and Windus, 1990), p. 15.
10. *Ibid.*, pp. 8–9.
11. Robert W. Gregg, *About Face?*, pp. 7, 8.
12. Herbert L. May, 'The international control of narcotic drugs', *International Conciliation*, **441** (May 1948), 349.
13. Leland M. Goodrich, *The United Nations* (London: Stevens, 1960), p. 104.
14. Kettil Bruun, Lynn Pan and Ingemar Rexed, *The Gentlemen's Club: International Control of Drugs and Alcohol* (Chicago: University of Chicago Press, 1975), p. 114.
15. William O. Walker III, 'International collaboration in historical perspective', in Peter H. Smith (ed.), *Drug Policy in the Americas* (Boulder: Westview Press, 1992), p. 271.
16. Bruun, Pan and Rexed, *The Gentlemen's Club*, p. 142.
17. Paul Kennedy, *Rise and Fall of the Great Powers*, p. 461.
18. Charles Siragusa, *The Trail of the Poppy* (Englewood Cliffs, NJ: Prentice-Hall, 1966), p. 212. Cited in Ethan A. Nadelmann, *Cops across Borders: The Internationalization of U.S. Criminal Law Enforcement* (University Park: Pennsylvania State University, 1993), p. 134.
19. Personal and confidential letter from Sharman to Anslinger, 20 April 1945, Anslinger Papers (hereafter cited as AP), Pattee Library Labor Archives, Penn State University, Pennsylvania, Box 2: File 9, and personal letter from Anslinger to Sharman, 24 July 1945, AP Box 2: File 19.
20. In fact, claims made by the Women's Christian Temperance Movement (WCTU) that the United States had opposed the control of opium at San Francisco were met with harsh rebuttals. The State Department claimed that 'whoever circulated that falsehood was an unmitigated liar'. *Foreign Relations of the United States*, **1** (1945), 1391.
21. *Traffic in Opium and Other Dangerous Drugs*, for the year ended 31 December 1946 (Washington, DC: US Treasury Department Bureau of Narcotics, 1947), p. 12.
22. Letter from Mrs Howell Moorhead to Mr Rogers, 16 March 1948. AP Box 2: File 17.
23. *Ibid.*
24. William O. Walker III, *Opium and Foreign Policy: The Anglo-American Search for Order in Asia, 1912–1954,* (Chapel Hill: University of North Carolina Press, 1991), p. 165.
25. Letter from State Department to Anslinger, 22 November 1946. National Archives, Washington, DC, Record Group 501.BN NARCOTICS (hereafter cited as NA), and *New York Times*, 10 December 1946.
26. Confidential Department of State Memorandum of Conversation, Office of Eastern Affairs, Mrs Howell Moorehead, Harry J. Anslinger and Mr Penfield, 5 February 1947, pp. 2–3, NA 501.BD NARCOTICS.
27. Report on the Third Session of the CND, 3–22 May 1948. Harry J. Anslinger to the Secretary of State, NA 501.BD NARCOTICS.
28. Department of State Memorandum of Conversation, Harry J. Anslinger and Mr George A. Morlock, 7 March 1946, NA 501.BN NARCOTICS.

29. Letter from Anslinger to Sharman, 16 March 1948, AP Box 2: File 17.
30. Report on the Third Session of the CND, 3–22 May 1948. Harry J. Anslinger to the Secretary of State, p. 9, NA 501.BN NARCOTICS.
31. *Ibid.*, p. 11.
32. Foreign Service Dispatch, 17 April 1956, regarding the candidacy of Mexico for re-election to the CND. Note from the Permanent Mission of Mexico to the UN, Luciano Joublanc Rivas, to Henry Cabot Lodge, Jr, Permanent Representative of the USA to the UN, NA 340.19.
33. 'Twenty years of narcotics control under the United Nations: review of the work of the Commission on Narcotic Drugs from its 1st to its 20th Session', *Bulletin on Narcotics*, **17**(1) (January–March 1966), 14.
34. Department of State Office Memorandum, Anslinger to Morlock, 10 September 1948, NA 501.BD NARCOTICS.
35. Letter from Anslinger to Sharman, 16 March 1948, AP Box 2: File 17.
36. Letter from Mrs Howell Moorhead to Mr G. Rogers, *op. cit.*, p. 2.
37. Letter from Mr George A. Morlock to Anslinger, 16 December 1952, AP Box 2: File 13.
38. The term 'Anslinger's Army' is used by McWilliams to describe the commissioner's large body of support. John C. McWilliams, *The Protectors: Harry J. Anslinger and the Federal Bureau of Narcotics, 1930–1962* (Newark: University of Delaware Press, 1990), p. 57.
39. Letter from Executive Secretary J. W. Dargavel to G. Humphrey, 2 December 1952, AP Box 2: File 13.
40. One letter claimed that 'Anslinger has contributed more toward the control of narcotics than any other person in the world – in fact he could well be called "Mr. Narcotics" ... when the UN began dealing with the narcotic problem in their meetings they looked to him for guidance and leadership.' See letter from J. Hill Junior to G. Humphrey, 4 December 1952, AP Box 2: File 13. Also see letter from Burroughs Wellcome and Co. to Mr R. W. Albright, Distillation Products, Rochester, New York, 22 December 1952, AP Box 2: File 13, and letter from Karl Bambach of the ADMA to Mr Elmer H. Bobst, President Warner-Hudnut Inc., New York, 12 December 1952, AP Box 2: File 13.
41. Rufus King, *The Drug Hang-Up* (Springfield, IL: Charles C. Thomas, 1974), p. 208.
42. Report from the UK delegate, Mr T. Hutson, on the third session of the CND, 3–22 May 1948, p. 1. From Foreign Office documents held at the Public Record Office, Kew, London (hereafter PRO) (FO371).
43. Extensive correspondence between Anslinger and Sharman over a considerable length of time demonstrates the similarities in their approaches toward drug control. Also see Bertil A. Renborg, *International Drug Control: A Study of International Administration by and through the League of Nations* (Washington, DC: Carnegie Endowment for International Peace, 1947), p. 10.
44. Report from the UK delegate, Mr T. Hutson, on the third session of the CND, 3–22 May 1948, *op. cit.*
45. *Ibid.*, p. 4.

46. Confidential letter from P. W. J. Buxton to M. W. Errock at the UN Department of the Foreign Office, undated, PRO (FO371).
47. Foreign Office telegram, from the UK delegate of the CND in Geneva to the Foreign Office, 30 July 1958, PRO (FO371).
48. From an interview with Tom C. Green, October 1993. Hereafter I/TCG.
49. Letter from Tom Green, UK delegate to the UN, New York, to Sam Hoare, Foreign Office, 16 May 1957, PRO (FO371 129987).
50. *Ibid.*
51. Confidential letter from UK delegate to the UN, New York, Sir Peter Dixon, to Sam Hoare, Foreign Office, 21 May 1957, PRO (FO371 129987).
52. Bruun, Pan and Rexed, *Gentlemen's Club*, pp. 128, 118.
53. John Hadwen and Johan Kaufman, *How UN Decisions Are Made* (Leyden: A. W. Sythhoff; New York: Oceana Publications, 1962), pp. 14, 54.
54. Peter D. Lowes, *The Genesis of International Narcotics Control* (Geneva: Libraries Droz, 1966), pp. 66, 163, 181. Cited in Bruun, Pann and Rexed, *The Gentlemen's Club*, p. 88.
55. Bruun, Pan and Rexed, *Gentlemen's Club*, p. 122.
56. Although Anslinger did not retire from the CND until 1970, his appearances at the annual meetings became less frequent during the 1960s. Tom Green recalled that 'being virtually the last survivor of those who had met to produce the earlier drug conventions, he belonged to a very different generation from the other representatives on the Commission'. Accordingly, during Green's era, 1957–64, Anslinger 'did not mix much with them'. Letter from Tom Green to author, 24 September 1994.
57. Robert W. Gregg and Michael Barkun (eds), *The United Nations System and Its Functions: Selected Readings* (New York: Van Nostrand, 1968), p. 36.
58. Letter from Anslinger to Dr Victor Hoo, Assistant Secretary-General of the UN, 1951, AP Box 2: File 14.
59. Letter from unnamed individual to Anslinger, 29 July 1956, AP Box 2: File 10; and see letter from Anslinger to Mr Penteado, 26 November 1951, AP Box 2: File 14.
60. Letter from Sharman to Anslinger, 13 August 1957, AP Box 2: File 10.
61. Bruun, Pan and Rexed, *Gentlemen's Club*, p. 129.
62. Letter from Anslinger to Sharman, 20 August 1957, AP Box 2: File 10.
63. State Department Memorandum of Conversation with Anslinger, from Mulliken to Hanes, 11 March 1958, p. 1, NA 340.19.
64. Letter from Sharman to Anslinger, 13 May 1958, AP Box 2: File 19.
65. Confidential letter from P. W. J. Buxton to M. W. Errock, UN Department British Foreign Office, undated, PRO (FO371).
66. See personal letter, 13 August 1957, AP Box 2: File 10, and personal letter from Sharman to Anslinger, 13 May 1958, AP Box 2: File 19.
67. Letter from Lande to Anslinger, 14 October 1962, AP Box 2: File 2. In the letter Lande also remarks, 'I do not have to tell you that I shall always do all in my power to deserve your trust.'
68. Rosemary Righter, *Utopia Lost: The United Nations and World Order* (New York: Twentieth Century Fund Press), p. 99.
69. *Ibid.*, pp. 98–9.

70. See letter from Lande to Anslinger, 14 October 1962, AP Box 2: File 4; confidential letter from Lande to Anslinger, 26 October 1962, AP Box 2: File 4; letter from Lande to Anslinger, 17 December 1962, Harry J. Anslinger Papers, Harry S. Truman Library (hereafter cited as HTL), Independence, Missouri, USA; confidential letter from Lande to Anslinger, 13 August 1963, AP Box 2: File 3; letter from Lande to Anslinger, 23 August 1963,
AP Box 2: File 3; and letter [marked 'Highly Confidential'] from Lande to Anslinger, 10 June 1964, AP Box 2: File 2.
71. Letter from Lande to Anslinger, 14 October 1962, AP Box 2: File 4.
72. Confidential letter from Lande to Anslinger, 26 October 1962, AP Box 2: File 4.
73. Confidential letter from Lande to Anslinger, 5 November 1965, HTL. Lande noted that information in a DND document (E/CN7/474), claiming that individuals experienced no physical or mental changes as a result of use of the drug, would be 'dangerous ammunition in the hands of our enemies'. Also see confidential letter from Lande to Anslinger, 17 February 1965, p. 4, HTL.
74. Letter from Adolf Lande to Anslinger, 5 August 1962, AP Box 2: File 4.
75. Letter from Lande to Anslinger, 7 August 1962, AP Box 2: File 4.
76. According to communications between British diplomats in Hong Kong and Macau, they were told by the State Department that 'the FBN was sending a Mr. Wayland Spear [sic], who was described as one of their "field supervisors of Enforcement Activities" on a trip to the Far East' and it was his 'chief purpose to collect information for the use of the US representative at the meeting of the UN CND in April' 1954. See correspondence between E. J. Cowen, of the British consulate in Macau, and P. G. F. Dalton, Political Adviser Hong Kong, undated, PRO (FO371 129983).
77. Ibid.
78. Letter from E. J. Cowan, the British consulate in Macau, to Peter G. F. Dalton, Political Adviser, Hong Kong, 9 March 1954, PRO (FO371 129983).
79. 'Twenty years of narcotics control', p. 34.
80. Ibid., p. 33.
81. Rufus King, The Drug Hang-Up, p. 97.
82. 'Twenty years of narcotics control', p. 34.
83. Ibid.
84. Report on the Second Session of the CND, 24 July–8 August 1947. Harry Anslinger to the Secretary of State, p. 2, NA 501.BN NARCOTICS.
85. Department of State Memorandum of Conversation, United Nations Commission of Inquiry on the Coca Leaf. Mr Victor W. von Hagen, Latin American adviser, Encyclopedia Americana, and Mr George A. Morlock, 6 October 1949, NA 501.BD NARCOTICS.
86. For details see Antonil [pen name of Anthony Henman], Mama Coca (London: Hassel Free Press, 1978), pp. 23–7.
87. New York Times, 30 April 1952.
88. Antonil, Mama Coca, p. 24.
89. 'Twenty years of narcotics control', p. 31.

90. *Ibid.*, p. 31.
91. UN document E/CN.7/SR119, December 1950, p. 7.
92. CND 11th Session, UN document E/CN.7/SR295, 1956.
93. CND 7th Session, UN document E/CN.7/ SR 176, 1952, p. 12.
94. 'Twenty years of narcotics control', p. 32.
95. Letter from Lande (European Office of the United Nations) to Anslinger, 17 December 1962, HTL.
96. Report on the First Session of the CND of the UN, held at Lake Success, New York, 27 November–13 December 1946, submitted by Harry J. Anslinger to the Secretary of State, p. 8, NA 501.BD NARCOTICS.
97. UN document E/CN.7/75, November–December 1946, p. 26.
98. Report of the Third Session of the CND, (3–22 May 1948), p. 13, NA 501 BD.NARCOTICS.
99. 'Twenty years of narcotics control', p. 14.
100. UN document E/CN.7/SR 78–99, September 1949, p. 118.
101. 'Twenty years of narcotics control', p. 29.
102. UN document E/CN.7/SR 78–99, September 1949, p. 65.
103. CND 5th session, UN document E/CN.7/SR 108, December 1950, p. 12.
104. CND 6th Session, UN document E/CN.7/ SR 160, April 1951, p. 11.
105. 'Twenty years of narcotics control', p. 16.
106. S. K. Chattergee, *Legal Aspects of International Drug Control* (Martinus Nijhoff, 1981), pp. 334, 336.
107. Statement of the Hon. H. J. Anslinger, chief representative on the US delegation to the International Opium Conference, UN, New York, 23 June 1952. Drug Enforcement Administration (DEA) Library, Washington, DC.
108. *Ibid.* Also see Anslinger's response to the protocol in *New York Times*, 24 June 1954.
109. *Ibid.*
110. *Ibid.*
111. *Ibid.*
112. Letter from Anslinger to Judge William T. McCarthy, 17 June 1953, AP Box 3: File 21.
113. Letter from Richard S. Wheeler, Acting Chief, Division of International Conferences, for the Secretary of State, to Anslinger, 18 August 1953, AP Box 2: File 12.
114. Harry J. Anslinger and W. F. Tompkins, *Traffic in Narcotics* (New York: Funk and Wagnalls, 1953), p. viii.
115. CND 12th Session, UN document E/CN.7/SR334, April 1957, p. 11.
116. CND 12th Session, UN document E/CN.7/SR336, May 1957, p. 12.
117. David Musto, *The American Disease: Origins of Narcotic Control* (Oxford: Oxford University Press, 1987), p. 231.
118. CND 14th Session, UN document E/CN.7/SR417, April 1959, p. 2.
119. See the annual reports of the CND sessions submitted to the Secretary of State by the chief US representative Harry Anslinger (HTL). As examination reveals, the reports consistently show US dominance.

CHAPTER 3

PROHIBITION DEFERRED:

Harry J. Anslinger, the United States and multilateral drug control during the Cold War, 1950–1958

> [W]e have seen on a number of occasions that bilateral anti-drug actions can be hampered by political concerns. This is not the case with a multilateral approach.
> Secretary-General Javier Pérez de Cuéllar, General Assembly Special Session on Drugs, 20 February 1990

> For more than forty years the struggle between the two superpowers and the coalitions they built and armed in this era of bipolarity was the single most important factor of the international system.
> Robert W. Gregg, *About Face? The United States and the United Nations*, 1993

In 1945, the disappearance of any hopes for a continuation of the wartime alliance between the United States and the Soviet Union ushered in a new era in East–West relations. Without the common threat from the Axis powers to unite them, the USA and the USSR adopted a polar rivalry within the restructured international system. The desire for national security and the survival of two different political ideologies resulted in the evolution of icy diplomatic relations between the countries. The creation of the People's Republic of China in October 1949 was also to heighten fears in the United States that Western democracy was under attack from a global communist conspiracy. The confrontational atmosphere of this Cold War affected all aspects of diplomacy, not least activities within the fledgling UN. Since the organization was designed to play a crucial role in the operation of the post-war international community, it was inevitable that it would become embroiled in any East–West dispute. The UN became a major arena for struggle, with strained American–Soviet and Sino-American relations influencing many of its endeavours. The area of drug control was not excluded from this process.

As we have seen, US hegemony ensured that Washington was the dominant force within the UN narcotic control system, playing a major role in determining the formulation of international legislation and hence the creation of a global norm. The political climate of the Cold War, however, often led US policymakers to allow wider foreign-policy concerns to take precedence over issues of international drug control. American fears of expansionist communist regimes controlled by Moscow played an important role in determining the character of US behaviour within the UN. The State Department's determination to check perceived communist aggression, and stand firm and contain any encroachments of what Washington viewed as a vast and belligerent Red monolith, resulted in matters of international narcotic control being subordinated to other foreign-policy concerns. Drug control issues, however morally righteous the US rhetoric may have been at the CND, could not compete with a realist concern for national security. In circumstances where the pursuit of drug policy was seen to conflict with American diplomatic interests, the State Department chose to override issues of narcotic control.

Of course, the influence of non-drug-related matters upon the American approach to international control was not a new phenomenon. It will be recalled how in the early years of the movement the United States had used the issue of opium control in China to enhance its trading opportunities in the East. At that time American control strategies had coincided with economic concerns. After 1945, however, conflicts between foreign policy and narcotic control made the self-righteous American rhetoric at the UN sound empty.

This chapter addresses one of the main themes of this book: the multiple motives underpinning America's quest for international drug prohibition. It examines the conflicting factors that influenced the formulation of US narcotic foreign policy at the UN during a period when the United States looked to contain communism around the world. The chapter focuses upon cases where the US government subordinated its mission for narcotic control at the UN to wider foreign-policy concerns, particularly in the important opium-producing area of the Middle East. Harry Anslinger's role within the US delegation to the CND is also scrutinized. His use of political issues to secure his own position will be shown. The commissioner's attempts to charge communist China with illegal narcotics trading in the 1950s is used as an example of this process. However, Anslinger's reputation as the controlling force of all US narcotic foreign policy is also questioned.[1] The commissioner's prominence within the US system will be shown, but examples will be used to demonstrate that Anslinger was permitted complete control of US narcotic foreign policy only when his actions did not conflict with the wider goals of the State Department. In this case, the United States' pursuit of political considerations over narcotic control will be used to provide evidence of Anslinger's genuine position. Consequently, the chapter will show that Anslinger did not possess unfettered control of America's policies towards international narcotic control at the UN.

ANSLINGER AND THE STATE DEPARTMENT

During his long career at the UN, Harry Anslinger played an important role in the construction and implementation of US international drug control policy; of this there is no doubt. There is abundant evidence to show that Anslinger operated effectively both with, and independently of, the US State Department. As we have seen, such behaviour led influential people such as Adolf Lande to believe that the commissioner was in overall control of US involvement with the UN narcotic framework.

British reports from CND sessions also seem to substantiate such an assessment of the commissioner's role within the US drug foreign-policy process. In fact in 1957 British diplomats noted that 'Anslinger is very much a law unto himself ... the State Department either cannot, or does not attempt to, keep control of him.'[2] A letter from Tom Green to Sir Samuel Hoare of the Foreign Office further illustrated Anslinger's apparent domination within the American delegation. Green reported at the twelfth session of the CND that despite the arrival of Gilmore Flues, the Assistant Secretary to the Treasury, and Dr Nathan Eddy of the WHO's Expert Committee, the US delegation was still, outwardly at least, under the control of Harry Anslinger. He noted:

> At the end of the first week of the Commission I feel able to forecast that it is likely to go down in history as one of the worst sessions on record. One of the main troubles is the weakness of the American delegation. This has now been reinforced numerically by a gentleman called Flues, who according to the list of delegates is *the* US representative, but who has put in only one appearance and has said half a dozen words, and Dr. Eddy, making a delegation of six. One gets the impression that each one of them is watching the others and that no one dares to do anything constructive lest it should turn out to be the wrong thing and incur the wrath of Mr. Anslinger.[3]

Anslinger's strong position in both the CND and the US delegation is further illustrated by an incident in May 1957 when he was voted into the chair of the commission for that session. Tom Green displayed his concern, and informed the Home Office that

> Anslinger has turned out rather worse than was feared and we are proceeding at a fine pace, but in a considerable state of confusion. Although there is a State Department man sitting behind the USA label, he gets no chance to speak and Anslinger speaks indiscriminately as Chairman and as US representative without making it clear which hat he is wearing.[4]

Tom Green was to provide some explanation for Anslinger's behaviour when he recalled that Anslinger was not a 'good committee man ... once he had made up his mind he resented explaining his decisions to other members of the CND', or for that matter the State Department. His standard response to questioning is said to have been, 'I've made up my mind, don't confuse me with the facts!'[5] However, his personal prominence in the CND, and the US position of strength, apparently ensured that more often than not he did not have to explain his actions if he chose not to.

Anslinger's tendency to challenge, or simply ignore, the State Department has therefore been interpreted on some occasions as a manifestation of his complete control of US narcotic policy at the CND. Indeed, it has been 'generally acknowledged' by those who have studied the United States' international control efforts that 'Anslinger was the most dominant figure in the CND for many years after the Second World War'.[6]

However, it is important to make the distinction between Anslinger's dominance at the CND and the extent of his control over US narcotic foreign policy. It is vital to note that the commissioner's status in the CND was largely the product of US ascendancy within the organization. Although he did not create the American prohibitive approach to international drug control, Anslinger found himself in a position where he was able to export successfully such ideas to the rest of the world. He, like Brent, Wright and Porter before him, worked to create an international regime based on American prohibitive ideals. The significant difference, however, was that Anslinger's career included a period when the United States was the dominant nation on the international stage. This was particularly true of his work in the CND in the twenty years after 1945. Accordingly, he achieved considerable success, whereas previous US exploits had been restricted by the nation's relatively weak status within the international community.

Nevertheless, this does not mean that Anslinger necessarily possessed complete control of US narcotic foreign policy. Unlike the domestic situation in the United States, Anslinger's actions at the UN were limited significantly by the constraints of wider American foreign policy. Although Anslinger worked for the Treasury Department, while he was at the UN he was constantly kept in check by the Department of State. In theory, the Department had the final word on all decisions at the UN. This restricted Anslinger's ability to act with as much freedom as he had while developing US domestic prohibitive legislation. At that time his manipulation of the press and Congress had given him great scope. Therefore, although Douglas Clark Kinder and William O. Walker III have noted that a study of Anslinger's reports for the commission 'indicate[s] the increase of his control over narcotics foreign policy',[7] it would be wrong to assume that the commissioner commanded absolute authority over US narcotics policy at the UN. We should guard against the assumption that Anslinger's dominance in the CND reflected complete control of the US policies adopted at the UN. Despite this, scholars have consistently misinterpreted Anslinger's role within the development of US policy at the UN. Indeed, Walker's observation that 'Anslinger had dominated *all* [emphasis added] aspects of US drug policy'[8] between 1943 and 1953 should not be used as an interpretative model for his entire international career.

Investigation shows that Anslinger's unilateral control over US narcotic policy at the UN only ever existed to the point where it did not dramatically conflict with the State Department's concerns for foreign policy. In cases where interests collided, the State Department always prevailed. Anslinger, ever conscious of his need to survive in the competitive bureaucratic environment of Washington, DC, would never jeopardize his career in the quest for his own objectives. The State Department's control of the commissioner can be seen in its assessment of the illicit international drugs traffic.

Closely monitoring Anslinger's actions in the CND, the Department was keen to screen any potentially damaging statements that he proposed to make at sessions of the Commission. Such a process can be seen clearly with Anslinger's approach to the People's Republic of China in the early 1950s. Here the commissioner's charges against the PRC were scrutinized by the State Department to ensure that any claims did not needlessly antagonize other nations represented at the CND.[9] In 1957 the Department also noted that the commissioner did 'not propose to cite any nation as a violator of the narcotics treaties' at the next session. However, it was recommended that 'This should be confirmed in order to avoid the possibility that he may cite a nation without obtaining the necessary clearances from the geographical bureau concerned.'[10] Anslinger's accusations at the CND therefore appear to have been authorized by the State Department before the sessions in order to avoid any conflict of interest. The Department consequently played a crucial role in determining Anslinger's activities at the CND. Although a Departmental memorandum admitted that 'the basic responsibility for narcotics control rests with the Treasury Department', and that the State Department's own interests concentrated on 'political considerations',[11] these political considerations ultimately took precedence over issues of drug control.

Accordingly, it was the Department's job to see that US 'narcotics policy' was 'coordinated with our [US] general foreign policy'. In 1958 a State Department document explained:

For example, nations are usually sensitive regarding charges that they are lax in administering narcotics laws and treaties. One of the main jobs of the international narcotics bodies is to determine what the weak spots in the control system are and to name them. The Department attempts to assure that the US Representative's observations on such matters are in line with our foreign policy.[12]

Anslinger was therefore constrained inasmuch as his policies for the creation of an international control system had to coincide with general US foreign policy. When they did not, there would inevitably be conflict between the two branches of government. Nevertheless, Anslinger was shrewd enough to appreciate that alienating the State Department would not have been good for the longevity of his career at both the FBN and the CND. A memorandum in 1958 described the commissioner's working relationship with the State Department and confirmed that his activities, as far as the Department was aware, were generally satisfactory. The State Department observed that

> Mr. Anslinger's relations with the Department have generally been good. In general, he recognizes the Department's interest in narcotics and consults with the Department when appropriate. In almost all of his dealings with the Department, Mr. Anslinger has shown a constant willingness to reach an agreement with the Department in a spirit of accommodation and friendliness. The differences the Department has had with him result from a tendency occasionally to overlook the political implications of some of his statements and actions and also to deal directly with his colleagues abroad on matters of interest to the Department as well as to the Commissioner. These differences have been more frequent in the past two or three years and have been due principally to Mr. Anslinger's natural inclination to approach any narcotics question from the standpoint of control and to underestimate other considerations.[13]

Therefore, according to the State Department, Anslinger generally cooperated with it on issues of narcotic control. Although admittedly operating within informal channels, with individuals such as Sharman and Lande, in an attempt to further the international prohibitive cause or his own goals for self-preservation, the commissioner usually remained within the confines of State Department policy. His survival instincts ensured this. It can be assumed that for most of the time the actions of the United States at the UN were the result of general agreement between Anslinger and the State Department.

A major difference of opinion, however, was to surface when the UN discussed the passage into law of the long-awaited Single Convention on Narcotic Drugs in 1961. This issue will be the focus of the next chapter. Nonetheless, Anslinger's charges against the People's Republic of China at the CND provide an example of a coincidence of interest between the commissioner and the State Department. It also shows that Anslinger, much like the State Department, often approached drug control at the UN with multiple motives.

ANSLINGER ACCUSES RED CHINA AND SAFEGUARDS HIS OWN POSITION

As the United States was gripped by Cold War anti-communist hysteria during the early 1950s, Anslinger effectively harnessed American paranoia to enhance his position at the FBN and push for stringent drug controls in the USA. Events abroad – Mao Zedong's communist victory in the civil war on mainland China in 1949 and communist North Korea's invasion of South Korea in 1950 – went a long way to convincing Americans that the communist bloc had plans for world domination. In the United States the claims of Wisconsin's Senator Joseph McCarthy that 'Reds' had infiltrated the State Department also heightened anxiety that there was a global communist conspiracy being led by Moscow. The Senator's rhetoric produced an upsurge in paranoia, and the phenomenon known as McCarthyism helped to ensure that all US government policy remained ardently anti-communist.

Using the CND as a platform from which to attack the People's Republic of China (PRC), the commissioner claimed that the Communist government was supporting the illicit exportation of narcotic drugs in an attempt to undermine the free world and raise vital revenue for world revolution. Despite a lack of substantiated evidence, Anslinger regularly accused the PRC of illegal activities at Commission sessions. In continuing to charge Communist China during a period when the United States had sent troops to the Korean peninsula and the PRC had joined the conflict on the side of North Korea, Anslinger shifted the policies of the FBN into line with wider American foreign policy. This had the effect of helping to make the FBN part of the US government's anti-communist strategy and safeguarded the Bureau's and therefore Anslinger's own position, within the aggressive bureaucratic environment of Washington. It also added to American anti-communist feelings, and hence assisted the State Department in the pursuit of an anti-Soviet and anti-Chinese foreign policy during the early years of the Eisenhower administration. The search for a plausible explanation for the lack of successful drug control in the region made Red China an ideal scapegoat for both Anslinger and the State Department.

By following the contours of US foreign policy towards what was perceived to be the Red menace, Anslinger exploited American xenophobia and fear of communism. In doing so he repeated the methods he had used against another foreign menace a decade earlier when he had made accusations regarding illegal Japanese narcotic trafficking before American entry into the Second World War in 1942. This had drawn on widespread anti-Japanese sentiment and produced popular support for the bureau. His charges against mainland China in the 1950s dovetailed with the pervasive and rampant anti-communism present in the United States at that time. This again heightened his prominence within Washington and provided him with a solid position from which to pursue strict drug prohibition. Anslinger's exploitation of American anti-communist paranoia was an influential factor in the passage of the strict 1951 Boggs Act and the 1956 Narcotic Control Act. Linking illegal drug use with communist drug trafficking proved to be a successful strategy and helped to ensure that, as Bonnie and Whitebread have noted, 'the punitive approach to narcotics use and dependence reached its zenith in the 1950s'.[14] However, despite a real, if misplaced, concern regarding Communist Chinese narcotics trafficking, Anslinger's charges against the PRC can be seen as the exploitation of a political issue for the safeguarding of his own interests.

The commissioner's charges against mainland China were to become notorious in the CND, with other delegates resigning themselves to the fact that they would have to listen to pages of accusations targeted at a nation which was not even represented in the UN.[15] It had been assumed that Communist China would have joined the UN in early 1950. However, its admission had been delayed owing to US–Soviet disagreements concerning the status of both Nationalist and Communist China within the organization. The United States consistently argued that the Communist Chinese should not be permitted membership of the UN, with Anslinger being given strict instructions to this effect at the CND. In the USA there was a great deal of anti-Chinese lobbying, with the Committee of One Million being particularly active. This committee, which was set up to lobby against the PRC's admission to the UN, drew heavily on Anslinger's statements concerning Communist China's drugs trafficking. The commissioner's evidence that communists were using drugs to subvert the free nations of the world was frequently used to support the committee's claims that the PRC should be kept out of the world organization.[16] At meetings of the CND, Russian representatives continually opposed Anslinger's behaviour on the grounds that it was largely political in nature and therefore outside the competence of the commission. The Soviets claimed that the American charges were a 'baseless fabrication from start to finish'.[17] However, the US representative proceeded annually to recount in detail Communist China's alleged activities. Anslinger's claims included the locations of Communist factories, smuggling routes and, incredibly, many of the specific individuals involved with the illegal trade. Using his status at the CND to influence his domestic position, the commissioner succeeded in bolstering support for both the FBN and its prohibitive legislation. Few politicians or journalists were to challenge his claims while McCarthyism maintained a tight hold on America, and Anslinger consequently developed a loyal following on Capitol Hill.

The commissioner's actions at the CND not only produced political support, but also received favourable coverage from the press. Indeed, as a study of both the *New York Times* and *The Times* of London shows, coverage of the activities of the UN narcotic control system between 1951 and 1954 was dominated by US charges against the PRC. For example, in May 1954 the *New York Times* stated that according to Harry Anslinger the PRC wanted to 'demoralize the free people of the world' and that 'fanatical Communist traffickers have resorted to the extreme measures of cutting off the ears of small time sellers who reveal the identity of the suppliers in Communist China'.[18] Later that month an editorial in the newspaper reported that in a response to such charges the 'Russians ... promptly protested ... that Anslinger was dragging in political issues'. However, maintaining strong backing for the commissioner, the *New York Times* continued,

> If the political issues appear, they are certainly no fault of a United Nations organization. ... If Red China chooses to be an international dope peddler it is hardly an improper 'political' step to bring that fact to the attention of the World Body.[19]

Anslinger's statements at the CND therefore appeared to become almost the official UN stance on the issue, and displayed his dominance within the commission. Citing Anslinger as the source of the claims gave the accusations an air of authenticity. As a result *The Times* ran pieces headed 'China Flooding U.S. with Narcotics'[20] and reported during the Korean War that the CND had been 'informed by an American federal agent ... that communists in the Far East, directed from Peking, are operating a vast dope ring essentially aimed at the morale of American troops and the accumulation of large sums of dollars'.[21] Favourable newspaper coverage essentially became US anti-PRC propaganda. In accepting Anslinger's claims without question, newspaper editors obediently duplicated Anslinger's blatant anti-communist stance. Reporting on the commissioner's claims in 1952, *The Times* wrote that the PRC had

> totally reversed the policies of the Nationalist Government concerning the growth of opium. While General Chiang Kai Shek's Government had reduced opium production to a minimum, which had led to the reduction of

smuggling, the growth of poppies had expanded in direct proportion to the communist military advance. ... Mr. Anslinger quoted from an official report dated March 10 from General Ridgeway's H.Q. in Tokyo which said 'investigations of arrests and seizures in Japan in 1951 proved conclusively, that the communists are smuggling heroin from China to Japan and using the proceeds to finance and obtain strategic materials for China'.[22]

In this way Anslinger, helped by newspaper coverage, ensured that his narcotic policies followed broader US foreign policy. The commissioner's claims that Chiang Kai-shek's Nationalist government had made efforts to eliminate opium production complemented the pro-Chiang sentiment within the United States.

Despite the lack of solid proof that the Mao Zedong's Communist Chinese government was sponsoring the export of narcotics, Anslinger persistently and resolutely claimed that the PRC was involved in flooding America with drugs. When asked by Senator Estes Kefauver in 1953 if he believed that an increase in addiction on the West Coast of the United States was attributable to the 'Red Chinese supplies', Anslinger replied, 'by all means ... we have very definite proof of that. We know exactly where it comes from and who's getting it'; Red China is 'selling poison to our fellow man for profit'.[23] Nevertheless, the commissioner still had no definite evidence to provide substance to his claims. He relied upon reports from his own FBN agents, biased information from Nationalist China[24] and hysteria of the time to perpetuate his accusations. The PRC responded to Anslinger's charges by issuing denials in the press, claiming that 'Our country has suffered from the evils of opium for over a hundred years since its forcible importation into China as a result of imperialist invasion.'[25] The Communists even took the unusual step of cabling the Secretary-General of the UN, Trygve Lie, to deny the accusations. However, the argument that Anslinger had no corroborated evidence did little to stem the flow of accusations levelled at mainland China.

His statements in the CND also had the effect of alienating the British authorities in Hong Kong, a region that Anslinger claimed to be a major point of transit for the Communist-supplied narcotics. Anslinger's comment, quoted in the *South China Morning Post* in 1953, that 'Japan is getting the first wave of this traffic, all channelled through Hong Kong'[26] was a point of great concern for the British government. Keen to appear vigilant in the fight against illicit traffic, the British were unhappy with the commissioner's insinuations of inadequate control in the territory. This was a point brought up in 1954 with the publication of a pro-FBN[27] book by Richard L. Deverall entitled *Mao Tse-tung: Stop This Dirty Opium Business!*[28] Deverall's work included references to British complacency concerning control of illicit narcotic traffic through the island and the involvement of British seamen in the illegal trade. The book was seen by John Henry Walker of Britain's Home Office as little more than 'a crude pastiche culled mainly from press reports and Harry Anslinger's annual onslaughts on Red China' at the CND.[29] Appreciating the erroneous nature of Anslinger's claims, Walker noted that there was little substantive evidence to corroborate Communist China's role in the strategic export of narcotics to the West. He noted that 'Mr. Frank McGrath, the representative in Hong Kong of the US Treasury, has no information to support these statements and certainly passed none to the Hong Kong Government.'[30] The Foreign Office concurred with Walker on his assessment of Anslinger's statements, adding that the 'sources of his sources, e.g. Chinese National Press and statements by arrested traffickers in Japan, seem to us to be very dubious'.[31] In assessing the possible impact of Anslinger's charges against the PRC, and by association Hong Kong, the British government displayed a holistic appreciation of the commissioner's motives. Referring to Anslinger's tactic of harnessing US domestic anti-communist fears, the British consul-general in San Francisco perceptively commented in 1954 that such blatant and unsubstantiated charges were 'fresh grist ... for the McCarthy mill'. Illustrating his understanding of Anslinger's strategy, he concluded that 'this suits Chiang Kai Shek admirably', and that individuals such as the ardent anti-communist Senator Joseph Knowland were 'liable to take up the matter even if McCarthy'[32] did not. Although Walker had noted that there had been good relations between the Hong Kong authorities and Anslinger in the past, he commented that 'I am not too hopeful of making very much progress since he has strong motives for emphasising the responsibility of other countries for illicit traffic in the US and for attributing this traffic to Communist sources.'[33] According to Walker, Anslinger's motives at the UN were mainly domestic in origin. He believed 'Mr. Anslinger is under pressure in Washington and having to fight to keep his job.' Despite appreciating that there was most likely some smuggling taking place within the Hong Kong region,[34] the British authorities concluded that 'It is deplorable that an American official should lend his name to such an unconvincing rehash of this old tale.'[35] However, despite a serious lack of evidence, Anslinger was to continue to claim that Red China was responsible for illegally exporting narcotics.[36] Even statements from US officials in the Far East which suggested that the commissioner's claims were not based on solid facts did little to deter him.[37]

After Anslinger's retirement from the FBN in 1962 many Bureau agents sought to distance themselves from his wild accusations. An ex-Bureau agent neatly summed up the commissioner's approach to the issue in 1971, the year the PRC was eventually admitted to the UN. He recalled that 'everywhere Anslinger spoke he said the same thing, "the Chicoms are flooding the world with dope to corrupt the youth of America." There was no evidence for Anslinger's accusations but that never stopped him.'[38]

Shortly after the PRC became a member of the UN, a State Department spokesman also confirmed that Anslinger's charges had been baseless fabrications, just as the Soviets had claimed. Having re-evaluated Beijing's relationship with Moscow, the US government had concluded that the PRC and the Soviet Union should not have been regarded as a giant Red monolith. Far from their uniting against the capitalist world, tensions had developed between the two countries. Territorial and ideological disputes between the Soviets and the Chinese encouraged a change in US foreign policy towards Communist China. This meant that any anti-Chinese sentiment produced by Anslinger's accusations was no longer beneficial. On the contrary, it was damaging to efforts to improve US relations with the PRC. As a result, a State Department spokesman stated that

There is no reliable evidence that the Communist Chinese have ever engaged in or sanctioned the illicit export of opium or its derivatives. Nor is there any evidence of that country exercising any control over participating in the Southeast Asia opium trade.[39]

Anslinger's anti-communist activities at the CND during the McCarthy era displayed his willingness to exploit political issues to pursue his own interests. Soviet claims that the US representative was using the CND as a forum for political issues were essentially correct, in that Anslinger subordinated narcotic control to other concerns. Although he was undoubtedly fearful of increased drug trafficking and addiction, Anslinger's primary motive for harnessing anti-communist paranoia in the United States was to safeguard his own position and that of the FBN in Washington. Such a strategy was not confined to the McCarthy era, with Anslinger continuing to use the tactic of linking the FBN's drug policy with American foreign policy after the wave of McCarthyism had subsided. When American overseas attention moved away from Korea to the vacuum left by the French withdrawal from Vietnam in 1954, Anslinger promptly testified in Senate hearings that illegal heroin production was taking place in Cambodia, Thailand, Vietnam and Laos. Although there was undoubtedly some truth in his testimony, the commissioner appreciated the political gains that could be made by highlighting the existence of illicit drug production in these strategically important nations. He was also to claim that in the early 1960s Fidel Castro's Cuba was a source of illicit narcotics.[40] In this way Anslinger again exploited domestic antagonism towards nations perceived as a threat to the United States. His tactic of shadowing American foreign policy during the years of the Cold War ensured that he was seen as an unrelenting crusader against not only the evil of drugs, but also the evil of communism. As McWilliams notes, Anslinger's longevity can thus be attributed to his perceived role as an indispensable protector of American interests at both home and abroad.[41] By locating the source of the United States' drug problems in nations with a political system different from that of the USA, Anslinger succeeded in the eyes of many in combining the evil of drugs with that of communism. Naturally, he benefited greatly from this process. His own well-entrenched hatred of communism coincided with American diplomatic concerns during the Cold War and provided the impetus for Anslinger's continuing quest to blame other countries and ethnic groups for many of the United States' own drug problems.

Anslinger's use of an American fear of communism to further his own interests also mirrored the multiple approach adopted by the US government towards international drug trafficking and control. While benefiting from his accusations of communist involvement in the illegal narcotics trade at the UN, the US authorities actively pursued a policy of complicity themselves. Permitting foreign-policy objectives to override any concerns for drug control, the US government used the Central Intelligence Agency (CIA) to help Chiang Kai-shek in his fight against the communist regime on the Chinese mainland. As Alfred McCoy demonstrates in *The Politics of Heroin: CIA Complicity in the Global Drug Trade*, in supporting the National-ist Chinese forces, the Kuomintang (KMT), the CIA itself became involved in the trafficking of opium, an important source of revenue for the KMT.[42] Therefore, despite Anslinger's claims that the Communist Chinese were exporting illicit narcotics, the USA actually contributed to a rise in illegal drug trafficking by assisting the Nationalist Chinese. In 1954, American involvement with the drug trade in Southeast Asia grew ever deeper as Washington stepped into the void left by the French in Vietnam. In order to provide support for anti-communist elements in the region, the United States sponsored activities funded by revenue produced from opium. As a result, and despite Anslinger's pious anti-narcotic rhetoric at the UN, the US government permitted foreign-policy goals to entice it into active involvement with the illicit drug trade in the so-called Golden Triangle of Laos, Burma and Thailand.[43] Debate does exist as to whether Anslinger had any knowledge of the CIA activities in Southeast Asia. However, research conducted by John C. McWilliams[44] shows Anslinger and the FBN to have been deeply involved with counter-intelligence operations. To judge from his intricate involvement with the US intelligence services, it is hard to imagine that Anslinger did not know what was going on in the region. It is therefore likely that the commissioner's own fear and hatred of communism, and his bureaucratic survival instincts, led him at least to tolerate, if not condone, the CIA's activities.

The political atmosphere created by the Cold War played a crucial role in the development of America's international drug control policy. Fears of communist expansionism meant that decisions were often taken for political reasons rather than reasons of narcotic control. In the case of Communist China, Anslinger's activities coincided, or at least did not conflict, with those of the US Department of State, thus perpetuating his image as the central focus for US policy at the UN. However, this was not always the case. It is possible to find examples of instances where the State Department's decisions to pursue paths dictated by foreign-policy interests revealed the commissioner's vulnerability within the US drug control system. American concern for Cold War politics was often to override efforts for international drug control. This process not only demonstrates how US action in the field of transnational drug control consisted of a number of different, often conflicting, elements, but also illuminates Anslinger's sometimes precarious position in relation to the rest of the US establishment. Although a dominant force in the CND, Anslinger was compelled to balance his desires for strict international control with his wish to keep his job secure. Consequently, despite opposing some policy decisions, Anslinger was forced to watch the State Department make choices that he felt would undermine effective international drug control.

THE DIVISION OF NARCOTIC DRUGS MOVES TO GENEVA

The commissioner's fight to prevent the move of the UN's Division of Narcotic Drugs to Geneva provides an example of State Department ascendancy. As noted earlier, during the Second World War Anslinger had been very keen to ensure that the drug control machinery of the League of Nations was moved to the United States. After 1945 some of the UN's control apparatus remained in the USA, convincing Anslinger that the American public, press and government would influence its decision-making. Anslinger claimed that the result would ensure that the UN followed strict prohibitionist policies under the scrutiny of the American people. However, in 1954, when Lie's successor as Secretary-General of the UN, the Swede Dag Hammarskjöld (1953–61), decided to relocate the DND in Geneva, Anslinger's plans for continuing American influence were jeopardized. Hammarskjöld, who like Lie had been a compromise candidate for the post of Secretary-General, retained the predominantly American senior international civil service employed by Lie. However,

Hammarskjöld was less susceptible to pressure from the United States than his predecessor.

The proposed move of the DND, and hence the CND meetings, from New York to Geneva met with a great deal of public hostility in the United States. Many letters were consequently sent to the Secretary of State, John Foster Dulles (1953–9), from concerned members of Congress and the Senate who were expressing the fears of their constituents. A letter to Dulles from Congressman John F. Baldwin of California was typical of such correspondence. Baldwin wrote:

> In my opinion the present location of this Division in the US has been a proper location, and I fail to see any justifiable reason for moving it to Geneva. It is well known that the people of the US feel very strongly on the subject of the control and regulation of narcotics trade, and for that reason the location of that Division in this country has been quite desirable.[45]

In addition, many Congressmen received correspondence from members of the Women's Christian Temperance Union (WCTU), who placed a great deal of pressure on Washington to resist the move. The organization believed that there was a very real 'threat to our American children of drug addiction if this change is made'.[46] It also raised points concerning a possible increase in the influence of Communist China on the UN if the DND was moved to Geneva. Exploiting a politically hot issue of the time, the WCTU based such an argument on the premise that European nations were going 'soft on' the Communist regime in China, while the United States stood alone and solid against such a threat to world democracy. The WCTU had been in Anslinger's camp for many years, and consequently it is hardly surprising that such a powerful regiment in Anslinger's army was mobilized in the fight to keep the DND in New York. It also comes as little surprise that another of Anslinger's allies, the American Drug Manufacturers Association (ADMA), also vigorously opposed the move.[47]

In the United States there was clearly a great deal of orchestrated opposition to the proposal. However, it is also essential to note that most of the high-profile rhetoric originated from staunch Anslinger supporters. Consequently, both the WCTU and the ADMA had been largely motivated by propaganda emanating from Anslinger's FBN. In the true American tradition, an ADMA resolution opposing the move placed the blame for any drug problems within the United States on external groups and cited the USA as a victim nation.

So on the surface of the issue it appears that Anslinger had a great deal of support for his resistance to the relocation proposal, both from the general public and on Capitol Hill, including the influential Senate Foreign Relations Committee.[48] However, as a reading of the records shows, the commissioner was up against the manifestations of a broader foreign-policy approach as adopted by the State Department.

The State Department's stance on the issue became clear in 1955 when Anslinger's supporters on Capitol Hill made plans to flex American muscles and withdraw US funds. The discovery of the threat to cut the US contribution to the UN by the amount that it took to run the DND proved to be too much for the State Department to accept. The news was relayed to the State Department in January 1955. The commissioner claimed that Elizabeth Smart, the Director of the WCTU, had informed him that if the DND was moved, Senator Byrd of Virginia, the new chairman of the Senate Finance Committee, would stop the relevant funds being made available to the international organization.[49] Such a proposal appears not to have been merely an idle threat, with the chairman of the Subcommittee for the Department of State on Appropriations, John J. Rooney, proposing an amendment to restrict the use of appropriations for the contribution to the UN. The move would obviously have had serious international implications. The fears that such action would harm US–UN relations were so great that the US ambassador to the UN, Henry Cabot Lodge, Jr, was asked to inform Rooney of his views on the issue. Lodge consequently made his feelings abundantly clear in a statement prepared for the Subcommittee on Appropriations. The Ambassador, in a statement that illustrates the differences that exist between the contemporary US stance on UN contributions and that held four decades earlier, argued that the proposal:

1. ... would be a clear violation of our treaty obligations for us to default on our contribution to the UN and, of course, to violate any treaty obligation injures our standing in the world.
2. Failure to send our contribution would deprive us eventually of the privileges of membership and consequently of influences in the UN. As the Soviet Union has not defaulted, and presumably will not default once it realizes that we have defaulted, this would mean an enormous increase in Soviet influence.
3. If we default on our contribution whenever the UN Secretariat contemplates some action with which we disagree, then we cannot deny the right of others to do the same thing. This would be a serious blow at the existence of the UN and would be against our own long term interests.
4. The failure to make our contribution to the UN would give a pretext to enemies of the US to say that we are trying to dictate the International Narcotics Control Program and were using the money power to blackjack the rest of the world.
5. A member of the legislative body does not withdraw from the legislative body because it happens to pass a bill with which he disagrees. The UN is

not a legislative body, and has none of the powers of government, so there
is even less reason for a state to withdraw from the UN because of some
action with which it disagrees.[50]

Ambassador Lodge's response to the proposal provides a crucial insight
into the rationale behind the State Department's strategy on the situation.
Concerns regarding the image of the United States at the UN, particularly
in front of the Soviets, were to be of paramount importance. The chilly
diplomatic atmosphere during the early years of the Cold War had an
effect on all US decisions at the UN, even at the expense of what Anslinger
perceived to be effective international drug control.

Nevertheless, despite the position taken by the State Department,
Anslinger displayed his tenacity and still worked energetically to prevent
the Secretary-General's proposal from going into operation. At a meeting
at the Department of State he argued his case for US opposition and
demonstrated why he felt the move was ill-advised, albeit in the manner of
a desperate man. Having been asked to express his views on the issue,
Anslinger said 'he was in weekly communication with the UN Secretariat.
If the Division was transferred, three experts on the staff would not go to
Geneva. The Division would lose its efficiency because people do not work
as hard in Geneva and production is not the same', and said that he saw
'no economy in the proposed transfer because it would take ten years to
amortize the cost of transferring the Secretariat to Geneva'.[51] In reply, Mr
Phillips of the State Department stated that 'he thought the comparative
costs should be considered and another point which interested him was
whether the location of the Secretariat in Geneva might influence the
apathy of the European countries toward narcotics control which Mr.
Anslinger had reported'. Anslinger's response was that 'the United States
does most of the investigation work abroad and that he did not see the
slightest possibility of increasing the interest of the European countries in
narcotics control'. In backing up his case Anslinger further stated that
'when meetings of the Commission were held in New York representatives of other countries, not members of the Commission, could attend
meetings ... there was great advantage to [this] personal discussion' and
'most of the research work on narcotics addiction was carried on in this
country and that the hospitals [here] had been studied by the Secretariat'.
Anslinger was of course referring to research that supported FBN policies.
Phillips's questioning continued along the same lines. He stated that the
'Department was obviously most seriously concerned that there be effective narcotics control work and that if the transfer of the United Nations
Secretariat was going to weaken the efficiency of narcotics control, he
would certainly be opposed to it, but he could not see that this was the

case'. In countering this argument, Anslinger displayed the existence of a continuing distrust of Europeans in the control framework. He noted that he had received a letter from Colonel Sharman 'who agreed with him that the Secretariat would not perform its duties as well in Geneva as in New York because of the Geneva atmosphere'. He also recalled that Gilbert Yates, head of the Division, 'had suggested to him that the PCOB and the DSB be brought back to New York'.

As the commissioner began to realize from the tone of the conversation that the State Department was not willing to support him on this issue, he began to make some interesting claims. These were concerned with the pro-American stance of the previous Secretary-General, Trygve Lie. Anslinger stated that 'he had some inside information as to what had brought about this whole issue and it would not have arisen if Mr. Lie had been Secretary-General'.[52] The commissioner's suggestion that Lie would not have permitted such a situation to develop adds credence to the argument that the UN's first Secretary-General had a special relationship with the United States. Anslinger's good working relationship with the UN secretariat during the first eight years of its life had done a great deal to enhance his own influence within the organization. However, Anslinger's relations with Dag Hammarskjöld do not appear to have been so good. Despite continued efforts by the commissioner to have Hammarskjöld reverse his decision, the Secretary-General stood firm.

Because of pressure from Anslinger, the State Department decided that it would make tentative moves to try to halt the relocation process. It was decided that the best strategy was to make a top-level approach to the Secretary-General by American officials with a view to 'inducing' Dag Hammarskjöld 'to drop the transfer on his own initiative'. This approach was because the State Department believed that the 'General Assembly endorsed [the] Secretariat reorganization plan only in general terms'. To further the US case, the Department suggested to the US team in New York that it should be pointed out that the 'US [was the] chief target of the illicit traffic', which 'could be better fought if the Division remains in New York'. 'This', they claimed, was 'one of the few instances in the economic and social field where [the] US directly benefited from the operations of the UN in New York'.[53]

In reply, the US delegation at the UN, clearly concerned by the wider political implications of US opposition and consequent actions to prevent the move, pointed out the difficulties of raising the issue either at the CND or at ECOSOC.[54] Having approached the Secretary-General and informed him of the US view that he should drop the transfer proposal, Hammarskjöld's stance on the position became clear. Accordingly, the

Secretary-General did not feel [that] he could drop [the] transfer on [his] own initiative at this time because of [the] endorsement of [the] proposal by both ECOSOC and the General Assembly. Also, he did not believe [that] he would be justified in dropping the transfer in [the] absence [of] 'substantive' evidence [that the] transfer would really have an effect on fighting [the] illicit narcotics traffic in [the] U.S.[55]

In conclusion, and 'In view of [the] considerations mentioned by [the] Secretary-General', the American UN team in New York believed that US

action in ECOSOC could be successful only if major pressure was exerted on other delegations. We seriously doubt whether this matter is important enough to involve the US prestige in ECOSOC and [the] General Assembly. Accordingly we most seriously doubt advisability of placing the matter on [the] Agenda [of] ECOSOC.[56]

So apparently, the United States did have the option of using pressure tactics to encourage other nations to support their position on this issue. However, according to a State Department memorandum of a conversation between Phillips and Anslinger, the Department had realized that it would have needed to 'develop sufficiently persuasive arguments *which could be used publicly* [emphasis added] so that the Narcotic Commission would recommend that the Division would be kept in New York'.[57] In the event, the issue was deemed unworthy of risking general US prestige in the organization as a whole. Nevertheless, regardless of the State Department's official stance, Anslinger still pushed to prevent the move. He went so far as to have a meeting with Dag Hammarskjöld himself, but made no further progress towards the satisfactory resolution of the issue, the Secretary-General using much the same arguments as before to counter Anslinger's equally recognizable lines of attack.[58]

It becomes evident therefore that despite Anslinger's feelings on the issue, broader foreign policy interests, particularly with regard to the Soviet Union, had to overrule a purely drug control standpoint. In this case, regardless of the US potential to apply pressure on other nations and to withdraw money from the UN, the State Department felt that too much prestige was at stake. Despite Anslinger's rigorous arguments, the narcotic control lobby was to be disappointed. The commissioner continued to display his dissatisfaction with the situation, the State Department noting in 1957 that 'Mr. Anslinger consistently opposed the transfer of the Narcotics section from New York to Geneva and has on several occasions since the transfer expressed his resentment over the transfer'.[59] Anslinger also tried to blame what he saw as the breakdown in efficiency in the DND on its move to Geneva.[60]

The State Department's politically oriented stance on the relocation of the DND was a clear demonstration of the primacy it gave to issues not directly related to narcotic control. As an example of such an approach it was not unique, with American involvement in the Middle East illustrating further US concerns for foreign policy over drug control.

THE UNITED STATES AND UN NARCOTIC CONTROL IN THE MIDDLE EAST

The Middle East had been a point of attention for the UN since 1946 and the creation of its narcotic control apparatus. The region's status as a source of illicit opium meant that the area remained under constant scrutiny, with various proposals being put forward by the CND to control the illegal flow. One such scheme was the Egyptian proposal in 1957 for the creation of a UN Middle East Anti-Narcotics Bureau or Agency. The purpose of the plan was to co-ordinate the actions of the nations in the region and at the UN, and therefore increase the efficiency of control in the area. Yet the proposal can be seen as another illustration of the United States' proclivity for placing political considerations above those for narcotic control. The impending discussions of the issue at the twelfth session of the CND led the US State Department to instruct its delegation that

the US position remains the same as it has in the past, as being opposed to the establishment of a regional agency of this kind. Such an agency is regarded as being too operational in character for the UN and having political implications which it is desirable to avoid.[61]

The political considerations were, as will become clear, more to do with American–Arab–Israeli diplomatic relations than with the control of illegal drugs in the Middle East. Such a US stance consequently played an important role in the postponement of discussions of the issue until the thirteenth session of the commission. However, the US authorities continued to assess the impacts of the proposal and the political implications that accompanied it. Communication from the State Department to the US embassy in Cairo provides a picture of the substance of US opposition to the scheme. It confirmed that 'For the information of the Embassy the US position is to oppose the establishment of a regional agency of this kind', despite being 'sympathetic to the special difficulties faced by members of the League of Arab States in their struggle against drug addiction.'

Justifying its position, and in doing so ignoring Anslinger's past use of CND meetings as a forum for politically motivated attacks against the PRC, the State Department claimed that 'for the Narcotics Commission to make such a recommendation would involve the departure from its long established policy of concentrating on legislative and policy problems'. In this way it was argued that discussion of the proposed Bureau would have been a 'political' issue. The Department added that a recommendation from the CND would also 'throw open the question of the establishment of similar bureaus in other regions'. It therefore argued that the

> project would involve the UN Secretariat in operational activities of a type which it has not previously undertaken and would evoke a series of complex constitutional problems in regard to the working relationships between UN officials and the governments concerned and between the regional part of the UN Secretariat and the Central Secretariat.[62]

Consequently, it was recommended that

> probably the best course would be to seek to have the Egyptian proposal voted down. If this does not appear feasible, the US could support a compromise proposed by the UN Secretariat whereby an exploratory commission would be appointed to study the needs of the area and to make recommendations to the Narcotics Commission.[63]

The State Department argued that a more suitable approach would be to follow the decisions 'taken by the Commission on Narcotic Drugs at the 1956–57 meetings'. At the time it appeared 'probable that if the members of the League of Arab States might establish a regional system of co-operative policing they could secure UN technical assistance', which was 'more appropriately within the framework of the UN activities'.[64]

However, a crucial factor within the State Department's opposition to the scheme was tied up with the important alliances maintained by the United States in the region. Washington viewed the proposal as 'wholly unacceptable to the US because of its political nature (Egyptian-dominated)'.[65] The US embassy in Cairo was therefore informed that 'the Arab League proposal would exclude Israel and thus evoke political implications which it is desirable to avoid'.[66] In this instance the United States consequently ignored an opportunity to enhance the efficiency of UN co-ordinated drug control in the Middle East. The security considerations of a volatile region, and the existence of a powerful Jewish lobby in the United States, both ensured that an international bureau that excluded Israel was not to be on the American agenda.

Anslinger did make limited moves to oppose the State Department's strategy on the proposed bureau, but his efforts were futile. The Department initially noted that 'Mr. Anslinger appeared to agree with this course of action', but observed that he had since

> written a letter to the Lebanese Ambassador ... suggesting that Lebanon support the ... proposal. This would appear to forestall any attempt to dispose of the issue finally at the forthcoming session and is a good example of the difficulties we encounter in trying to obtain agreement with Mr. Anslinger.[67]

Despite the commissioner's opposition towards the policies adopted by the State Department, the US was successful in preventing the creation of a Middle East control agency. Anslinger's opinions were not considered.

The relations of the United States with both Afghanistan and Iran can also be seen to demonstrate the State Department's subordination of narcotic control in the Middle East to other, apparently more pressing foreign policy concerns. A discussion of events in the region also introduces contemporary examples of US subordination of drug control to wider foreign policy.

Although a source of illegal opium for some time, Afghanistan had declined an invitation to attend the conference for the completion of the 1953 Opium Protocol. However, despite an apparent lack of interest in the UN's opium control framework as created by the protocol, the Afghan government requested inclusion among the authorized producer nations in 1956. This suggestion created much debate in the CND, some delegates claiming that it would be unfair to exclude Afghanistan from having a producer status simply because it had not attended the conference. Regardless of this opinion, Afghanistan's request was to be greatly influenced by the opium situation of its neighbour Iran.

The Iranian government had been traditionally opposed to controls on opium production because it was an important source of revenue. However, its stance changed dramatically after Mohammed Mussaddiq's government was overthrown with American support in 1953. American pressure thereafter led to the adoption of laws that were completely in line with US prohibitive ideals. In 1955 Iran consequently outlawed all production of opium. According to Anslinger, in his 1962 book *The Murderers*, the policy had been put into effect by the work of his agent Colonel Garland Williams.[68] The Iranian authorities argued that permission for opium production in Afghanistan would have a deleterious impact upon Iran. In the first case, it would have appeared inconsistent if the CND had urged nations to ratify the 1953 legislation and simultaneously allowed Afghanistan to produce even more opium. Second, opium production in the neighbouring nation might have hindered Iranian attempts to reduce addiction.

The United States, the motivating force behind the 1953 Opium Protocol, and a great believer in the idea of control at source, would have been expected to support Iran's efforts for control and oppose Afghanistan's request to become another opium producer, especially as the Iranians had adopted a US-style control regime so wholeheartedly. However, this was not to be the case. Although the USA maintained close diplomatic links with Iran, a country with an important strategic role to play in the region, the State Department's policy on opium did produce tension between the two nations.

American interest in the strategically crucial Baghdad Pact ensured that US–Iranian relations were intimate. The pact, originally made between Turkey and Iraq in 1955, and joined by Pakistan, Britain and Iran later in that year, aimed for mutual co-operation against left-wing militants in the region. Although the pact's structure altered after the Suez crisis in 1956 and the withdrawal of Iraq in 1958, it remained central to Western security considerations in the important area. The pact was to become the basis of the Central Treaty Organization (CENTO), which, with increased US involvement, sought to provide an integrated defence policy against the Soviet Union. Yet despite such shared strategic concerns, the United States was to side with Afghanistan on the issue of opium production.

Despite evidence from the US embassy in Teheran suggesting that opium was being illegally smuggled from Afghanistan into Iran,[69] the United States appeared to turn its back on Iran and supported the Afghan government's request. Evidence, as we shall see, suggests that this decision was motivated by fears of an Afghan move towards the Soviet sphere of influence.

The policy did not go unopposed. Concerns regarding the impact of the US government's actions on Iran were voiced by the American embassy in Teheran. In a revealing confidential telegram to the Secretary of State, John Foster Dulles, the American Ambassador outlined his fears. Noting the 'psychological problem created by [the] US attitude', Mr Chapin observed that US action would damage the stability of the Shah's government and undermine Teheran's faith in US support.[70] Striking at the crux of the issue, the Ambassador drew attention to the fact that the American decision in favour of Afghanistan would ultimately harm US interests, 'because [the] Iranians believe US motivation may have been ... a bid to keep Afghanistan from sliding further behind the Iron Curtain'.[71] Clearly, then, Teheran had no illusions regarding superpower politics in the region. Evidence also suggests that the Iranian Minister of Health, Dr Sahel, 'felt very strongly' that the United States 'had let him down'. He 'stressed the great economic loss his country was suffering as a result of its enlightened, though highly unpopular, decision' to introduce US-initiated legislation to prohibit opium smoking in his country. Displaying the Iranian government's bemusement with the American stance, Sahel also pointed out that the United States 'had voted with those profiteers who were not members of the Baghdad Pact, although there was every humane and moral reason for voting to outlaw the growth of the poppy seed'.[72]

Indeed, the conflicting aspects of the American approach to the issue placed the USA in an awkward position in the region. The United States wanted Afghanistan to become a listed legitimate opium producer nation under the terms of the 1953 Opium Protocol, but simultaneously supported Iran's domestic opium prohibition programme, even though the two schemes were in direct conflict with one another. Nevertheless, instead of supporting the Iranian government in its efforts to eliminate illegal opium production, the State Department chose to back the Afghan authorities, thus theoretically increasing the amount of opium that could be diverted into illicit channels and the Iranian black market. It should be remembered that such action would arguably have also increased the flow of illicit opiates to the rest of the world, including paradoxically the United States itself.

The Iranian authorities were understandably aggrieved by the lack of US support for what was in essence a US-style prohibition scheme. Washington's support of the Afghan request, although evidence suggested that the Afghan government was doing nothing to stop opium smuggling into Iran,[73] appeared irrational. The State Department's desire to appease the Afghan regime, owing to security interests in the region, appeared to override any concerns for drug control in what today is known as the Golden Crescent (Afghanistan, Iran and Pakistan).

The UN's arduous ratification procedures ensured that the 1953 protocol did not come into force until the early 1960s when the necessary number of nations had acceded to the legislation. In 1957, therefore, despite US efforts to get the 1953 law ratified, the protocol remained to be implemented. For this reason, and despite hindering the US policy to reduce opium production at source, the State Department was permitted the luxury of supporting the continuing Afghan claim to produce opium, without having to contend with Iranian opposition on a formal basis in the UN. The Americans noted that 'since the Opium Protocol of 1953 is not yet in force, Afghanistan requires no permission to produce and export opium for medical and scientific purposes'. However, as a caveat they also noted that Iranian claims regarding smuggling were of a serious nature and Afghan reports to the UN regarding opium production were being challenged as less than adequate. Consequently, the US representatives were instructed by the State Department to 'temporize the issue', and invite the governments of Iran and Afghanistan to submit to the Commission [CND] ... in 1958 'all information which they [were] in a position to furnish ... which would be of assistance to the Commission [CND]'.[74] In essence, therefore, the Americans continued to support the positions adopted by both Afghanistan and Iran, although they appeared to be in conflict. Because of the State Department's stance, the US representative supported the proposed UN technical assistance to nations, notably Iran, thus continuing in some way to provide backing to a nation sympathetic to US narcotic policies and Western influence in the region.[75]

Thus despite antagonizing a trusted ally in the region that was adopting a domestically unpopular and essentially US-style scheme to prohibit poppy cultivation, the State Department continued to back the Afghan plan to produce opium. It is perhaps possible to argue that the State Department merely wished to legalize and monitor production that was already under way. However, the political considerations that dominated the atmosphere of the period are more likely to have been the motivation behind the contradictory US behaviour.

To be sure, the mid-1950s saw a dramatic shift in US attitudes towards Afghanistan. Since the end of the Second World War, the State Department had chosen to ignore repeated Afghan requests for economic, political and military support, preferring instead to strengthen Pakistan as a buffer against Soviet influence in the region. Long-standing Afghan–Pakistani tensions concerning territorial disputes made significant US aid for Kabul undesirable and impractical within the strategic context of the US relations with Karachi. Washington consequently paid Afghanistan little attention and, as Henry S. Bradsher notes, US foreign policy experts regarded Afghanistan as 'merely an exotic land beyond the Northwest frontier'.[76] Thus, while US attention focused upon Iran and Pakistan, the latter becoming a member of the South East Asia Treaty Organization (SEATO) in 1954 as well as the Baghdad Pact in 1955, Kabul moved ever closer towards the Soviet sphere. Accordingly, in 1953 Afghanistan became the first non-communist recipient of Soviet aid. Massive investment from Moscow funded much-needed civil engineering projects and strengthened traditionally strong ties between the nations. Although the early 1950s saw the USSR move to increase economic leverage upon Afghanistan, it was not until 1956 that Moscow agreed to significant military aid for Kabul. A $32.4 million Soviet loan in July thus altered the pattern of communist aid, giving Moscow considerable sway over the Afghan army and air force. Realization of increasing Soviet influence in the region understandably forced Washington to reassess its strategic calculations. Indeed, soon after the arms deal, the US National Security

Council (NSC) found that 'the capability of the United States to shape events in South Asia is severely limited'. The NSC recommended US efforts to resolve the Afghan dispute with Pakistan and 'to encourage Afghanistan to minimize its reliance upon the communist bloc ... and look to the United States and other Free World Sources for military training and assistance'.[77]

While US efforts to reverse the years of neglect focused primarily upon military assistance, Washington also moved to improve relations with Kabul through co-operation and aid in other fields. In 1956, the State Department accordingly designated the nation as an 'emergency action area'. This move initiated a search for ways to ameliorate US–Afghan relations and maintain Afghanistan's precious neutrality.[78] One method was the adoption of the US 'civil aviation program', which aimed to compete with the USSR in the field of commercial aviation in Afghanistan.[79] The timing of the US decision concerning Afghan opium production therefore makes it highly probable that American support on this issue was also at the vanguard of the new policy towards Afghanistan. The State Department no doubt hoped that the US stance would place Washington in a more favourable light in Kabul. It is also likely that American policymakers hoped that any revenue from the lucrative licit opium crops would lessen Afghan reliance upon Soviet economic support. Potential increases in the illegal opium traffic and strained relations with a valuable ally both seemed to be bearable costs of a hastily refashioned, though ultimately futile, regional containment policy.

The United States was fortunate in that the complex issue resolved itself in 1958, thus avoiding further complications in relations between the USA, Afghanistan and Iran. To use official UN parlance, at the Thirteenth Session of the CND 'the observer of Afghanistan declared that his country in the interests of humanity and in the spirit of international co-operation had decided to revive its policy of complete prohibition of cultivation, trade, purchase, sale, import, export and use of opium'.[80] Evidence suggests that CND support for UN technical assistance and financial assistance under the programmes of individual governments and private organizations had been enough to encourage the Afghan government to reverse its policies and move towards a prohibitive strategy on opium.[81] Ironically, this was the case despite earlier US support for increased production of the drug.

The Golden Crescent is today one of the world's major sources of illegal heroin. Although it would be absurd to blame contemporary conditions in the region upon US action, or perhaps more appropriately inaction, in the 1950s, it is interesting to note that US drug control efforts there remained tied up with foreign-policy concerns well into the 1980s. After Soviet troops entered Afghanistan in December 1979, the United States, through CIA channels, provided the Afghan Mujaheddin rebels with military supplies to fight the Soviets and the pro-Soviet Afghan regime led by Prime Minister Babrak Karmal. US support, however, also stretched to the toleration of *Mujaheddin* opium production, a traditional source of revenue for many Afghan tribes. Thus in a similar fashion to events in Southeast Asia in the 1950s, the American willingness to support anti-communist factions in the region conflicted with the long-term US desire to control the illegal production of opium at source. Such events were not isolated incidents. Washington's energetic anti-communism has produced a number of similar situations elsewhere. As we shall see, while later examples have involved a different drug and a different continent, the duality inherent within US policy remains fundamentally the same.

The American stance on drug control in Iran and Afghanistan in the late 1950s, like the USA's convoluted policies of the 1980s, must therefore be assessed in relation to the regional foreign policy goals of the United States during that period. Although three decades separate the incidents discussed here, the motivation remains the same. Fears that nations such as Afghanistan were falling into Soviet spheres of influence appeared to have taken precedence over all other policies. Such a reaction is understandable when assessed within the framework of the Cold War. However, it is crucial to note that the subordination of US narcotic foreign policy in both the Middle East and Southeast Asia could have undermined the same national security that Washington sought through its strategy of seeking to contain perceived communist expansion. Increasing drug addiction in the United States was seen as a real threat to national values during the 1950s. A US government subcommittee concluded in January 1956 that drug addiction was causing half the crimes committed in metropolitan areas, and a quarter of all reported in the entire nation. Drug use was found to be 'contagious' and addicts at large were seen to be spreading the habit with 'cancerous rapidity'.[82] Official anxiety manifested itself in the passage of the draconian 1951 Boggs Act and the 1956 Narcotics Control Act discussed earlier. Thus, while Washington's actions adhered to the complex principles of Cold War diplomacy, they ran counter to US measures against drug abuse both at home and abroad.

CONCLUSION

American Cold War foreign policy concerns produced a contradictory approach to international narcotic control at the UN. Despite US dominance in the CND and a public drive for international prohibition, the

State Department was to ensure that narcotic foreign policy did not conflict with the wider concerns for American security. Anslinger and the US delegation's search for narcotic control, and the consequent application of pressure on nations to follow the US policy for prohibition, was therefore only one component of a multifaceted American approach towards international control. The perceived threat from communist expansion ensured that foreign policy took precedence over narcotic policy, even though the United States boldly proclaimed its desire for strict international legislation and pushed for measures such as the 1953 Opium Protocol.

The State Department's subordination of narcotic control to other interests, more precisely a fear of communism, was in some ways mirrored in the behaviour of Harry Anslinger. He exploited political issues to enhance and safeguard his own position in Washington, DC, and thus also adopted a varied approach to the issue of control. However, his actions were constrained by the State Department. Consequently, despite some occasions when the FBN chief appeared to be operating independently of the US government, Anslinger ensured that he remained within the confines of State Department policy. He thereby made sure that his position as US representative to the CND remained secure over many years. As a result, Anslinger was indeed a successful 'bureaucratic Cold Warrior', as Douglas Clark Kinder has labelled him.[83]

Nonetheless, Anslinger's awareness for bureaucratic survival ensured that he was not the single controlling force behind US narcotic foreign policy at the UN. Although this is in no way intended to deny Anslinger's importance, it does attempt to place the commissioner in the context of the United States' long-term quest for international drug prohibition. He was an important factor in the US crusade for international prohibitive policies. His lengthy tenure at the helm of the FBN, his supposed expertise and his forceful personality made this inevitable. However, the commissioner's instincts for self-preservation resulted in the pursuit of what can be termed a path of least resistance. He would ultimately concur with the wider foreign-policy concerns of the State Department, so he cannot be held to be completely responsible for the formulation and control of US narcotic foreign policy at the UN. It is true that while at the UN Anslinger pushed for narcotic prohibition, even if this meant some conflict with the State Department. Nevertheless, he was never to push so hard as to risk his own position. His relationship with the Department was also affected by his complex and sometimes contradictory belief system. This included both a desire for prohibitive narcotic policies and a fear and hatred of communism. During his career such beliefs were to coincide and collide, thus revealing another aspect of the United States' discrepant approach to international narcotic control. The contradictions inherent in Anslinger's approach to the issue of drug control are, as have been discussed, well illustrated in his charges against the People's Republic of China.[84]

However, as will be shown in the next chapter, an accurate picture of the commissioner's role within the US system for drug control at the UN can be seen in his actions concerning the creation of a Single Convention on Narcotic Drugs. The US government's stance towards the legislation illuminates its concern for political issues and Anslinger's weakness in relation to the State Department. The passage into international law of the Single Convention also demonstrated that, despite contradictions and conflicts, the United States remained the dominant force in the UN narcotic control framework. The result of this was the continuing creation of US-style prohibitive international control legislation.

NOTES

1. See, for example, Rufus King's comments that the commissioner 'dominated most policy deliberations on the international scene'. Rufus King, *The Drug Hang Up: America's Fifty-Year Folly*, 2nd edn (Springfield, IL: Charles C. Thomas, 1974), p. 71. An article in the magazine *Grit* in 1961 was also a typical example of the media's portrayal of Anslinger as the controlling force of all US narcotic foreign policy. In March, it noted that 'Through his chairmanship of the UN commission, Anslinger keeps the war against dope neatly coordinated around the world.' (The magazine was incorrect to state that Anslinger was chairman of the CND in 1961. This was in fact a position he last held in 1956.)

2. Letter from Samuel Hoare (Home Office) to Mr G. R. Gauntlet concerning British comments on synthetic drugs, 6 March 1957, Public Record Office, Kew, London, UK, hereafter PRO (FO371). A State Department representative often accompanied Anslinger to the meetings of the CND, but, was there only to advise the commissioner on political statements and appeared, according to Tom Green, to have had little, if any, influence over Anslinger. From an interview with Tom C. Green, October 1993 (hereafter I/TCG.)

3. Foreign Office telegram from the UK representative on the CND to the Foreign Office, 2 May 1958. PRO (FO371).

4. Letter from Tom C. Green to Sam Hoare, 4 May 1950, UNS1815/26, PRO (FO371 129987).

5. Information from I/TCG.

6. Kettil Bruun, Lynn Pan and Ingemar Rexed, *The Gentlemen's Club: International Control of Drugs and Alcohol* (Chicago: University of Chicago Press, 1975), p. 124.

7. Douglas Clark Kinder and William O. Walker III, 'Stable force in a storm: Harry J. Anslinger and US narcotic foreign policy 1930–1962', *Journal of American History*, 72 (March 1986), 922.

8. William O. Walker III, *Opium and Foreign Policy: The Anglo-American Search for Order, 1912–1954* (Chapel-Hill: University of North Carolina Press, 1991), p. 213.
9. See correspondence between Anslinger and the State Department 1955. Telegrams 20 April 1955, 22 April 1955, 26 April 1955, regarding proposed statement on illicit narcotic traffic in the Far East. National Archives, Washington, DC, USA (hereafter NA), 340.19.
10. Office memorandum concerning a conversation with Mr Anslinger on certain problems in the field of narcotic drugs, from Mr Ottis E. Mulliken to Mr John W. Hanes, 11 March 1958, p. 4, NA 340.19.
11. Memorandum of meeting with the Hon. A. Gilmore Flues, Assistant Secretary of the Treasury, from Mr Ottis E. Mulliken to John W. Hanes, 16 April 1958, p. 2, NA 340.19.
12. *Ibid.*
13. *Ibid.*, p. 3.
14. Richard J. Bonnie and Charles H. Whitebread II, *The Marihuana Conviction: A History of Marihuana Prohibition in the US* (Charlottesville: University Press of Virginia, 1974), p. 204.
15. Remarks of Harry Anslinger regarding the PRC at the Eighth Session of the CND, 1953 (24 pages), PRO (FO371 129983), and also the remarks of Harry J. Anslinger concerning the illicit narcotic traffic in the Far East, pp. 1–11, Ninth Session of the CND, 1954, PRO (FO371 129983), and remarks at the Tenth session of the CND, 1955. Speeches of Anslinger, Drug Enforcement Administration Library, Washington, DC, USA (hereafter DEAL).
16. See *The Committee on One Million – Against the Admission of Red China to the UN: A Brief History of an Authorized and Effective People's Movement* (New York), p. 5, Harry J. Anslinger Papers, Harry S. Truman Library (hereafter cited as HTL), Independence, Missouri, USA. Correspondence Folder 6.
17. William O. Walker III, *Opium and Foreign Policy*, p. 197.
18. *New York Times*, 5 May 1954, p. 8.
19. *Ibid.*, p. 14.
20. *The Times*, 27 June 1955, Reuter, p. 6.
21. *The Times*, 16 April 1953. UN correspondent.
22. *The Times*, 6 May 1952, p. 5. The title of the piece was 'Chinese accused in UN commission'.
23. South China Morning Post, 'Dope from Red China channelled through Hong Kong flooding US', 25 November 1953. Additionally see *South China Morning Post*, 27 November 1953.
24. According to British authorities, 'Mr Walker believes that a good deal of the information in Mr. Anslinger's statements was furnished by National Chinese sources.' Letter from British embassy, Washington, DC, to H. F. Bartlett, Far East Department, 21 January 1954, PRO (FO371 129983).
25. 'Political affairs: Yuan issues decree regarding suppression of opium and narcotics'. From Peking (Beijing), 26 February 1950, PRO (FO371 88823), and extracts from daily news release, 3 July 1954, PRO (FO371 129983).
26. Letter from John H. Walker, Home Office, to H. F. Bartlett, 14 January 1954, PRO (FO371).

27. Letter from Herbert E. Gaston to Anslinger, 27 July 1954, AP Box 2: File 12, 1954. Gaston notes that Deverall's book was 'well documented', and, because much of the information was from FBN sources, was therefore legitimate.

28. Richard Deverall, *Mao Tse-tung: Stop This Dirty Opium Business!*, (Tokyo, 1954).

29. Letter from John H. Walker, Home Office, to Miss I. Mackie, Foreign Office, undated, PRO (FO371 129983), and Foreign Office to Chancery, British embassy, Tokyo, 6 October 1954, PRO (FO371 129983).

30. Letter from John H. Walker, Home Office, to H. F. Bartlett, 14 January 1954, PRO (FO371).

31. Letter from B. C. Macdermot, Foreign Office, to A. Dudley, Singapore, PRO (FO371 129983).

32. Letter from R. H. Hadlow, British consulate-general, San Francisco, to A. Campbell, 6 April 1954, PRO (FO371 129983).

33. Letter from John H. Walker, Home Office, to Miss D. G. Hallet, Colonial Office, London, 2 February 1954, PRO (FO371 129983).

34. Secret telegram from Humphrey Trevelyan, British Embassy, to Colin T. Crowe, Foreign Office, 11 October 1954, PRO (FO371 129983).

35. Letter from H. F. Bartlett, Far East Department, to British embassy, Washington, DC, 21 January 1954, PRO (FO371 129983).

36. Anslinger continued to stand by his claims into the 1960s. In 1964, in his book *The Protectors*, Anslinger reiterated his long-standing charges, stating that 'The record is clear. Communist China, with the greatest land mass in Asia at her disposal, has been flooding her neighbouring countries with drugs. Japan, once herself a despoiler of the moral fibre of China during the 1930s, has been a major target of the Communists.' Harry J. Anslinger, *The Protectors* (New York: Farrar, Straus, 1964), p. 223. Also see correspondence between Anslinger and Mr David Ward. Anslinger states that 'throughout the Communist Chinese regime we have received many authoritative reports from sources, both official and unofficial, which amply confirm every statement that we have made'. Letter from Anslinger to Ward, 23 September 1963, HTL.

37. See memorandum of conversation regarding Anslinger's proposed statement concerning illicit traffic in the Far East, between George A. Morlock and Colonel Robert E. Sullivan, Office of the Provost Marshall, 2 May 1955, NA 340.19. Marshall noted that the 'Office has never been able to find documentary proof that communist China has infiltrated communism into our armed forces in the Far East. Their investigations in 1952 and 1953 came to naught.' He also remarked that 'Of course some of the peddlers of narcotics in the Far East are communists.'

38. Douglas Clark Kinder, 'Bureaucratic Cold Warrior: Harry J. Anslinger and illicit narcotics traffic', *Pacific Historical Review*, **50** (May 1981), 171.

39. US House of Representatives, 1972, *Congressional Record*, 29 March 1972, cited by David F. Musto, 'The rise and fall of epidemics: learning from history, in Griffith Edwards, John Strang and Jerome H. Jaffe (eds), *Drugs, Alcohol, and Tobacco: Making the Science and Policy Connections* (Oxford:

Oxford Medical Publications, 1993), p. 282. It is also interesting to note that, having reached a low point in diplomatic relations with the PRC, the Soviet Union began to charge the Communist Chinese with drug smuggling. Despite the State Department's statement, books still appeared in the United States in the 1970s that accused the Communist Chinese with using drugs to undermine Western nations. See, for example, A. H. Stanton Candlin, *Psychochemical Warfare: The Chinese Communist Drug Offensive against the West* (New Rochelle, NY: Arlington House, 1973), and Gerd Hamburger and Rudolf Shermann, *The Peking Bomb: The Psychochemical War against America* (Washington, DC: Robert B. Luce, 1975). Both books borrowed heavily from Anslinger.

40. See Report to Secretary of State from Anslinger of the US delegation to the Eighteenth Session of the CND, 28 June 1963, p. 6, Anslinger Papers (hereafter cited as AP), Pattee Library Labor Archives, Penn State University, Pennsylvania, Box 10: File 11.

41. John C. McWilliams, *The Protectors: Harry J. Anslinger and the Federal Bureau of Narcotics, 1930–1962*, (Newark: University of Delaware Press, 1990), p. 154.

42. It was becoming clear to some authorities in the region that, despite Anslinger's protestations to the contrary, it was the Nationalist Chinese forces, not the Communists, who were heavily involved with the illicit drug trade. For example, in 1957 the British government acknowledged the KMT's involvement in the illegal opium trade and noted that 'As we understand it, opium is an important source of revenue to the KMT.' Confidential telegram from Gauntlet, Foreign Office, to Tom Green. From a report from HMG consul, Chiang-mai, Thailand, 15 March 1957, PRO (FO371 129979).

43. For an account, see Alfred W. McCoy, *The Politics of Heroin: CIA Complicity in the Global Drug Trade* (New York: Lawrence Hill, 1991), pp. 127–493.

44. For an account of Anslinger and the FBN's involvement with the intelligence community, see John C. McWilliams, 'Covert connections: the FBN, the OSS, and the CIA', *Historian*, **53**(4) (1991), 657–78. McWilliams also describes FBN agent George White's activities with CIA mind control experiments in 1952, the so-called MK ULTRA project (pp. 669–71).

45. Letter from John F. Baldwin to John Foster Dulles, 12 January 1955, NA 340.19. Also see letter from William B. Windall (Rep., New Jersey) to Dulles, 4 January 1955, NA 340.19, and letter from Gracie Pfost (Rep., Idaho) to US UN ambassador Lodge, 6 January 1955, NA 340.19, and letter from Senator Thomas H. Kuchel to Dulles, 28 March 1955, NA 340.19.

46. Letter from Ross Adair (Rep., Indiana) to John Foster Dulles, 10 January 1955, NA 340.19.

47. Letter from Karl Bambach, Executive Vice-President ADMA, to John Foster Dulles, 27 January 1955, NA 340.19.

48. See Letter from Chairman Walker F. George to Dulles, 2 April 1955. (Senate Resolution 87, 84th Congress, First Session, 1 April 1955), NA 340.19.

49. State Department memorandum of conversation between Anslinger and George A. Morlock, 5 January 1955, NA 340.19.

50. Letter from David McKey, Assistant Secretary State Department, to Mr Rooney, 14 April 1955, NA 340.19.

51. State Department memorandum of conversation between Anslinger and Mr Phillips, 20 January 1955, NA 340.19.

52. *Ibid.*, pp. 1–4. Anslinger also went on to claim that he had discussed the issue with the Mexican ambassador and that he was 'all in favor of going to Geneva because his wife was interested in visiting Geneva!'.

53. Telegram from US delegation at the UN to State Department, 3 March 1955, NA 340.19.

54. Telegram from US delegation at the UN in New York to Secretary of State, 9 March 1955, NA 340.19. According to the telegram, the 'US ... expressed reluctance to raise the question in ECOSOC because of consequent embarrassment to both Secretariat and US. Bunche [Fr] indicated strong personal view desirable avoid ECOSOC or NC [Narcotic Commission] action if possible since Secretariat would probably have to support transfer if Hammarskjold unwilling to act on basis of US informal approaches.'

55. Telegram from US delegation at the UN in New York to Secretary of State, 12 March 1955, NA 340.19.

56. *Ibid.* Also see State Department memorandum of conversation, 12 March 1955, NA 340.1.

57. Memorandum of conversation between Anslinger and Mr Phillips of the State Department's International Office, 20 January 1955, p. 5, NA 340.19.

58. Anslinger met the Secretary-General on 30 March 1955. See letter from Philippe de Seyenes, Under-Secretary, Department of Economic and Social Affairs, to Mr Preston Hotchis, US Representative to ECOSOC, NA 340.19, and telegram from the US delegation at the UN in New York to State Department, 5 April 1955, NA 340.19.

59. Memorandum of meeting between Anslinger and the Hon. A. Gilmore Flues, 16 April 1958, *op. cit.*, p. 3.

60. See memorandum to Assistant Secretary of the Department of State Kendal from Anslinger, 11 August 1956, AP Box 2: File 10.

61. Department of State position paper for the Twelfth Session of the CND, 24 April 1957, p. 3, NA 340.19.

62. Telegram from Dulles, State Department, to US embassy, Cairo, 23 May 1957, NA 340.19.

63. *Ibid.*, p. 3.

64. Telegram from Dulles, State Department, to US embassy, Cairo, 23 May 1957, NA 340.19.

65. *Ibid.*, p. 3.

66. Telegram from Dulles, State Department, to US embassy, Cairo, 23 May 1957, NA 340.19.

67. *Ibid.*, p. 3.

68. Harry J. Anslinger and Will Ousler, *The Murderers* (London: Arthur Baker, 1962), p. 204.

69. Confidential telegram from Mr Chapin, US embassy, Teheran, to Secretary of State, 2 July 1956, p. 1, NA 340.19.

70. *Ibid.*

71. *Ibid.*

72. Letter from H. Leonard Warres, MD, Baltimore, to J. F. Dulles, 25 July 1956, NA 340.19.
73. Confidential telegram from Mr Chapin, US embassy, Teheran, to Secretary of State, 2 July 1956, p. 2, NA 340.19.
74. Department of State position paper, for the Twelfth Session of the CND, 24 April 1957, item 6, p. 5, NA 340.19.
75. Department of State position paper, for the Twelfth Session of the CND, 24 April 1957, item 16, p. 2, NA 340.19.
76. Henry S. Bradsher, *Afghanistan and the Soviet Union*, (Durham, NC: Duke Press Policy Studies, 1983), p. 19.
77. *Ibid.*, p. 28.
78. See 'Expansion of Soviet influence in Afghanistan and U.S. countermeasures', 11 May 1956, report by the Operations Co-ordination Board, National Security Council, cited in Henry S. Bradsher, *Afghanistan and the Soviet Union*, p. 29.
79. *Ibid.*, and confidential telegram from Mr Chapin, US embassy, Teheran, to Secretary of State, 2 July 1956, p. 2, NA 340.19.
80. UN Secretariat, 'Twenty years of narcotics control under the United Nations: review of the work of the Commission on Narcotic Drugs from its 1st to its 20th session', *Bulletin on Narcotics*, **18**(1) (1966), 30.
81. 'The thirteenth session of the Commission on Narcotic Drugs and the twenty-sixth session of the Economic and Social Council', *Bulletin on Narcotics*, **10**(4) (1958), 45.
82. Rufus King, *The Drug Hang-Up*, p. 142.
83. Douglas Clark Kinder, 'Bureaucratic Cold Warrior', pp. 169–91.
84. There is also evidence to suggest that Senator Joseph McCarthy, the source of much of the American anti-communist hysteria in the early 1950s, was himself addicted to morphine, a habit Anslinger apparently secretly supplied to prevent the revelation from becoming public. Anslinger, the great crusader against both narcotics and communism, was therefore simultaneously exploiting the communist paranoia of McCarthyism and helping to supply the Senator with drugs – a twisted irony that demonstrated the commissioner's opportunistic nature. John C. McWilliams, *The Protectors*, pp. 98–9.

CHAPTER 4

THE SPURNED PROGENY:
Harry J. Anslinger, the United States and the 1961 Single Convention on Narcotic Drugs

This Convention was the crowning result of over half a century of persistent efforts to create international legislation that would bring under effective national and international control all narcotic substances.
Leon Steinig of the International Narcotic Control Board, *Bulletin on Narcotics*, 1968

The 1961 Single Convention on Narcotic Drugs occupies an important place in the history of international drug control and the American crusade. It plays a central role in the creation and perpetuation of the global prohibitionist norm discussed in earlier chapters. And therefore warrants our attention.

The convention was designed to tidy up and increase the efficiency of the international control system that had developed since 1912. Ultimately, however, it did not merely bring together disparate pieces of international legislation that preceded it; the convention also included new provisions not contained in earlier treaties, creating a stricter system for control. As noted in the Introduction to this book, the legislation obliges signatory nations to limit exclusively to medical and scientific purposes the production, manufacture, export, import, distribution of, trade in, use and possession of drugs; eradicate all unlicensed cultivation; suppress illicit manufacture and traffic; and co-operate with each other in achieving the aims of the convention. The international text completed in 1961 has been described by Gianfranco Dell'Alba, Olivier Dupuis and Jean-Luc Robert as 'the basis for the prohibition and repression of illicit drug use at a global level'.[1]

The significance and contemporary relevance of the Convention is enhanced when we recall that it has also provided the foundations for all subsequent UN narcotic control treaties. The 1971, 1972 and 1988 UN drug control conventions, which will be discussed at more length in the next chapter, were all constructed upon the provisions contained within the 1961 document.

For many proponents of transnational narcotic prohibition the convention

represented a high point in the international process that began in Shanghai in 1909. This was a view espoused by the secretariat of the UN drug
control apparatus. It claimed in 1964, the year the convention came into
force, that 'opium eating and smoking, coca-leaf chewing and cannabis
consumption will finally be outlawed throughout the world'. The convention, the secretariat concluded, 'represents a major step in the struggle of
mankind against one of the most insidious and destructive of all evils –
narcotics abuse'.[2] By depicting the legislation as an important advance for
the protection of humankind against the 'evils' of non-medical and non-
scientific drug use, the UN has successfully placed pressure upon nations
to comply with the legislative ideals of the convention. States that deviate
from the provisions of the 1961 legislation, and consequently fail to
conform to the international prohibitive norm, can be portrayed as a
menace to humankind. Commenting on the impact of the UN system, and
particularly the Single Convention, upon the formulation of national drug
control legislation, Rufus King notes that 'for better or for worse, the
remarkable phenomenon of direct international manipulation in this
domestic field, and manipulation significantly dominated by the United
States besides, is apparently going to remain with us'.[3]

King is right to acknowledge the important role the United States
played in the formulation of the Single Convention. American interest in
some form of consolidating convention to update, and where necessary
replace, the earlier international legislation had been apparent since 1948.
At that time, as King notes, 'the CND adopted a US drafted and US
sponsored resolution addressed to the ECOSOC requesting the Secretary-
General to commence work on a Single Convention'.[4] The convening of
the Plenipotentiary Conference for the Adoption of a Single Convention
on Narcotic Drugs in New York in 1961 undoubtedly owed a great deal to
the work of successive US delegations to the CND since 1948. The convention could be seen, therefore, as the successful conclusion of over a decade
of US endeavour. Indeed, provisions concerning the international pro-
scription of the use of cannabis, coca and opium reflect the inclusion in the
convention of several long-term American prohibitionist aims. In many
respects, the convention can be seen as the handiwork of the United States,
with its predominantly prohibitive perspective resulting from American
involvement in the drafting process.

However, any interpretation of the Single Convention as simply the
triumphant culmination of persistent US endeavour is inadequate. Many
accounts, including King's appraisal, fail to acknowledge that the United
States ultimately appeared dissatisfied with the final terms of the treaty.
American unease with the convention did not escape the attention of
Adolf Lande. He noted in 1962 that after the conference in New York the

'representative of the United States ... expressed the view that the Single Convention should be amended to make it more effective before it came into force'.[5] Harry Anslinger, who was predictably the US representative mentioned by Lande, also grasped every opportunity to affirm the USA's apparent discontent. In a 1964 article in the UN *Bulletin on Narcotics*, Bertil Renborg noted that Anslinger had made it clear that 'both his Government and himself' were 'firmly opposed to its [the Single Convention] coming into force'.[6] This was because, Anslinger believed, several provisions in the convention, far from tightening control, actually weakened aspects of the international system as it stood before 1961. Thus, although US influence in the UN's narcotic control machinery led to the creation of legislation based predominantly upon a belief in prohibition, the recognition of American opposition to the convention shatters the conceptually neat image of the Single Convention as an American success story. However, the history of the US relationship with the 1961 legislation is also complicated by the discovery of a conflict of interest that existed between Anslinger and the US State Department. Investigation reveals that Anslinger's comments in 1964, which gave the impression that both he and the State Department opposed the Single Convention, were misleading. In reality, as will be shown, Anslinger attempted to undermine the legislation, while the State Department privately supported it.

The aim of this chapter, therefore, is not to scrutinize the structure and individual provisions of the Convention. Others have ably completed this task.[7] It is the intention here to re-evaluate the differences in stance adopted by Harry Anslinger and the US State Department during the course of the 1961 legislation's passage into international law. The chapter will begin by reviewing the state of the international control system before 1961 and then examine the relationships that existed between the different power blocs that attended the conference for the adoption of the Single Convention. The final legislation produced by the conference will also be examined briefly. Next, by viewing the American position on this legislation as the product of intragovernmental conflict and political compromise, the chapter will highlight significant, and hitherto unexplored, facets of the relationship that existed between Anslinger and the US State Department.

In corroboration of the evidence put forward in earlier chapters, Anslinger's image as the dominant force in US narcotic foreign policy at the UN will be challenged. Anslinger's collision of interest with the State Department provides an example of his proclivity to pursue his own objectives. However, his efforts, and ultimately failure, to prevent the convention from coming into force will be used to illustrate Anslinger's inability to produce the results he desired when they conflicted with the wishes of the State Department. Such an interpretation of Anslinger's role therefore contrasts with that put forward by other scholars. For example, William O. Walker III has said, 'as a lasting testimony to Anslinger's tenure as narcotics commissioner ... nations from around the world ratified the 1961 Single Convention on Narcotic Drugs'.[8] As will be shown, the widespread ratification of the convention was not at all what Anslinger wanted.

It will also be shown how Anslinger believed that the convention's control of certain drugs, particularly the production of opium, was weaker than for previous treaties, notably the 1953 Opium Protocol. As a result he worked hard to encourage other nations to withhold support for the 1961 legislation. Despite Anslinger's activities, however, we will see how the State Department preferred not to use American dominance within the UN to pressurize other nations to oppose the legislation. This was a decision influenced by the wider diplomatic implications of the Cold War.

PRELUDE TO THE 1961 CONVENTION

Before we embark on an analysis of the activities of Anslinger and the State Department, it is useful to summarize the state of the international control system as it stood before 1961. It should be recalled that the system operated on several premises. These had been established through the implementation of transnational treaties since 1912. After extensive pressure from the United States, the central tenet of the control framework was that narcotic drugs were to be used only for medical or scientific purposes. In order to attempt to achieve this provision, the system maintained that each nation's narcotics trade had to have a government licence and records of all transactions. These regulations were contained in the 1912 and 1925 conventions. In addition, as a means to control stocks worldwide, the narcotics supplies of each country or territory obtained from either manufacture or import had to be limited to the quantities needed for medical and scientific purposes. According to the provisions of the 1931 convention, these needs were to be computed from estimates made by the governments concerned. In addressing the illicit side of the narcotic issue, the 1936 convention had introduced measures aimed at ensuring prosecution and effective punishment of illicit narcotic traffickers. In accordance with the 1931 convention, governments within individual states were under an obligation to organize their narcotics control services in line with treaty requirements. This included furnishing, to the appropriate international bodies, annual reports on control in their territories, the state of laws and regulations, information on seizures, statistical data, and estimates of narcotic requirements. The intention, therefore, was that the international framework could review and regulate the world narcotic situation. This included making evaluations and recommendations that would in theory facilitate the running of the international system – although admittedly, then as now, the effectiveness of its operation depended a great deal upon the co-operation of national governments.

The UN drug control framework's gradual and piecemeal development over the space of nearly fifty years had inevitably resulted in incon-sistencies and shortcomings. The existence of six pre-war treaties, and an additional three under the aegis of the UN, had understandably produced an unwieldy and over-complicated framework for international control. As a result, moves were made to put into force a treaty that would simplify the international system, and increase its effectiveness by strengthening any perceived weaknesses. What was required, it was argued, was a new single convention to replace and improve the efficiency of the preceding *ad hoc* transnational framework.

The process of drafting a universally acceptable document was long and arduous, requiring a great deal of revision on its way to becoming international law. The different interests of the various nations participat-ing in the drafting process ensured this. Nonetheless, having begun work in 1948, the UN secretariat's first draft of the Single Convention was made available to the Commission on Narcotic Drugs (CND) between its fifth and tenth sessions, that is to say during the period 1950–5. Because of comments and responses to the document from members of the commis-sion during this time, a second draft was produced in 1956. This dropped controversial provisions such as the establishment of an international opium monopoly and clearing-house that had been included in the first draft. These were intended to regulate imports and exports of narcotics, and were rejected by many nations because of their possible infringement upon national sovereignty. However, the draft retained the provision of prohibition on narcotic raw materials. Thus, with the inclusion of some transitional clauses, the absolute prohibition of marijuana and coca was for the first time written into the text of an international treaty. (The consequences of this will be explored in the next chapter.) Adolf Lande of the secretariat had proposed two alternative drafts of the convention which differed in the way in which they treated cannabis. The first proceeded from the assumption that cannabis had no medical value and should therefore be prohibited. The second outlined strict control if it was found that cannabis was medically valuable. Considering the rigid anti-cannabis stance held by the powerful US lobby and influential members of the WHO, it was inevitable that the first proposal became part of the final text. Despite some reservations from nations where cannabis was used medicinally, US pressure ensured that the drug came to be placed in the same addicting class as opium.

Opposition to US moves to strengthen the prohibitive nature of the proposed legislation did exist, however. On occasions this came from the UK, a nation that, as has been noted and as a reading of the records will show, usually argued for a regulative approach rather than prohibition.[9] As a result of conflicting views, the commission continued to review the second draft, and a third version was discussed in 1957 and 1958. Still containing some provisions that lacked widespread support, this draft became the main working paper of the Plenipotentiary Conference for the Adoption of a Single Convention on Narcotic Drugs, which was held in New York from 24 January to 25 March 1961. A critique of the conference can be used to provide an insight into the circumstances that produced the conflict of interest between Anslinger and his colleagues at the State Department.

THE 1961 CONFERENCE

Like the drafting procedure that preceded it, the Plenipotentiary Conference for the Adoption of a Single Convention on Narcotic Drugs can be viewed as a struggle of interests between different power blocs, each striving to achieve the best results for their national conditions. As William B. McAllister notes, each state attending the conference 'came to the meeting with an agenda based on its own domestic priorities'. McAllister identifies two principal interest groups: the organic group and the manufacturing group.[10] These, as the labels imply, consisted first of nations involved in the production of organic narcotic raw materials (cannabis, opium and coca), and second, the industrialized Western nations and their allies. The organic group[11] favoured weak controls because its members not only gained revenue from the production of organic drugs but, as McAllister notes, were also 'culturally predisposed to view organic drugs in a favourable light, having had daily experiences with the substances for centuries'. The manufacturing group,[12] on the other hand, had no cultural affinity for organic drugs and suffered to a certain extent from problems related to illegal drug use. Consequently, they were keen to enact strict controls on the production of organic materials, but opposed undue restrictions placed on the course of medical research or on the fabrication and distribution of manufactured drugs. It should be remembered that these nations were the major producers of the world's supply of synthetic drugs. The result of such an alignment of groups was a striking conflict of interest between many states in the East, South America and Southeast Asia with many in the West, particularly the United States.[13]

The inevitable outcome of such conflict, however, was a compromise in the final terms of the convention. As McAllister notes, the organic group was able to dilute the language of the international treaty by 'injecting exceptions, loopholes and deferrals into the wording'.[14] As a result, and in order to ensure that the majority of the provisions favoured by the manufacturing group made it into the final document, nations including the United States had to agree to make limited concessions to the organic group. The British delegate was aware of this fact, and to that effect stated that 'for the Single Convention to be effective, it had to be universally acceptable'.[15] When speaking at the 1961 conference, Tom Green displayed his appreciation of international diplomacy and reminded the conference that it 'should not forget that it was preferable to leave out even desirable provisions, if they were likely to prove unacceptable to a substantial number of States'.[16]

Ultimately the provisions sacrificed on the altar of universal acceptability concerned the control of opium production; more precisely the strict controls contained within the 1953 Opium Protocol. It will be remembered that the protocol permitted nations to grow opiates for domestic medical purposes, but restricted the exportation of opium to seven listed producer countries. A relaxation of these rules in the Single Convention was therefore seen by the organic group as a great improvement upon what it regarded as the onerous terms of the 1953 legislation. The protocol, although it had yet to come into force, would have seriously damaged the potential for nations not listed by the UN to create revenue from opium production. It should be recalled, however, that the protocol had been seen by Anslinger as a major advance in the international control of drugs. And as we shall see, Anslinger's personal dissatisfaction with the Single Convention's treatment of opium production provided the basis for his conflict with the State Department.

Nevertheless, despite this weakening in the control of opium production at source, the powerful position held by the manufacturing group ensured that the convention ultimately remained based upon predominantly prohibitive principles. To quote McAllister once more,

> the manufacturing states largely managed to have their cake and eat it too, as it were. By threatening nonagreement, utilizing their economic power, and using political pressure, the manufacturing group inserted enough loopholes, favorable language, and bureaucratic safeguards ... to protect the majority of their interests.[17]

Although the organic group's opposition to extensive strict controls had essentially been placated by the relaxation of the limitation on opium production, Western industrialized nations, especially the United States, ensured that indigenous drug use in places like South America became the subject of proscriptive international legislation. Consequently, the finished document reflected the participation of the UN's dominant, particularly American, Western membership.

THE POST-1961 SYSTEM FOR INTERNATIONAL DRUG CONTROL

So, after years of discussion in the CND, and two months of intensive deliberation at the New York Conference, the Single Convention on Narcotic Drugs finally became open for signature on 30 March 1961. The US-initiated ECOSOC resolutions in 1948 had directed the new convention to achieve four main goals, and this, as we shall see, was a task that the Single Convention, for the most part, achieved. In fulfilling its first objective, the convention successfully codified almost all previous pieces of international control legislation.[18] The second goal of the new treaty, the simplification of the international drug control machinery, was achieved with the creation of a new body, the International Narcotic Control Board (INCB). This was the product of the amalgamation of the Permanent Central Opium Board (PCOB) and the Drug Supervisory Body (DSB). The third aim of the convention was the extension of the control system to the cultivation of other natural products, in addition to opium and poppy straw, which produced narcotic effects. This meant that the convention for the first time subjected the harvesting of cannabis, cannabis resin and coca leaves (unless the leaves were used for flavouring beverages) to the same requirements as opium. The final goal of the legislation was the adoption of appropriate measures for the treatment and rehabilitation of drug addicts, and this was covered by article 38 of the convention.

Although some provisions were new as treaty obligations, others, such as the estimates and statistics system established by the conventions of 1925 and 1931, remained virtually unchanged. Consequently, having completed the tasks it had set out to achieve in 1948, the UN drug control apparatus viewed the convention as a major milestone in the history of international narcotic control.[19] This was a view shared by the press, with *The Times*, for example, noting that the convention represented a climax of ten years of efforts, and would aim to 'ensure an adequate supply of narcotics for medical and scientific use, while at the same time preventing the spread of drug addiction'.[20]

The Single Convention, therefore, made moves to fill the gaps left by the previous international treaties. The most serious shortcoming from the prohibitionists' perspective had been the lack of provisions for effective control of the production of opium, coca leaves and cannabis. However, as noted, although the Single Convention greatly strengthened the international control of cannabis and coca, it did weaken the provisions for the control of opium as contained within the 1953 Opium Protocol. Reflecting the compromise present in the text of the convention, the UN Secretariat noted in 1961 that the Single Convention was a flexible and generally accepted treaty that represented the 'highest common denominator for the acceptance of international obligations by sovereign countries'. Nevertheless, it also acknowledged there had been 'misgivings' expressed concerning the convention's provisions for the controlling of opium production.[21] As mentioned earlier, the source of these misgivings was Harry Anslinger, who claimed to be representing the opinions of the US government, including the State Department. This, as we shall see, was not completely accurate. The issues that lay behind such a predicament will be explored in the next section.

THE WAYWARD CHILD: THE SINGLE CONVENTION, ANSLINGER AND THE US STATE DEPARTMENT

The Single Convention's mandate to supersede all previous international treaties meant that when it came into effect the Convention would replace the 1953 Opium Protocol, although in 1961 the protocol itself was yet to have attracted enough ratifications to become international law. The protocol, it will be remembered, had been regarded by many, particularly Anslinger and his US delegation, as a great step forward in the control of opium production at source. Consequently, 'it was hoped that' such provisions contained in the protocol 'would not be deleted from the Single Convention'. The American delegation to the conference in 1961 had therefore been anxious that the new convention did not 'weaken the international control system'.[22] Henry Giordano, Anslinger's deputy at the FBN and his alternate at the conference, pointed out that 'the US government would support in principle, the provisions of the draft Single Convention placing opium production under international control as a necessary requirement for an effective instrument'.[23] However, as noted, the Single Convention's controls over opium production did in fact represent a relaxation of those arrived at in the 1953 Opium Protocol. This proved to be a major disappointment for Anslinger, whose goal it was to create a stricter international control system. This was particularly true for the control of opium at source; a long-time US aim. His report in 1961 on the Single Convention to the Secretary of State clearly revealed his dissatisfaction with the new legislation. Anslinger stressed his opposition to several points within the finalized draft, although it is clear that his main point of contention concerned the provisions for the control of opium. This is ironic when recalling Anslinger's inactivity regarding Afghanistan's plans to produce opium in 1957. Having successfully achieved strict international control for cannabis and coca, the commissioner expressed his fears that the measures for the control of opium smoking were not stringent enough.[24] He also raised points concerning the provision of treatment for drug addiction. Accordingly, he noted that 'The language of the Third Draft ... recommended compulsory treatment for drug addiction in a closed institution which was strongly favored by the United States as being the most successful method of treatment.' Anslinger continued by stressing that the convention, however, 'contains an article recommending only that the parties having a serious addiction problem provide adequate treatment facilities if they have the economic means to do so.' This, in his opinion, was 'meaningless and one of the unfortunate developments of the Conference'.[25]

With regard to the convention's approach to opium control, he observed that 'the limitation of production of opium is considerably weaker than the provision in the 1953 Protocol which limited lawful exporters of opium to six [sic] named parties'. It was Anslinger's conviction that the Single Convention's treatment of opium was a compromise provision 'resulting from the insistence of the Soviet Bloc, countries of the British Commonwealth and some African countries'.[26] Displaying his single-minded attitude and his refusal to accept the compromises incurred during the Convention's passage to law, Anslinger continued to inform the Secretary of State that

> It is clearly apparent from the atmosphere of the Conference that many delegations were intent upon producing a document based mainly on recommendations and universally acceptable principles rather than on binding obligations which have customarily been the basis of existing narcotic treaties.

As a result, he claimed, the 'United States Delegation is as a whole of the opinion that this Single Convention is not as strong as would have been desired and that it does not offer any real improvement over existing multilateral treaties'.[27] Such a belief rested on the fact that the convention permitted the production of up to five tons of opium by any nation for legitimate medical and scientific purposes. The more stringent Opium Protocol, although awaiting the necessary number of ratifications to bring it into force, was for Anslinger a preferable piece of control legislation.

Anslinger's reaction to the UN's move to implement the 1961 convention was to express his dissatisfaction at the seventeenth session of the

CND in 1962. Here he claimed that the Single Convention should be amended to make it more effective before it came into force. Keen to publicize his views against the convention, the US representative also used UN publications to broadcast his sentiments, expressing his ardent opposition to the legislation in the *Bulletin on Narcotics* in 1963. A piece entitled 'The United States' views on the Single Convention on Narcotic Drugs' had been requested by the chief US representative to make it perfectly clear to the international community that the USA did not favour the ratification of the new legislation. Earlier UN literature had, against Anslinger's will, given the impression that the United States supported the Single Convention. Besides putting on record his complaints concerning opium control, Anslinger in this instance also made a case against the convention's provisions dealing with the estimates and the statistics system.[28] In conclusion, it was once again unequivocally stated that the United States would not ratify or accede to the Single Convention and opposed its coming into force as it included 'objectionable features' that would cause 'a retrocession of international narcotic controls'.[29] The State Department, however, had other ideas.

Study of the Department of State's evaluation of Anslinger's views on the convention in the late 1950s exposes the difference in objectives between the US government and its chief delegate to the CND. Anslinger's comments in *Food, Drug and Cosmetic Law Journal* in November 1958 make it clear that, publicly at least, the commissioner was supportive of a convention to 'simplify and improve the existing international instruments'.[30] However, in March of that year State Department officials had become aware of his private concerns. At that time a Department memorandum noted that 'Mr. Anslinger no longer appears to favor the inclusion of all international narcotic provisions in one convention.' In explaining the Department's position on the issue, it continued,

> Since we were largely responsible for suggesting this reform of the present piecemeal approach, perhaps we should explore with him the depth of his current opposition, his reasons, and what he proposes to do about the Convention ... he may use his influence to delay action on the Convention.

Finally, in a decisive statement of intent, it noted that 'The Department favors a rapid conclusion of the Single Convention as an administrative and substantive reform of the international control system.'[31]

Nevertheless, despite such wishes, the commissioner was already attempting to use his influential position at the CND to determine the future of the proposed Single Convention; a procedure not sanctioned by his own government. Evidence shows that even during the drafting stages the commissioner was not happy with the direction that the Single Convention was taking. As early as 1957 he employed a top FBN agent, Charles Siragusa, to apply pressure on national delegations to support the 1953 protocol. Despite the State Department's desire to give the convention US backing, Anslinger remained unenthusiastic. Alfred L. Tennyson, one of Anslinger's alternates at the 1953 conference and a man who had assisted in the third draft of the Single Convention, illustrated Anslinger's position. He recalled in 1961 a statement that the commissioner had made at the closing meeting of the CND's 1957 session, at which Anslinger was chairman. The commission had been reviewing part of the third draft of the convention, and several provisions that Anslinger considered to be 'unwise and not conducive to effective international or national control' had been adopted by a majority vote. A question was presented regarding the possible allocation of additional time to complete the review of the draft. According to Tennyson,

> The Commissioner, after allowing a number of delegations to speak on this, electrified the meeting by stating ... that the lack of progress toward drafting an effective control measure to date convinced him that there should be no concern about devoting additional time to a fruitless task at the next session, but that the Parties could more effectively control the traffic under existing conventions and protocols, including the 1953 protocol. There was an unusually long and eloquent silence following this statement, finally broken up by some delegates with speeches seeking to mollify the Commissioner and hoping that the Chairman did not seriously consider the progress futile, etc., but they realized from the Chairman's expression that he meant exactly what he had said.[32]

Tennyson also noted that Anslinger's stance on the finalized draft of the convention had been equally uncompromising. He stated in 1961 that 'one must be convinced that the principle of the Commissioner's position at the twelfth Session [1957] is even more applicable to this latest draft; that it would be better to continue under present conventions and protocols, including the protocol of 1953'.[33] Such an admission clearly runs counter to the image put forward by Rufus King and others who have depicted the Single Convention as Anslinger's 'grand project'.[34] Disheartened with its development, Anslinger was in fact to disown the legislation that the United States had had such a major role in initiating, and concentrate his efforts upon fulfilling the potential of the Opium Protocol.

THE RESUSCITATION OF THE 'VIRTUALLY OBSOLETE'
1953 PROTOCOL

Anslinger and his US delegation went to great lengths to enlist the support of other nations in opposing the Single Convention. Discussions between Americans and other national representatives during the 1962 session of the CND display Anslinger's determination to prevent the Single Convention from obtaining the necessary number of ratifications for it to come into force. On Anslinger's instructions, John T. Cusack, a senior FBN agent, and James P. Hendrick, the Deputy to the Assistant of the Treasury, met various delegations at the session in order to ascertain their intentions towards the new legislation. Their aim was to persuade other nations to follow Anslinger's line against the convention.

According to the two Americans, of the delegations approached most seemed to have serious reservations concerning the 1961 legislation. This can be seen through an examination of the documents relating to the activities of Cusack and Hendrick. It appeared, for example, that the Spanish government believed that the convention lacked the efficiency of some of the existing agreements, and considered an important defect of the legislation to be the 'failure to include the provisions of the 1953 Protocol'.[35] Other national delegations were also particularly wary about the possible implementation of the 1953 protocol. Several states, including Greece, Italy, Denmark, Portugal and the United Arab Republic (UAR), argued that if this piece of international legislation came into effect they would not, according to the opinions of the delegates involved in the discussion, feel the need to ratify the Single Convention. Dr Danner, the Federal Republic of Germany's delegate, illustrated this stance when he told Cusack, 'Well, you know we ratified the opium protocol of 1953, and if it comes into force we don't need the single convention.' According to the American delegate, Danner had laughed and said, 'Tell me do you know something? Do you have the 1953 protocol in your pocket?'[36] Cusack's cautious reply was that there was always the possibility that Greece or Turkey, or both, might ratify.

In fact, frantic US backstage activity was under way to ensure that either Greece or Turkey, or ideally both, would indeed ratify the 1953 Opium Protocol. According to the terms of the legislation, the protocol required the ratification of 25 states, including three of the seven listed opium-producing countries. As it stood, only two producing countries had ratified the Protocol. Consequently, the ratification by either Greece or Turkey, both listed nations, would have been sufficient to bring the Protocol into effect. This was Anslinger's objective since, in his opinion, it would have strengthened the international control of opium and undermined the Single Convention. Anslinger had obviously been considering such an option for some time. In his report to the Secretary of State in 1961 he had noted that the '1953 Opium Protocol needs only the ratification of one more opium producing country to bring the instrument into force'. He had suggested that

> the urging on the part of the United States for either Turkey or Greece to ratify the 1953 Opium Protocol would together with existing treaties, provide more effective worldwide control of narcotic drugs than would have been possible under the Single Convention on Narcotic Drugs.[37]

Despite never apparently receiving clearance from the State Department to pursue the ratification of the Opium Protocol by Greece or Turkey, Anslinger made it his priority.

Like other national delegations at the 1962 CND session, the Turks received a visit from Cusack and Hendrick; although in this instance there was a great deal more at stake for the Americans. Success in their attempts to persuade Turkey to ratify the 1953 protocol would have been a great step in the march to undermine the Single Convention. According to Cusack and Hendrick, the Turks were concerned with the scope of the Single Convention because they 'knew it would endanger Turkey's opium market'. Such concern also meant that the country had not ratified the Opium Protocol after the 1953 conference. It transpired, however, that by 1961 Turkey had the Single Convention under study, but agreed with Anslinger that there were, owing to its universality, weaknesses. The Turks' position was, therefore, that they would 'continue to study the treaty'. A decision whether to ratify would 'be made later'. Having discussed the issue with the Turkish delegates, Cusack noted that they had abstained from a CND resolution urging governments to ratify the 1961 convention. He consequently concluded from 'private conversations and official statements' that the Turkish delegates, Mr Oskol and Mr Aoba, hoped that the Single Convention would not come into force. Despite this fact the US delegate still believed that they 'may prefer to take their chances with it rather than the 1953 protocol which they view as completely unacceptable'. Cusack also stated that he believed that the Turks felt 'that Turkey could not comply with the opium control measures required by the opium protocol of 1953 and would soon run into serious international difficulty'. On this point he agreed that there was 'sound basis for this opinion'. Consequently, Cusack suggested linking Turkey's ratification of the 1953 protocol with the incentive of economic aid. He concluded, therefore, that 'perhaps if the Turkish Government agreed to ratify the opium protocol of 1953 our government might consider some special aid to enable Turkey to implement the control measures'. The adoption of a familiar US tactic to achieve prescribed aims was not a new initiative. It was, however, indicative of the FBN agent's keen desire to get the 1953 legislation operational. Cusack's concern regarding the state of the international control of opium was evident in comments on the Turkish stance on opium regulation. He noted that

> I am not so sure whether Oskol and Acba really care whether Turkish opium affects Americans, Iranians or Arabs as long as it does not affect the ... Turks .... On the other hand from the United States' point of view, unless the Opium protocol of 1953, is implemented, or similar provisions in another treaty implemented, the tremendous annual diversion of Turkish opium – averaging at least 100 tons – will continue to adversely affect the United States, the UAR, Iran, Syrian Arab Republic, and Lebanon, and some European countries. Only the 1953 protocol or its provision inserted in another treaty will force the Turkish Government to go from their 'paper control of opium' to actual control.[38]

It was Cusack's belief that the proposed US financial aid would encourage the Turkish delegation 'to recommend ratification' to its government, especially since this would have allowed Turkey to sell home-produced opium on the world market. Cusack perceptively noted that

> Although Oskol's long opposition to the 1953 Protocol is well known, he has a face-saving device for reversing his stand in seeking ratification by taking the position the protocol is now needed in view of the inherent weaknesses of the Single Convention.[39]

While Cusack and Hendrick worked to encourage Turkey to support the Opium Protocol, they also made efforts to obtain the Greek government's ratification of the 1953 legislation. Cusack's confidence that the US delegation's activity for this goal would prove to be fruitful was clearly shown in his comments concerning Turkey and the protocol. He noted that Turkey could opt for the 1953 protocol instead of the Single Convention 'when the Protocol comes into force with the Greek ratification'.[40] Such confidence was indeed well placed. As we shall see, pressure placed upon the Greek government did bring about its ratification of the 1953 protocol.

During Cusack and Hendrick's survey of delegations at the 1962 session of the CND, it had been noted by the Americans that 'As already known, the Greek Government supports our position on the Single Convention.'[41]

The government of the United Kingdom, a supporter of the Single Convention, naturally regarded Anslinger's approaches to the Greek delegation unfavourably. The British view of US attempts to persuade the

Greek delegation in Geneva to ratify the 1953 protocol was therefore unsympathetic. Correspondence between the British embassy in Washington, DC, and the Foreign Office on the topic illuminates both the US tactics and the UK reaction. British diplomats noted in 1962 that when they asked the US delegation whether it 'intended to seek a substitute for the Single Convention' the Americans had responded that 'they thought that it would be better to have the 1953 Opium Protocol'.[42] This provoked an understandably concerned British reaction. The UK delegate reported to the Home Office that 'the US Government are being rather tiresome in refusing to ratify the Single Convention of 1961 and insisting instead on trying to bring the 1953 Protocol into operation'. The report concluded by stating that

> Briefly we feel that as the 1961 Convention was drafted to supersede all previous agreements on control of narcotics, it is absurd to work for the bringing into force of the 1953 Protocol which is unacceptable to the great majority of states.[43]

American pressure on Greece, which, like Turkey, was technically listed as an opium-producing nation, was a central part of Anslinger's strategy. Its ratification of the protocol would have had the effect of bringing the opium legislation into operation. The British were aware of this fact and privately noted that the '1953 Protocol, which is now virtually obsolete', was preventing the Single Convention from coming into force quickly. The British observed that

> The ratification by the Greek Government of the 1953 Protocol will, by virtue of the fact that Greece is listed as an opium producer, though it has in fact not produced any in the last five years, bring the 1953 Protocol into operation and may delay the coming into effect of the 1961 Convention which was intended to supersede it.[44]

However, despite such an observation it had already become clear that American pressure on the Greek government to follow the US line on the Single Convention was producing results. The British government discovered in late June 1962 that 'It was no longer true to say that the Greek Government' supported the 1961 convention. Athens still 'favoured a Single Convention, but in more stringent terms and hoped that the Single Convention might be amended accordingly'. The Head of the Economic Department of the Greek Foreign Ministry, Mr Xydis, 'volunteered however that the main factor in the Greek decision to ratify the 1953 Protocol had been heavy and prolonged US pressure'.[45] In response to this turn of events the British appeared greatly disheartened. 'The situation seems to be very much as we expected,' wrote Tom Key of the Foreign Office in June 1962; 'it appears that the Greeks have succumbed to US pressure ... there does not appear to be very much more we can do.' Key continued to describe his view of events by stating that

> at the last session of the narcotics commission it was clear that the only real opposition to the Single Convention comes from the US. We believe that the US attitude on this matter is a mistaken one, and it was quite clear that the great majority of countries represented on the commission took the same view. It is regrettable that the US should have used its influence with other nations in an effort to prevent the Single Convention from being brought into effect.[46]

Consequently, the British believed that such an American approach would undoubtedly affect the ratification of the Single Convention, and 'if the 1953 Protocol comes into effect it may well produce confusion in the minds of other countries which are considering whether they should ratify the Single Convention. This is no doubt what they are hoping for.'[47]

The fact that the Greeks appeared to have conceded to pressure from Anslinger to ratify the 1953 legislation understandably created a certain amount of speculation among the other delegations. For example, the Indian delegation, despite being initially in favour of the Single Convention, did not seem as certain 'after picking up rumours that either Greece or Turkey, or both, might ratify the 1953 Protocol'. As a result, according to the US delegation, the Indians 'exhibited much interest ... and indicated that should the 1953 protocol enter into force this would greatly influence their final decision as to whether or not to seek ratification of the Single Convention'.[48] Speculation about the Greek decision was therefore sufficient to create uncertainty within the international community. This looked likely to undermine support for the Single Convention, which, as noted earlier, was exactly what Anslinger had been working for, although it was an aim that ran counter to the wishes of the US State Department.

Anslinger's activities at the 1962 session also produced comment from some of his old colleagues in the international system. Colonel Sharman, who retired from his work at the UN in 1958, commented from the sidelines on the wranglings within the Commission. He noted that 'the old wheels creek and grind in much the same manner as twenty years ago'.[49] It comes as no great surprise to discover that Anslinger's position on the 1961 legislation was supported wholeheartedly by Sharman. Accordingly the Canadian informed his trusted ex-colleague that 'As you can imagine, I agree 100% in relation to your position on the Convention.' Clearly appalled by the attitude of his national delegation in Geneva, Sharman noted that he was astonished to see that Canada was the first to ratify, particularly when only countries like Thailand and Morocco saw fit to follow her example ... . Canada was the first country to tie itself to the Single Convention which is purely destructive in relation to so many of the safeguards still existing.[50]

However, Anslinger did not receive support from another 'old hand', Herbert May. May noted that 'I know that the U.S. is not satisfied with the Convention.' This, he believed, was largely due to the invitation of mainland China to the Single Convention Conference and the extension in the number of countries that were permitted to cultivate and export raw opium. However, he remarked that 'My feeling is that, on a worldwide humanitarian matter, every country should be invited. With prewar China left out the Convention cannot fully operate.' May also perceptively noted that 'an international convention is a compromise: it practically never gives everyone all that it wants [sic]'. This point, as we have seen, was dismissed by Anslinger in his blinkered approach towards strict international narcotic control.

In his 1962 annual report concerning the CND session to Secretary of State Dean Rusk, Anslinger recounted events relating to the convention. He noted that a resolution sponsored by Canada, India and the Netherlands, inviting governments to ratify the Single Convention, ended in a result of 12 for (Brazil, Canada, Hungary, India, Japan, Morocco, Netherlands, Poland, Switzerland, the USSR, the UK and Yugoslavia), 2 against (Mexico and the USA), and 5 abstentions (China, France, Iran, Turkey, the UAR). The Mexican representative apparently voted against it because he 'felt that the resolution was premature'.[51] However, such a Mexican decision could have been expected bearing in mind the Mexican delegation's proclivity for voting along lines similar to those of the United States. Events at the CND meeting also provided solid proof of the success of US efforts to persuade Greece to ratify the 1953 protocol. Accordingly, at the session the observer for Greece 'announced that his Government would ratify the 1953 Opium Protocol'.[52] As a result, the US and the UAR representatives expressed their 'satisfaction with this announcement'. However, it was noted by Anslinger that the decision 'was not met with any great enthusiasm by the majority of the Commission'. This, he believed, 'could have the effect of accelerating ratification of the Single Convention'.[53] The official explanation for the American delegation's opposition to the convention was that 'it would encourage opium production, which would go completely out of control, and thus result in an increase in illicit production'. Consequently, the US delegation

urged governments to consider carefully all provisions of the Single Convention before deciding to ratify it. It hoped that at some time in the future the Single Convention could be revised so as to retain and strengthen, rather than weaken, the control measures of the existing treaties, including the 1953 Protocol.[54]

Despite Anslinger's efforts to scupper the convention, the majority of nations in the CND were in favour and urged its ratification. National representatives generally agreed that the Single Convention was an improvement on the 1953 protocol for a number of reasons; notably its provisions covering cannabis and coca, and its universality. The protocol's rigid terms, as noted earlier, had proved unacceptable to the organic drug-producing nations. Consequently, many of its essential provisions were transferred to the Single Convention, while those that were too strict to be widely accepted were omitted. Many strict controls as favoured by Anslinger had to be weakened to gain universal acceptance. The convention therefore proved to be acceptable to a wide array of nations. For example, the representative of the UK stated that his government intended to ratify it as soon as domestic legislation necessary to carry out the provisions of the convention could be enacted. The Canadian representative pointed out that his government had already ratified. The Indian representative, apparently disregarding remarks made privately to Cusack, stated that the provisions of the Single Convention were realistic and wider than those of the 1953 protocol. Additionally the convention drew considerable support from the Netherlands, Yugoslavia, Switzerland, Morocco and Poland, with the observer of Afghanistan considering it to be a 'major United Nations achievement'.[55]

Because of such support, a resolution addressed to ECOSOC inviting all governments to ratify the Single Convention was introduced and adopted. This signalled a major setback in Anslinger's attempts to affect the shape of the international control system. Yet Anslinger reported to the Secretary of State that, as in previous years, 'the United States was able to maintain leadership and substantial support throughout the session', except in the case of the discussions on the Single Convention.[56] This resulted in a paradoxical situation where, according to Anslinger, the United States sustained support from members of the commission in all areas of the CND's work, except in the opposition to the Single Convention; a piece of legislation which, it should be remembered, was proposed by Anslinger and the United States in 1948.

The existence of such a bizarre situation left Anslinger open to attack from some quarters within the United States. Such criticism of the way the US delegation handled the 1961 meeting on the convention led Anslinger to admit to the Assistant Secretary of the Treasury, James A. Reed, that 'we did a bad job'.[57] Reed, as a member of the US department responsible for the FBN, was keen to strengthen the transnational system for the control of drugs. A strict UN framework which included the provisions of the 1953 Opium Protocol would have benefited his work by, in theory, reducing the quantities of illicit narcotics available globally, especially those likely to enter the United States. Anslinger's failure to prevent the Single Convention's approval in Geneva therefore proved disappointing to the Department of the Treasury. In defence, Anslinger offered the following reasons for his delegation's poor performance. First, Anslinger claimed that the State Department had limited his options at the conference. He stated that 'Several months before the conference was to take place, Treasury found indications, through informal discussions, that agreement on our proposals would be found extremely difficult. Accordingly we asked State to try to postpone the conference for a year or so.' However, according to Anslinger, 'State said that it was impossible as the Single Convention was a United States proposal.' Elaborating on this point, Anslinger recalled that he had

> proceeded to line up the delegations to propose a recess until the atmosphere would be more favourable on our side . . . . We succeeded in getting a majority who felt that the conference was going badly. I made the recommendation for a recess but State rejected the idea, claiming that the United States never called for a recess at any conference.[58]

The State Department clearly felt that any postponement would have been greatly detrimental to the prestige that the United States held within the UN. More precisely, it is likely that the State Department believed that asking for a recess would have been interpreted by the Soviet delegation as a sign of weakness. This was an undesirable risk while the USA and the USSR maintained a confrontational Cold War relationship within all areas of the UN's work. In opposing the State Department's position Anslinger compared the control of narcotics to that of nuclear weapons. He consequently stated that 'In view of the many times a recess has been called at Geneva on nuclear discussions, such a proposal would have been the wise course.' However, unlike Anslinger, the State Department did not seem to feel the control of drugs to be as important as the control of weapons of mass destruction.

Second, Anslinger recalled that the US delegation had faced a great deal of resistance, particularly from the USSR, which he claimed had been controlling the proceedings. He consequently noted that

> When it became evident that the Soviets were running the show, and that the British Commonwealth, the neutrals and the small African nations were going along with the Russians, we had a meeting at the US mission in New

York, and officials of that agency joined with members of the delegation to try to line up votes on our side. After much backstage work, it was found that we could not line up one delegation.[59]

By claiming that the United States had faced opposition from such a powerful group of nations, the commissioner attempted to deflect any blame away from his own handling of affairs. It is likely that by stressing the involvement of the USSR within the proceedings, Anslinger was attempting to harness anti-Soviet feelings within the US government. Nevertheless, having pursued this tack and failed, Anslinger informed Reed that he had spoken to the top British diplomat Sir Samuel Hoare, and concluded that the USA would have to go along with the Soviets. The alternative would have been to 'come out with nothing'. Finally, therefore, Anslinger 'proceeded to whittle down Russian demands'. It was his belief that the Soviets had been exploiting the narcotics issue for political gain by

holding out as bait to the small nations a proposal to allow any nation to produce 100 tons of opium annually for the export market. The Russians pointed out to the small African and Asian nations that this could be their economic salvation.[60]

Anslinger was also greatly dismayed by the behaviour of the Canadian delegation at Geneva. Since the retirement of Colonel Sharman from the DND in 1958, Anslinger was left as the only 'old hand' working within the UN drug control system. This meant that Sharman was no longer active in encouraging the Canadian government to support US-backed policies. It should be remembered that since 1945 Sharman had supported Anslinger's stance on international control almost without exception. His retirement consequently resulted in a move away from unswerving Canadian support for US-initiated policies.

Anslinger's position of weakness in relation to the State Department can therefore clearly be seen in his attempts to undermine the Single Convention. Despite having the support of Reed at the Treasury, Anslinger could do little more than lobby other delegations and use unofficial pressure to slow the ratification process of the convention. The existence of intra-governmental conflict on the issue can also be identified in Anslinger's correspondence with Reed. The commissioner concluded by saying that he was 'happy to hear' Mr Reed 'tell Curren', the Canadian representative, 'that the United States intended to exert every effort to prevent the Single Convention from coming into operation'.[61] This may have been the view of Anslinger and the Treasury; it was not, however, the stance of the State Department.

As shown earlier, the Department was determined to have the Single Convention come into force as soon as possible. The British CND delegate confirmed this in 1962. Having discussed the issue of the Single Convention with US embassy officials, Tom Green noted that 'it became quite clear that ... the preference of the Narcotics Division of the American Treasury for the 1953 Opium Protocol' was 'embarrassing to the State Department'. The Department had been opposed to the US delegation's support for the 1953 protocol, and was 'apparently anxious for arguments to get the decision reversed'.[62]

Although at the age of 70 Anslinger retired as commissioner of the FBN in July 1962,[63] he remained US representative to the CND until 1970. In this capacity he continued to oppose the Single Convention. After a great deal of activity his efforts were to achieve limited success. Consequently, despite a lack of support from the State Department, Anslinger managed to get the 1953 Opium Protocol operational. With the crucial ratification of Greece, the protocol came into force on 8 March 1963. This was the culmination of many years' work for Anslinger, implementing the strict international opium control system that he had envisioned a decade earlier. Yet in order to complete his plan, Anslinger still had to undermine the Single Convention.

Once the convention had received the necessary 40 ratifications, it would supersede the 1953 legislation. As a result, Anslinger continued in his attempts to thwart support for the Single Convention. By the Eighteenth Session of the CND in 1963, seventeen nations had ratified the 1961 legislation. However, despite this, Anslinger optimistically noted that 'All of these, with the exception of Canada and Thailand, are small nations of minor importance in respect to narcotics problems.'[64] According to Anslinger 'a number of delegations announced their intention to ratify ... but evidently with tongue in cheek, as they privately stated that they would await the action of the US Government'.[65] During the session 'the Government of Turkey announced that ratification of the 1953 Opium Protocol was in process and would soon be accomplished'. This, according to Anslinger, caused 'keen disappointment among proponents of the ... Single Convention'.[66] Yet, despite such disappointment among the supporters of the Convention, they remained in the majority, with the obstructive activities of Anslinger doing little to halt the Convention's progress towards ratification.

On 13 November 1964, Kenya became the 40th country to accede to the Single Convention on Narcotic Drugs. Adhering to article 41 of the Convention, the legislation came into force 30 days later, on 13 December 1964. The Convention therefore superseded the 1953 protocol less than two years after it had come into effect. Despite all his concerted efforts,

Anslinger was forced to watch as the international system moved to follow what he perceived to be a greatly weakened course for control. Operating beyond the mandate of the State Department, Anslinger had failed to secure sufficient opposition to the Convention. He had displayed great tenacity in pressurizing the Greek and Turkish delegates to recommend ratification of the protocol. Nevertheless, acting without the full backing of his government, the chief US representative found it impossible to block a convention that had widespread support from nations with diverse domestic priorities.

It is likely that Anslinger's opposition to the Single Convention impeded US Congressional ratification of the legislation, which was finally received by the UN secretariat in 1967. The debate surrounding American ratification, however, also displayed Anslinger's proclivity to change his position on issues and use international legislation to affect US domestic drug control law. Despite opposing the convention at the 1961 conference, Anslinger used it in 1967 to counter moves in the United States to liberalize controls on the use of cannabis. In a hearing before the Senate Foreign Relations Committee on 27 April 1967, Anslinger stated that an 'important reason for becoming a party to the 1961 Single Convention is the marijuana problem'. He continued:

> Several groups in the United States are loudly agitating to liberalize controls, and in fact to legalize its use. In the convention it is very specific that we must prevent its misuse. If the United States becomes a party to the 1961 Convention we will be able to use our treaty obligations to resist the legalized use of marijuana.[67]

By using the familiar tactic of linking domestic policies to international commitments, Anslinger continued his battle against marijuana in the United States. Although he had vigorously opposed the Single Convention six years earlier, his support in 1967 undoubtedly helped to ensure congressional ratification. The Senate approved the decision without dissent, and the *New York Times*, for one, thought it unworthy of a mention. Much like the Harrison Act and Marijuana Tax Act before it, the ratification slipped into law without any significant attention. American pressure to include strict controls on the drug in the Single Convention therefore ultimately provided a mandate for rigid national legislation. Indeed, the ratification led Anslinger to note that 'We've got [the marijuana] laws so tightly tied up they'll never change them.'[68]

The coming into force of the convention was welcomed as a vast improvement of the UN narcotic control system. The UN secretariat regarded the convention as superior to the protocol in that it included the control of coca and cannabis. Indeed, despite Anslinger's opposition to the final draft of the convention, the 1961 legislation was indisputably a great advance in the cause of international narcotic prohibition. Although Anslinger had been opposed to the convention's provisions for opium control, American dominance of the UN control framework undoubtedly resulted in the creation of a wide-ranging piece of prohibitive legislation.

The importance of the USA's long-term interest in the convention was acknowledged by Adolf Lande, who noted in 1961 that

> when the Single Convention comes into force, efforts of half a century, and particularly those of the United States and its Narcotics Bureau as pioneer in the field, to establish a comprehensive and effective system of narcotics control will finally be brought to fruition.

This, he observed, would be the case 'despite all imperfections which may continue to exist and which seem unavoidable in a work which requires the constant consent of numerous states of different legal, administrative, social, and cultural backgrounds and having different degrees of interest in the problem'.[69]

CONCLUSION

As with any piece of international legislation that embraces nations from all around the world, the Single Convention was ultimately a compromise. It remained, however, the most prohibition-oriented transnational narcotic control law that had ever been created and is crucial to the story of the creation of an international prohibitive norm. Despite the inevitable reduction in severity that resulted from the need for universal acceptability, the convention retained US-influenced prohibitive characteristics. American political and economic prominence within the UN control framework ensured that the US perception of legitimate drug use and the best ways to control such use remained dominant. Consequently, as Rufus King has claimed, the convention gave the United States 'another way to push endeavours wherein it had previously failed', especially 'choking off sources of the coca leaf'.[70] In the control of cannabis it also signified a new policy: prohibition.

Commentators have questioned the effectiveness of the 1961 legislation, with criticism being levelled at its reliance upon the principle of voluntary adherence. However, the UN's perpetuation of a global prohibitionist norm and the organization's image as a guardian of humankind mean that its legislation often remains unchallenged. As noted earlier, any deviation from UN conventions marks the offending nation as a villain of the international system. The price of non-compliance can be costly.

Multiple motives determined the American stance on the Single Convention. What initially appeared to be a straightforward US approach towards the legislation was greatly complicated by Harry Anslinger's preference for the stricter opium provisions contained within the 1953 Opium Protocol. Nevertheless, his attempts to sabotage the convention had little effect in undoing the years of work the United States had devoted to the construction of a rigidly prohibitive international control system. Anslinger wanted strict international control for cannabis and coca, but felt that the Single Convention's provisions for opium were too weak to warrant his support. His stance illustrates the complex and often contradictory way he approached drug control at the UN.

The US State Department's opposition to Anslinger's anti-Single Convention stance illuminated the US government's willingness to defer the goal of stringent international prohibition to other foreign policy considerations. Despite Anslinger's fears that the Single Convention would weaken the international system, the State Department refused to permit the US delegation to undermine the prestige of the United States at the forum of the UN. Backing down on a US-initiated scheme would have given the impression of vacillation and weakness. This was particularly undesirable in front of the Soviet Union during a tense period of the Cold War.

The State Department, disagreeing with Anslinger, felt that the convention would not damage the UN system for international drug control. Anslinger's conflict of interests with the State Department and his failure to prevent the Single Convention from coming into force also displayed his own vulnerability within the US bureaucracy. Although occupying an important formative position within the US international narcotic control framework, Anslinger could not function effectively without the backing of the State Department. Consequently, although Anslinger's traditional image is one of all-controlling dominance, in reality he could operate effectively only when his policies coincided with those of the State Department. Incidents of collision of interest resulted in the head of the US delegation being overruled; as throughout US involvement with international drug control, concern for wider foreign policy always took precedence over issues of narcotic control.

Despite being the product of both compromise and political duality, US dominance in the UN control system ensured that the Single Convention created a Western-oriented prohibitive framework for international drug control. The convention provided the foundations for later UN legislation that has further strengthened the global prohibitive norm. This includes the 1972 Amending Protocol, which strengthened some provisions within the Single Convention. Like its predecessor, the 1972 legislation was an American-initiated scheme, and illustrated the continuing US influence upon the UN system. Consequently, as will be shown in the next chapter, the international drug control regime not only affects the national drug control policies around the world, but also provides US prohibitive rhetoric and actions beyond the multinational realm with a morally justified formal sanction.

NOTES

1. Gianfranco Dell'Alba, Olivier Dupuis and Jean-Luc Robert, 'For a revision of the United Nations conventions on drugs', in *Questioning Prohibition: 1994 International Report on Drugs* (Brussels: International Antiprohibitionist League, 1994), p. 213.
2. 'Coming into force of the Single Convention on Narcotic Drugs, 1961', *Bulletin on Narcotics*, **17**(1) (January–March 1965), 1.
3. Rufus King, *The Drug Hang-Up: America's Fifty-Year Folly*, (Springfield, IL: Charles C. Thomas, 1974), p. 220.
4. *Ibid.*, pp. 218–19, and *UN Conference for the Adoption of a Single Convention on Narcotic Drugs*, Vol. 1 (New York: UN Publications, 1964), p. 6.
5. Adolf Lande, 'The Single Convention on Narcotic Drugs, 1961', *International Organization*, **16** (1962), 798.
6. Bertil A. Renborg, 'The Grand Old Men of the League of Nations: what they achieved. Who they were', *Bulletin on Narcotics*, **16**(4) (October–December 1964), 10.
7. See S. K. Chattergee, *Legal Aspects of International Drug Control* (London: Martinus Nijhoff, 1981), pp. 343–448.
8. William O. Walker III, 'An analytical overview', in Rapheal F. Perl (ed.), *Drugs and Foreign Policy: A Critical Review* (Boulder: Westview Press, 1994), p. 24.
9. See 'Comments of the UK Government on the Second Draft of the Single Convention', UN document E/CN.7/AC.3/7, pp. 1–3: Article 2, 'Substances under control' and article 3, 'Changes in scope of control: new drugs'. Public Record Office, Kew, London, UK (hereafter PRO) (FO371 129982).
10. For a discussion on the dynamics of the Plenipotentiary Conference and the different groups operating to influence the design of the Single Convention, see William B. McAllister, 'Conflicts of interest in the international drug control system', in William O. Walker III (ed.), *Drug Control Policy: Essays in Historical and Comparative Perspective* (University Park: Pennsylvania State University Press, 1992), pp. 148–62.
11. The organic group was led by opium-producing states, such as India, Pakistan, Turkey and Burma, coca-producing states, such as Indonesia and the Andean region of South America, the opium- and cannabis-producing

states of South and Southeast Asia, and finally the cannabis-producing areas of the Horn of Africa.

12. The manufacturing group was led by the United States, the United Kingdom, Canada, Switzerland, the Netherlands, West Germany and Japan. The main clash of interests was between the organic group and the manufacturing group. Here different goals proved too much to overcome for mutual satisfaction on both sides.

13. It should, however, be noted that while the United Kingdom and the United States can both be classified as members of the manufacturing group, differences did exist in the approach that the two governments adopted towards the provisions of the Single Convention. As noted earlier, the British had displayed dissatisfaction with the prohibitive approach taken by the Americans. Differences in opinion at the conference remained based on the freedom of the British medical profession to determine which drugs could be used for the treatment of patients. See statement made by Tom Green, UK representative on the CND, 25 January 1961, p. 3, PRO (FO371 129982).

14. William B. McAllister, 'Conflicts of interest', p. 150.

15. UN Conference for the Adoption of a Single Convention on Narcotic Drugs, Vol. 1, p. 4.

16. Ibid.

17. William B. McAllister, 'Conflicts of interest', p. 161. To be sure, the British had been concerned about their freedom of action regarding the medical use of narcotics in the UK. However, the British government remained keen to support the control of drug production overseas. For example, see Foreign Office aide-mémoire, 30 June 1962, concerning the position of the Greek government towards the 1953 Opium Protocol. PRO (FO371 166947).

18. The only exception to this was the maintenance of many provisions of the 1936 Convention on Illicit Traffic. This was because the Single Convention was regarded by many nations as having weakened the system as established by the 1936 legislation. As Lande notes, 'It was for this reason that the [1961] conference decided that the new convention should not replace the 1936 Convention between parties thereto as it did in the case of the other narcotic treaties. The parties to the 1961 Convention would, therefore, be able to continue to apply among themselves its stronger provisions.' See Adolf Lande, 'The Single Convention on Narcotic Drugs, 1961', International Organization, 16 (1962), 792.

19. International Dug Control (New York: UN Publications, 1965, Sales No. 65.I.22), p. 21. For the official UN perception of the Single Convention, see pp. 20–4.

20. The Times, 27 March 1961.

21. International Drug Control, p. 23.

22. View of the US delegate at the 1961 Conference, UN Conference for the Adoption of a Single Convention, Vol. 1, pp. 52 and 6.

23. Ibid.

24. Anslinger consequently stated that 'Although transitional reservations are permitted concerning the smoking of opium in territories which permitted this vice on January 1, 1961, parties are not requested to prohibit the smok-

ing of opium by all persons not registered as opium smokers on January 1, 1964.' Report by Anslinger, 'The Single Convention on Narcotic Drugs of 1961: purposes and aims', 28 March 1961, p. 2, Anslinger Papers (hereafter cited as AP), Pattee Library Labor Archives, Penn State University, University Park, Pennsylvania, Box 10: File 11.

25. *Ibid.*, p. 5.
26. *Ibid.*, pp. 2–3.
27. *Ibid.*
28. 'The United States' views on the Single Convention on Narcotic Drugs', *Bulletin on Narcotics*, **15**(2) (1963), 9.
29. *Ibid.*, p. 11.
30. Harry Anslinger, 'Report of progress in drafting the Single Convention, a proposed codification of the multilateral treaty law on narcotic drugs', *Food Drug and Cosmetic Law Journal*, **13**(11) (1958), 692.
31. State Department memorandum, 'Conversation with Mr Anslinger on certain problems in the field of narcotic drugs', from Mr Mulliken to Mr Hanes, 11 March 1958, p. 3, NA 340.19.
32. Letter from FBN to Assistant Secretary of the Treasury, Mr Gilmore Flues. Remarks on a letter to the FBN from Alfred L. Tennyson, 11 September 1961, AP Box 2: File 6.
33. *Ibid.*
34. Rufus King, *The Drug Hang-Up*, p. 218.
35. Airgram from Robert Zimmerman, US embassy, Madrid, to Department of State, 6 July 1962, AP Box 2: File 5.
36. State Department confidential memorandum, 'Discussion of conversations of Mr James P. Hendrick, Deputy to the Assistant Secretary of the Treasury, and of Mr John T. Cusack, of the United States Delegation to the Seventeenth Session of the Commission on Narcotic Drugs, with delegations regarding the Single Convention on Narcotic Drugs, 1961, 31 May 1962', AP Box 2: File 5.
37. Report by Anslinger, 'The Single Convention on Narcotic Drugs of 1961: purposes and aims', 28 March 1961, pp. 5–6. AP Box 10: File 11.
38. *Ibid.*
39. *Ibid.*
40. *Ibid.*
41. *Ibid.*, p. 2.
42. Confidential letter from Gill Brown of the British Embassy, Washington, DC, to A. B. Horn in the UN Department of the Foreign Office, 1962, PRO (FO371 166947).
43. Minutes from E. E. Key, 15 June 1962, UN document UNS18112/9. PRO.
44. Confidential letter from P. H. Scott of the Foreign Office to J. N. O. Curle, Home Office, 16 June 1962. PRO (FO371).
45. Confidential letter from the British embassy, Greece, to the Foreign Office, 21 June 1962. PRO (FO371).
46. Letter from E. E. Key at the Foreign Office to the Home Office, 28 June 1962, PRO (FO371).
47. *Ibid.*

48. State Department confidential memorandum, 'Discussion of conversations of Mr James P. Hendrick, Deputy to the Assistant Secretary of the Treasury, and of Mr John T. Cusack, of the United States Delegation to the Seventeenth Session of the Commission on Narcotic Drugs, with delegations regarding the Single Convention on Narcotic Drugs, 1961, 31 May 1962', pp. 3–4, AP Box 2: File 5.

49. Letter from Sharman to Anslinger, 22 January 1962, AP Box 2: File 5.

50. Letter from Sharman to Anslinger, 20 February 1962, AP Box 2: File 5.

51. Report of US Delegation to the Seventeenth Session of the CND, Geneva, 14 May–1 June 1962. Anslinger to the Secretary of State of the United States of America, 15 August 1962, p. 6, Harry J. Anslinger Papers, Harry S. Truman Library (hereafter cited as HTL), Independence, Missouri, USA.

52. *Ibid.*, p. 9.

53. *Ibid.*, p. 10.

54. *Ibid.*, p. 12.

55. *Ibid.*

56. *Ibid.*, pp. 14–15.

57. US government memorandum from Anslinger to Mr Reed, 1 October 1962, HTL.

58. US government memorandum, from Anslinger to Mr J. Reed, US Department of Treasury, 1 October 1962, HTL.

59. *Ibid.*

60. *Ibid.*

61. *Ibid.*

62. Minutes of meeting between Mr Irving of the US Embassy and Mr T. C. Green, 1962, Undated, PRO (FO371 166947).

63. *New York Times*, 2 July 1962, p. 15. Although Anslinger, against his will, lost the leadership of the FBN, he remained active in the US delegation to the CND. The new head of the FBN, Henry Giordano, represented the United States at meetings as Anslinger attended fewer sessions. However, Anslinger continued to write the annual reports to the Secretary of State, illustrating his continuing prominence within the American delegation.

64. Report of the US Delegation to the Eighteenth Session United Nations Commission on Narcotic Drugs, Geneva, 29 April–17 May 1963, submitted by Anslinger, chairman of the Delegation, to the Secretary of State, 28 June 1963, p. 15, HTL.

65. *Ibid.*

66. *Ibid.*, p. 16.

67. David Soloman, *Reefer Madness: Marijuana in America* (New York: Grove Press, 1979), p. 227.

68. Anslinger quoted in *The New Republic*, **157** (July 1967), cited in Michael Schaller, 'The federal prohibition of marihuana', *Journal of Social History*, **4** (1970), 74.

69. Adolf Lande, 'The Single Convention', pp. 795–6.

70. Rufus King, *The Drug Hang-Up*, p. 218.

CHAPTER 5

THE GLOBAL DRUG PROHIBITION REGIME AT WORK

Folks, there is nothing new. You have just got to keep plugging away, putting money in the battle ... and pressuring the foreign governments to come on board.
Lawrence Smith, speaking about the US war on drugs in the Committee on Foreign Affairs, 1986

Drug abuse is now right at the top of the list of priorities requiring urgent attention from the international community. It is by its nature truly international; and it demands a co-ordinated international response. Only the United Nations can orchestrate that response.
Javier Pérez de Cuéllar, Secretary-General of the United Nations, 1990

The drug war overseas has always been an important element of US counternarcotics policy. America must be ready to look beyond its border for opportunities to combat the drug trade. Fighting the drug war overseas – where the most dangerous drugs used in the US, cocaine, heroin, originate – is the first line in defense in combating the scourge of drugs.
Senator Joseph R. Biden, Jr, Chairman of the Committee on the Judiciary of the US Senate, 1994

Solid in his belief that the internationalization of prohibition through the UN would solve the problem of drug addiction, Harry Anslinger remarked in a 1959 radio interview that 'if we didn't have UN control the world would still have millions and millions of addicts'.[1] Unfortunately, the all too obvious fact is that forty years on we have both a fully developed UN drug control programme and many millions of drug addicts. As I noted in the Introduction, despite the existence of an international regime to tackle the problem of illicit drug use, there has been an unprecedented increase in all aspects of the illegal drug issue at a global scale.

Up to this point, this study has concentrated on the evolution between 1909 and 1961 of the international drug prohibition regime. It has emphasized the important, though complex and often contradictory, role played by the United States in this process and Washington's part in determining the character of the multinational framework. The purpose of this chapter, then, is to bring events more up to date. Exploring the expansion and some of the consequences of the international regime since the creation of the Single Convention, the chapter shows how, despite the failure of current policies to produce a pragmatic approach to an individual's desire to use mind-altering substances, the UN remains a vehicle for the promotion and perpetuation of the prohibitionist ideal – an ideal that both historic and contemporary experience have shown to be bankrupt. After examining the post-1961 developments of the UN control system, the chapter discusses the impact of the global drug prohibition regime on different parts of the world. It closes by exploring US unilateral actions that operate within, and are effectively given legitimacy by, the international framework and the value system that surrounds it. Attention focuses predominantly on Latin America, a traditional focus of US supply-oriented strategies.

DEVELOPMENT OF THE GLOBAL DRUG PROHIBITION REGIME: EXPANSION OF THE UN FRAMEWORK SINCE THE SINGLE CONVENTION

Although there have been nominal moves towards the adoption of demand-side strategies, the late 1990s sees the organization continue to pursue an approach to drug use that is governed predominantly by supply-oriented thinking and the doctrine of prohibition. The United States, while consistently subordinating drug control to wider foreign-policy concerns, has helped to ensure this. As we have seen, American influence upon the formulation of the organization's policy on drug control has been enormous. Resulting similarities in approach between the United States and the UN can be recognized in the language used by the organization's drug control apparatus. Official UN literature which claims that 'countries all around the globe' are being 'contaminated' by the 'scourge'[2] of drug use readily evokes memories of the US campaigns against narcotic drugs of Richmond Hobson and Dr Wright in the early decades of the twentieth century. The US influence upon the UN system is not, of course, limited to the use of emotive language. The Single Convention has provided the keystone to the US dominated international regime, and subsequent UN-designed international efforts have followed this singularly prohibitionist route.

Consequently, since 1961 the system created by the Single Convention has been further strengthened by several treaties. In an effort to tighten international controls on synthetic drugs, the UN instigated the 1971 Convention on Psychotropic Substances. This extended control to a broad range of fabricated behaviour- and mood-altering substances that according to the UN could lead to harmful dependencies. These included hallucinogens such as lysergic acid diethylamide (LSD), stimulants such as amphetamines, and sedative-hypnotics such as barbiturates. Because the 1971 convention was largely designed by drug manufacturing nations, efforts were made to ensure that Western pharmaceutical interests were safeguarded. Indeed, its final provisions favoured nations that manufactured synthetic drugs. Although article 38 of the Single Convention had been a 'passing nod on the demand side'[3] of the drug control issue, for the first time in the history of international treaties the 1971 convention contained a provision concerning harm reduction. This was at least a symbolic departure from the predominant source-oriented prohibition ethos of the international regime. For as S. D. Stein notes, 'Paradoxical though it may seem, much of the history of national and international narcotics control can be written without reference to addicts or addiction.'[4] In broad terms, the convention called for the early identification of drug problems, treatment, rehabilitation and social reintegration. The 1971 legislation was nevertheless still based upon the control system established by the Single Convention.

The same year, 1971, also saw the creation of a new UN body to help in the international fight against drugs: the United Nations Fund for Drug Abuse Control (UNFDAC). Proposed by the United States and administered by the Secretary-General, UNFDAC is sustained by voluntary contributions from different sources, notably member nations. With an opening pledge of $2 million from the United States, the fund became another tool for the implementation of UN legislation. The product of another American initiative in the early 1970s was a protocol to strengthen the provisions of the 1961 legislation. This was the 1972 Protocol Amending the Single Convention, which came into force on 8 August 1975. It increased efforts to prevent the illicit production of, traffic in and use of narcotics. The protocol requires the prior authorization for the cultivation, production, manufacture, conversion and compounding of preparations, trade, distribution and the import and export of drugs. Although it also highlighted the need for treatment and rehabilitation of drug users, this option was seen as an alternative to, or, more importantly, an addition to, imprisonment for those who committed a drug offence. Thus the protocol also followed the prohibitive traditions of the Single Convention.

Despite such progress in strengthening the international framework, the fact that some states were still not parties to these treaties remained a concern to the organization. Consequently, in 1987 a UN International Conference on Drug Abuse and Illicit Trafficking worked towards increasing the scope of and participation in the existing treaty system. The conference aimed at the promotion and strict implementation of treaty obligations, at both national and international levels, and resulted in the Comprehensive Multidisciplinary Outline of Future Activities in Drug Abuse Control (CMO). The CMO consequently contained 35 targets defining perceived problems and suggesting specific courses of action at all levels. Although not legally binding, the outline persisted in urging nations to continue in the pursuit of the prohibition-based UN control system. The system itself was also extended one year later with the creation of the 1988 Convention Against Illicit Traffic in Narcotic Drugs and Psychotropic Substances. Its ancestry is beyond doubt, with the preamble stating that 'Recognizing the need to reinforce and supplement the measures provided in the Single Convention on Narcotic Drugs, 1961 ... '[5] As the title of the 1988 legislation suggests, the convention remains concerned with the supply-side of the drugs equation, giving force to the illicit trafficking recommendations contained within the CMO.

With such prohibitive legislation in place, the UN has continued to urge countries to follow its lead. In 1990, the General Assembly proclaimed the period 1991–2000 as the United Nations Decade Against Drug Abuse. Its goal was to 'intensify international co-operation and to increase efforts of States' to adhere to the principle that the 'destruction of the mind and body through the deliberate ingestion of drugs for non-medical reasons is dangerous and wrong'.[6] The 1990 Special Session of the General Assembly also produced the Political Declaration and Global Programme of Action to implement such aims. In reaffirming the principles of the 1961 Single Convention, the Programme of Action continued to build upon prohibitionist reasoning. Other moves for a restructuring of the control apparatus have also merely prolonged the pursuit of existing policies. The creation of the United Nations International Drug Control Programme (UNDCP) in 1991 was certainly an attempt to increase the efficiency of the current system. The UNDCP, which relies upon voluntary contributions from governments and other sources for approximately 90 per cent of its resources, amalgamated the DND, the UNFDAC and the secretariat of the INCB. This has centralized operations and in theory permits better co-ordination and 'expertise' in the operation of the UN's drug control efforts. Today, according to its own literature, the UNDCP addresses all aspects of the drug problem including 'crop substitution, drug law enforcement, prevention, treatment and rehabilitation of drug addicts and legislative and institutional reforms to enhance Governments' capacity to fight drug abuse'.[7]

Although some admissions have been made for the treatment and rehabilitation of drug users, the framework of the current international system is still firmly based upon a family of prohibitive UN conventions. As Richard Hartnoll notes, despite the relatively recent emergence at the international level of concern about demand reduction, the international framework remains very much about control ... the assumption of which has underpinned the historical emergence of this framework, which has been further elaborated in successive treaties ... is that the drug problem should be approached primarily through the suppression of supply and through the prohibition of possession for non-medical and non-scientific purposes.[8]

In fact the UN has consistently refused to consider any alternative approaches to the issue of drug use, and continues to urge nations to provide financial support for the UNDCP. Like the US authorities, the UN has persistently worked to undermine studies that contradict its own stance on drug control. A good example of this practice concerns a UN report on cocaine. This was undertaken between 1992 and 1994 by the WHO Programme on Substance Abuse (WHO/PSA) in association with the UN Interregional Crime and Justice Research Institute (UNICRI). The authors of the report, the largest global study on cocaine ever conducted, produced some unexpected conclusions. Among them was that occasional use causes 'generally few problems'; health problems from legal drugs are greater than those from cocaine; cocaine is not seen as 'invariably' harmful to health by many experts; the use of coca leaves has 'positive ... functions for indigenous Andean populations' and appears to have 'no negative effects'; education has hitherto tended to sensationalize and mythologize the properties of the drug; and the adverse effects of current drug policies need to be assessed. Obviously shocked by the report's findings, the UN was quick to issue disclaimers. In a press briefing it was stated that 'The sometimes unexpected conclusions of the study do not represent an official position of the WHO.' The report was also accompanied by a statement which announced that 'the material included does not represent' the official view of the body and 'in no way should it be read that WHO or UNICRI endorse the use of any psychoactive substance'.[9] On the other hand, the UN has always been quick to endorse studies that confirm the wisdom of the prohibitive approach to the control of drugs. The WHO's support for a 1995 study linking cancer to cannabis smoking is a case in point.[10]

It will be recalled how Anslinger and the FBN attempted to silence those who opposed official policies, a tradition that the US government is continuing today. Nadelmann has called recent American pressure upon Colombian politicians to stop open discussion of drug legalization 'part of a fairly systematic US government campaign to silence the debate on legalisation'.[11] Indeed, the WHO cocaine project findings also provoked an angry US reaction. Rumours circulating within the UN drug control framework at the time of the report's release suggested that the United States had threatened to withdraw funding from the WHO/PSA.[12] With the principal actor on the international drug control stage adopting such a rigid and obstructionist stance on the issue, it is perhaps inevitable that the UNDCP will also remain unswervingly in favour of prohibition. However, without moving to reform the international system, the UN's approach remains blinkered. The UN steadfastly adheres to the principle that if more time and money are invested in its current strategy, success will be inevitable.

A best-case scenario, one in which demand-side policies in reality represent at least an equal part of an integrated UN plan, may support such a position. The prohibition-based regime, however, does not look so promising. Despite stricter legislation at all levels, illegal drug use remains prevalent world-wide. In fact, the UN itself has gone so far as to admit to the failure of the war on drugs. A UN panel noted in 1993 that the effects of drug abuse remained grim world-wide.[13] The important US-influenced Single Convention is therefore, according to Anthony Henman and his co-authors, underlain with a critical paradox. 'How is it', Henman and colleagues ask, 'that an instrument designed to reduce the use of illicit drugs can ultimately have ushered in an age when the consumption of these substances has increased beyond even the most alarmist projections?' 'Is it not obvious', they continue, 'that the misconceived obsession with extirpating the use of certain drugs – those deemed illicit – greatly increases the profitability of their production?'[14] The answer to the conundrum would apparently be 'not'; at least with respect to those in charge of the UN drug control apparatus.

As it is, the UN has played an important role in creating and perpetuating a US-style international drug control regime – an approach that, whichever way it is examined, has failed disastrously on a national level. Despite the pursuit of a policy of drug prohibition for over 80 years, the United States remains a nation where illicit drug use is commonplace among all sections of society. This consequently provides little hope that the doctrine's globalization will prove to be any more of a success. Although direct parallels with drug prohibition should be avoided, the American experience with alcohol prohibition between 1919 and 1933 shows the unworkable nature of a policy that attempts to proscribe an individual's wish to consume a psychoactive substance. As David Boaz notes, 'alcohol didn't cause the high crime rates of the 1920s, prohibition did. And drugs don't cause today's alarming crime rates, drug prohibition does.'[15] The situation produced by the prohibition of drugs is, however, far worse than that created by fourteen years of alcohol prohibition in the United States. Comments made in 1931 by Senator Robert

Wagner of New York are consequently equally applicable to the approaches adopted by the United States and the UN today. Wagner asked, 'Why heap more sacrifice upon the altar of hopelessness?'[16]

Empty vessel? Does the UNDCP affect national drug control policies?

The international framework for the control of drugs clearly rests upon prohibitive foundations. However, critics of the UNDCP argue that this is of little consequence since the organization has no real impact on transnational control efforts. Various, usually American, pundits discount the UN as nothing more than a talking-shop with little tangible influence. The gradualist nature of the multilateral approach to drug control often appears to be too slow to satisfy an identifiable American impatience that demands rapid success. As we shall see, the US government has adopted aggressive unilateral and bilateral efforts to supplement the more gradual drug control work of the UN. Some observers consequently do not appreciate the varied and extensive influence that UN legislation has world-wide, or even misconstrue its role entirely. For example, Manuel Barbarena and Kevin N. Wright have made the mistake of viewing the UN as an ineffective organization that is opposed to the current US prohibitionist drug control policies. They have consequently claimed that

> Looking at the objectives proposed by the UN we see how this organization fantasizes by 'requesting,' 'suggesting,' 'emphasizing,' 'recommending,' etc., but it is not really telling us how these objectives are going to be achieved. Another problem is that the UN does not have the real power to force certain nations to comply with the resolutions. The UN is, then, an organization with good and sound ideas but without the force to accomplish them.

Barbarena and Wright therefore believe that 'The United Nations plays only a role as a figurehead against the drug war.'[17] They can be challenged on a number of counts: characterizing the UN's ideas on drug control as sound, the organization's lack of power and its purely emblematic status as a figurehead against prohibition.

First, as has been shown, the UN drug control programme is based upon prohibitionist assumptions. Although lip service has been given to demand reduction, treatment, rehabilitation and education, prohibition remains the central belief of the organization. As Richard Hartnoll notes,

> Although the Conventions do not stipulate that the use or misuse of controlled drugs must in itself be a punishable offence, they constitute to

delineate a policy that is clearly and essentially prohibitionist in character. The growing status attributed to prevention, treatment and rehabilitation should not be seen as a repudiation of that principle . . . . Rather it should be seen as the incorporation of an additional strand in an overall strategy whose goal is the elimination of illicit drug use. The rhetoric of the 'war on drugs on all fronts' accurately encapsulates the dominant theme of international policy.[18]

Second, as we shall see, the UN plays an active and significant, though differentiated and perhaps not always highly visible, role in the fight against drugs. Although it is easy to see why observers perceive the UN drug control framework as little more than a talking-shop, UN conventions and the organization's perpetuation of a prohibitionist norm do have an impact upon paradigms of national drug control. Indeed, it would be valid to highlight the UN's treaties' principle of voluntary adherence as an area of possible weakness. As the UN itself admits, 'It is important to realize that the UN and its drug control programmes can only be as strong and effective as the support given to them by Member States.'[19] A country's violation of a treaty, for example, may result only in recommendations that other nations cease their drug exports to that state, or the UN may call on a government for remedial measures to be taken. While the UN control framework can in some respects be regarded as what Donnelly terms a promotional regime, the organization's image as a benevolent movement whose mission it is to safeguard the well-being of *all* humankind gives the UNDCP and its associated legislation substantial moral influence and suasion. Hence a nation's refusal to adhere to a UN convention instantaneously results in its branding as an enemy of the international community, or even of humankind itself. This can result in a loss of prestige, not to mention economic opportunities and political influence. In much the same way as many nations perceive good relations with the United States to be more important than freedom to develop national drug policies, so countries voluntarily adhere to UN narcotic conventions. Thus, although UN conventions often only 'recommend' provisions, failure to comply with them can tarnish a nation's international reputation.

An example of the powerful nature of voluntary adherence was seen at the 1987 Conference on Drug Abuse and Illicit Trafficking. At the close of the proceedings, officials are said to have seen the conference as turning the moral screw on governments to join the co-ordinated 'counter-offensive against the insidious threat of drug abuse and against the organised forces of evil'. Mahathir Mohammed, the Malaysian Prime Minister and the conference president, accordingly noted that 'No nation or political leadership can now afford to ignore or stand in the way of the campaign to rid us of the scourge of drugs and drug traffickers.' The CMO, the president claimed, 'must ... be regarded as a morally binding pledge'.[20]

Consequently, when the moral voluntarism of the UN is combined with unilateral pressure exerted by Washington and US agencies, the international regime becomes more coercive than promotional. Nations need to withstand a great deal of persuasion if they wish to pursue alternative approaches to the issue of drug use within their own borders. To illustrate this point and demonstrate that not all American observers dismiss the impact of the UN, it is useful to recall the observations of Theodore Vallance on this issue. Recognizing the inertia created by the UN, Vallance notes that 'the interconnectedness of drug policies of more than one hundred countries' that are parties to UN conventions 'poses formidable obstacles to the advocacy of alternative drug policies in the United States'. Appreciating that UN conventions also limit other nations' freedom to alter control policies, Vallance continues, 'In spite of the arguments that can be offered in favor of one or another form of legalization, no one country could easily rear back and legalize drugs without provoking criticism and other possible consequences from other countries.'[21]

The actions of American drug control bodies, particularly the Drug Enforcement Administration (DEA), also become more pressing as a result of the UN's stance on the issue of control, as the last point illustrates. To state, as do Barbarena and Wright, that the UN is 'only' a figurehead is also very misleading. The position adopted by the UN and its conventions provides significant and symbolic legitimization for the continuation of the present crusade against drug use world-wide. As will be discussed later in this chapter, actions carried out in the name of the US war on drugs receive what amounts to a moral mandate from the ostensibly philanthropic United Nations. The UN plays a vital role in the creation of norms; that is to say, attitudes towards drug use and policies designed to address that issue. Through the development of an international system based upon prohibitive ideology, the UN has moved to standardize attitudes and reactions. Richard Hartnoll lucidly notes that the international system therefore

> must ... be seen as a persuasive and critical influence in shaping world-wide the ideological basis of how the 'drug problem' is characterized, in defining what are and what are not appropriate policy perspectives, and determining the parameters within which national policies, laws and other responses develop.[22]

By reinforcing the current prohibitive policy for drug control, the UN effectively perpetuates the implementation of a failed doctrine. The UN, therefore, can be seen to promote, perpetuate and legitimize the current US-style prohibitionist-based approach to drug use – an approach that, as we have seen, is based more on moralism, racism and pseudo-scientific evidence than reasoned debate on the most appropriate response to drug use.

The impacts and consequences of controls brought into operation by UN legislation do vary dramatically between nations; most notably between what can be inelegantly termed Western and non-Western countries. This is the result of several interacting factors. First, owing to their relative economic stability, and thus reduced dependence on the United States for financial aid, many Western (or, if you prefer, industrialized) nations can withstand American pressure at the UN. This can lead to the removal or dilution of unfavourable US initiated provisions. Thus, as we have seen, the United Kingdom for example has been able to resist US pressure and, to some extent, ensure that some alterations were made in the conditions laid down in international treaties. In these cases, the cost of non-compliance or incomplete compliance with the prohibitive regime is not excessively damaging to national well-being. On the other hand, less economically secure nations, such as many countries in Latin America, are more likely to follow the US line on drug control. Washington's policy of linking the provision of political support and much-needed economic aid to adherence to US schemes leaves little room for manoeuvre.

Second, and perhaps more important, is the issue of cultural identity and heritage. Because many Western nations share a common ancestry and consequently, to a large degree, the same moral value systems as the United States, any changes to domestic legislation that do result from US-designed UN law do not have a dramatically visible impact on the society of that nation. For example, since the 1971 Misuse of Drugs Act, the British, it can be argued, have been moving away from the traditional medico-centric approach to drug control. The adoption of a stronger crime control perspective can be seen as a move towards an American-style criminalization approach to the problem of drug use. Treatment and maintenance have continued, but they are now less prominent in policy and practice. State involvement and the increasing politicization of the debate on drugs have produced a situation where law enforcement and penal measures are taking centre stage. However, efforts to move British legislation into line with international trends are also likely to have had an effect upon the direction of the UK's drug control legislation. This has been the case for many years in the UK, with, as Philip Bean has pointed out, 'all of the major British Dangerous Drugs legislation from 1920–1964' being 'passed to fulfil international treaty obligations'.[23] Hartnoll also warns that

Any understanding of the development of both British and international policies must include an appreciation of the powerful and persuasive influence of the U.S. in vigorously exporting the prohibitionist model of a moral crusade against drugs, and in defining the parameters within which policies have evolved across the globe.[24]

Although this may be the case, such changes in UK legislation do not require a massive realignment in societal values or extensive cultural restructuring. The use of psychoactive substances other than alcohol, coffee and nicotine, for example, is not regarded as a morally acceptable form of behaviour in most Western nations. Changes in control strategies merely affect those who illegally use substances to alter their moods, and do not have a great impact upon the majority of the population. However, many non-Western countries, again for example those in Latin America, operate within totally different cultural and moral boundaries with regard to the use of psychoactive drugs. The definition of licit and illicit substances in those societies may vary greatly from the widely held norms in Western society. As a result, one can observe the dramatic repercussions of US-influenced UN drug control policies in nations with socio-cultural backgrounds different from that of USA.

CONSEQUENCES OF THE GLOBAL DRUG PROHIBITION REGIME: THE IMPACT ON NON-WESTERN NATIONS

A prime example of such a process can be observed when we look at the way in which Andean nations have been forced to alter their traditional patterns of drug use. For the inhabitants of the Andes region, chewing the coca leaf is a way of life, just as the social drinking of alcohol is, for example, in the United States and much of the Western world. The practice is not maintained merely to achieve a temporary 'high' or 'rush'. It is taken to fight the effects of altitude sickness, hunger and fatigue in order to continue work in inhospitable conditions. The coca plant also plays a massive symbolic role in the societies of the Andean region of South America. As well as having nutritional value, it is regarded as sacred owing to its medicinal, magical and religious qualities. Consequently, the coca leaf can be seen to represent the cultural identity of the people whose ancestors built the great pre-Columbian civilizations. To a Bolivian hill-farming family, for example, US domination of the multilateral treaty system has meant the attempted termination of an ancient and socially ingrained custom. Here coca chewing does not fit into the cultural and, more importantly, moral framework developed in and exported from the United States of America. Because the UN hosts a number of anti-drug bodies that follow the line dictated from Washington, the behaviour receives very little international toleration. Through the activities of the CND and resultant UN drug control legislation, most notably the 1961 Single Convention, the United States has applied pressure on the Bolivian and other Andean governments to phase out the legal production of the coca leaf and criminalize the traditional practice of coca chewing.

It was announced at the plenipotentiary conference in 1961 that 'all non-medical use of narcotic drugs', including not only the chewing of coca leaves, but also opium smoking, opium eating and the consumption of cannabis, 'will be outlawed everywhere'. This object, it was claimed, was a 'goal which workers in international narcotics control all over the world' had 'striven to achieve for half a century'.[25] More accurately, this goal had been predominantly an American objective. In one drastic action, the provisions of the Single Convention universally outlawed culturally ingrained paradigms of drug use. To allow for the phasing out of these patterns, the 1961 legislation included some transitional reservations under article 49. These permitted the temporary continuation of the practice of coca chewing and the use of cannabis, cannabis resin and extracts and tinctures of cannabis for non-medical purposes. However, under the terms of the legislation, coca leaf chewing had to be abolished within 25 years from the coming into force of the convention. Similarly, the non-medical or non-scientific use of cannabis was to be discontinued as soon as possible, 'but in any case within twenty-five years' from the date the convention came into force. This was, according to Dr Norman Taylor, a rather optimistic timetable when 'matched against three thousand years of use by untold millions'.[26]

Under article 22 of the convention, parties also obligated themselves to prohibit the cultivation of the coca bush, the opium poppy and the cannabis plant. This would be the case whenever the prevailing conditions in their countries or territories rendered the prohibition of the drugs' cultivation the most suitable measure, in their opinion, for protecting the public health and welfare and preventing the diversion of drugs into illicit traffic. Article 26 even stated that 'the Parties shall as far as possible enforce the uprooting of all coca bushes which grow wild. They shall destroy the coca bushes if illegally cultivated.'[27] Thus, the Single Convention became the first multilateral convention to make prohibitory provisions concerning the cultivation of the coca bush.

Today the 1961 Convention's approach towards coca chewing remains prominent within the organization, with UN literature referring to coca chewing as drug 'abuse'.[28] This is the case despite, as Nadelmann notes, the significant evidence that the practice is not only deeply rooted in the Andean culture but also not particularly harmful, and even moderately beneficial. Additionally, as Henman has commented, despite cosmetic changes in the 1988 convention, 'albeit with ambiguous wording', the official thinking on the legitimacy of 'traditional uses' continues to be underpinned by the concept of a war on drugs.[29] Consequently, although the text of the Vienna Convention admits that UN measures should 'take due account of the traditional licit uses [of coca] where there is historical evidence of such use', it has done nothing in practice to derogate the provisions of the Single Convention.[30] However, the ludicrously unrealistic and unworkable provisions of the UN's legislation remain plain to see, with the Single Convention's most visible failure being the continuing and widespread practice of coca chewing. This remains the case despite the fact that we are currently well over the 25-year deadline set for its abolition.

As they stand, current UN policies appear to struggle to make the distinction between cocaine and coca. Adhering to the misplaced findings of the American-dominated 1947 Commission, the UN continues to link the indigenous practice of coca chewing to the use of cocaine in the West. The enduring belief that problems associated with illegal cocaine use in countries like the United States are directly related to coca chewing in South America seems likely to ensure that there will be little change in UN policy in the near future. Such a situation, it will be recalled, was foreseen by the UK representative to the third session of the CND in 1948. Hutson's observations were therefore remarkably far-sighted, and foreshadowed the present predicament concerning the lack of distinction between coca and cocaine.

The UNDCP's attempts at crop substitution have also done little to alleviate the damaging effects of the war on coca. The development of programmes to encourage and assist Latin American farmers to replace coca crops with legal alternatives has met with little significant or long-term success. Poor results have been closely related to the instability present in the economies of many Latin American nations. The collapse of many traditional industries in the region has led to a massive decline in economic development. Mushrooming debt, wild inflation and endemic unemployment have forced a dramatic drop in the living standards of many people. This has all happened at the same time as the so-called narco-traffickers have been providing opportunities for employment, scarce hard currency, and prosperous business. Consequently, as Mark Heil has noted, 'This dynamic has strengthened the illicit drug trade in relation to governments preoccupied with crisis management.'[31]

The economic rewards to be gained by the production of raw coca for the cocaine industry often prove to be too great for a disadvantaged farmer to miss. For example, in Peru's Upper Huallaga Valley (UHV), a coca producer's gross income in 1985 was 10 times higher than that of a coffee grower and 21 times that of a rice farmer. The existence of high profits is without a doubt one of the biggest hurdles that has to be overcome in order to make crop substitution an attractive proposition. Although Latin America, and the Andean region in particular, is continuing to be a priority for the UNDCP, the organization does not appear to appreciate a farmer's predicament concerning crop substitution. UNDCP literature observes that 'the fact is ... the farmer is breaking the law and usually knows it'. The UNDCP also notes that 'The income received by the farmer for the illicit narcotics production, *unfortunately* [emphasis added], is higher than that received for traditional food crops.'[32] Such an attitude suggests that the UN programmes for crop substitution see the financial advantages of drug production as merely an unfortunate peripheral factor, rather than the central factor, in the coca problem. Myopia induced by the goal of coca eradication ensures that the UN fails to address the issue of crop substitution realistically. The fact that anti-coca sentiments remain entrenched within the dogma of the UN's drug control system reflects the endurance of questionable assumptions. It also demonstrates how the cultural standards of the UN's dominant Western membership are consistently imposed upon the societies of other nations.

American-influenced UN legislation, as shown, ensures that culturally ingrained patterns of drug use have become outlawed in some countries simply because they do not sit comfortably within a moral framework constructed by Western nations. Consequently, such a process of what is essentially Americanization should not be underestimated. As noted in the Introduction to this book, international prohibition regimes naturally tend to reflect the economic and political interests of the dominant members of international society. The United States has therefore greatly influenced the creation of an international regime. Indeed, during the period before the ratification of the Single Convention there was a feeling within the US-dominated UN drug control system that the rest of the world should strive to get its own domestic control system into line with that in the USA. For example, an article in the UN *Bulletin on Narcotics* noted:

> For a State that already possesses internal rules and institutions which have been developed and tried by experience, the implementation of the 1961 Single Convention calls for no innovations, while a State which has no such rules and institutions must establish them.[33]

Adolf Lande, the Deputy Executive Secretary of the UN secretariat at the conference in 1961 and one of the main architects of the legislation, also displayed his faith in the US-style prohibitive system for control. In 1962 he noted that to adhere to the conditions of the Single Convention, 'a number of countries will have to adjust their narcotics regime to the *higher standards* [emphasis added] prevailing in such countries as the United States'.[34]

In his lucid examination of this issue, Nadelmann states that 'moral and emotional factors', in combination with the desire to proselytize, can and do play an important role in the creation and evolution of international regimes. To be sure, as discussed earlier, the compulsion to convert others to one's beliefs and remake the world in one's own image has long played a role in international politics.[35] American involvement in the international drug control movement has therefore resulted in cultural intrusion on both counts. Consequently, the Andean nations, for example, are being forced to phase out and criminalize the consumption of coca and adopt a programme created outside their own cultural frame of reference. This is the case despite the fact that the social and ceremonial use of alcohol continues in most Western nations unhindered. The consumption of alcohol is seen to be a morally acceptable form of behaviour, and although it may not be practised in all nations around the world, it is given little attention on the international stage.

A good example of this cultural bias can be seen during the 1961 plenipotentiary conference for the adoption of the Single Convention. Then the Secretary-General and the conference chairman gave specific instructions that alcohol was to be outside the meeting's terms of reference. The UN's attitude towards alcohol was also clearly apparent at the CND in the same year. At the 1961 session the commission considered the control of cannabis. As Rufus King notes, an Interpol observer scolded commentators from the Netherlands who had challenged the UN's traditional stance on the drug and dared to make the 'heretical suggestion that cannabis addiction was no worse than alcoholism'. With support from a WHO spokesperson, it was claimed that cannabis should definitely be an internationally controlled substance. Despite opposition from nations such as India, this stance was backed by the familiar argument that there was the 'added danger that cannabis abuse is very likely to be the forerunner of addiction to more dangerous addicting drugs'.[36] Countering claims put forward by Anslinger and the US delegation that cannabis was a stepping-stone drug, the Indian representative noted that cannabis addiction, like alcoholism, did not constitute a serious social problem in a country where marijuana smoking did not lead on to the taking of heroin.[37] Nonetheless, the commission and the WHO's Expert Committee on Drugs Liable to Produce Addiction continued to follow US-influenced ideas concerning cannabis addiction, crime and the drug's proclivity for leading to more addictive substances. On the other hand, the social acceptability of alcohol use in most Western nations helped to ensure that the drug remained largely beyond the scope of UN control.

Like many of his beliefs, Anslinger's own stance on alcohol was confusing and contradictory. The great national and international anti-drug crusader is reported to have once said, 'You can't trust a man who doesn't drink.'[38] This is a strange conviction, bearing in mind that the early years of his career were devoted to the enforcement of alcohol prohibition. The irony of Anslinger's lack of understanding, or for that matter lack of interest, in cultural differentiation was well illustrated during an interview with Richard Cowan, the ex-director of the US National Organization for the Reform of Marijuana Laws (NORML). During the interview with the then retired FBN chief, Cowan recalled that Anslinger defended his ardent anti-marijuana stance while puffing on a large cigar and sipping an equally generous glass of brandy.[39] While adopting a similarly biased stance on indigenous drug use in South America and other parts of the world, the UN control policies can be validly seen as a form of cultural imperialism; or, at the risk of being too journalistic, narco-cultural imperialism.

CONSEQUENCES OF THE GLOBAL DRUG PROHIBITION REGIME: THE IMPACT ON WESTERN NATIONS

UN policies also affect nations of the Western industrialized world, although in a way that is not as simple to identify and define. The similarities between the powerful Western members of the UN control machinery undoubtedly mean that adherence to the UN-perpetuated regime has been less dramatic in the so-called developed nations of the world. Since 1961, nations have been moving to ensure that national drug control policies conform to UN specifications and recommendations. Although voluntary in nature, the UN's crucial use of moral suasion has resulted in widespread loyalty to the principles embodied in the organization's international drug control laws. Despite this, the highly visible failure of current drug control paradigms has produced intensive debate as to the integrity of the prohibitionist ethic. The damaging impact that the war on drugs is having upon societies throughout the world is forcing a re-evaluation of the central tenets of the prohibitive approach.

At the time of the construction of the Single Convention, many, particularly European, nations were content to follow the main thrust of the US-initiated prohibitionist strategy. Countries such as the United Kingdom and France were careful to ensure that their own interests, notably pharmaceutical investments in the case of Britain, were safeguarded.

However, provided the legislation's clauses did not threaten the structure of established drug control and societal attitudes towards drug use, opposition was limited. In 1961, Western nations did not have to make any dramatic changes in the way they approached the issue of drug control. Clauses referring to cannabis and coca had no immediate bearing upon the so-called industrialized countries of the West. For example, France and the UK believed that the cannabis problem was of little concern in their countries and were only concerned that national governments should be free to decide on complete prohibition at their own discretion.

The era of the Single Convention, however, was a time when drug 'abuse', as it is commonly regarded today, was an unfamiliar phenomenon in Europe. For example, the late Bing Spear, formerly the head of the Home Office Drugs Branch, is said to have known by name virtually every registered addict in London – an amazing state of affairs bearing in mind London's large addict population today. Such an escalation of the drug problem not just in the capital of the United Kingdom but throughout the Western world has resulted in the issue of drug use being pushed towards the top of many political agendas. Today, attempts by national governments to address what is undoubtedly a serious social, criminal and medical 'problem' are guided by international legislation that was signed in a different era of drug use. Any moves that are made to approach the drug issue from a more rational, dispassionate and pragmatic direction are met by counter-force from the UN's prohibitive legislation. Individuals and organizations that speak out against the damaging effects of the current war on drugs are faced with an official response stating that national policies are merely following internationally agreed legislation constructed by the United Nations. The inertia existent in many European national control policies can be attributed to an almost invisible barrier that is the UN legislative framework.

The United Kingdom has experienced a gradual, but steadily increasing, tide of opinion calling for some form of reassessment of the current approach to drug control. Politicians, from all sides of the political spectrum, church leaders, social workers and medical doctors have urged for the discourse on drug use to be widened to include strategies other than US-style prohibition. It is interesting to note that some senior police officers, those responsible for actually enforcing the current drug laws, are also speaking out against a rigidly prohibitive approach. Commander John Grieve, Director of Intelligence at Scotland Yard, recently stated that 'What we're doing at the moment simply does not work.'[40] Following this line, and echoing the words of August Vollmer in 1936, Chief Inspector Ron Clarke of the Greater Manchester Police has commented that 'there should be no place for the police in the control of drugs'. He continued to state that the problem is 'unpoliceable', with current policies 'not applying common sense'. Clarke, however, has taken the argument one step further by recognizing the restrictive nature of the UN, particularly the 1961 Single Convention. This, he believes, should be 'scrapped' along with all the conventions that are based on it. The United Kingdom's current predicament concerning illegal drug use is, according to Clarke, largely the fault of 'Uncle Sam' and the USA's influence upon the international system.[41] These arguments are all the more persuasive when it is remembered that Grieve and Clarke are both at the front line of the current war on drugs, while those who design policies frequently deal only with the theoretical side of the drug issue. Despite opposition from influential sections of society, it is true that British governments are currently choosing to follow UN policy and function within the confines of the international treaty structure. However, this is restrictive. Although the UK still clings to the remnants of the so-called 'British system', and consequently approaches many aspects of the issue from a pragmatic and humane standpoint, freedom to put more distance between British and American policies is greatly constrained by the UK's adherence to UN drug control conventions. Combined with American unilateral efforts to 'encourage' the UK to follow prohibitive legislation, British governments are greatly restricted in the ways in which they can approach drug control. Pressure from US agencies such as the DEA, which has agents assigned to 70 offices in 50 countries around the world, is, as noted, further legitimized by the rhetoric of and stance adopted by the UN.

Although the United Kingdom has appeared to be moving increasingly towards a drug control strategy that follows US ideals, there is no reason to assume that it is the best policy to adopt. The unique conditions of every nation mean that a single policy blueprint has no hope of effectively addressing the issue of drug use. For example, despite the 1980s media hype concerning the expected arrival of an American-style crack cocaine epidemic in the United Kingdom, US DEA officials were proved wrong when Britain did not duplicate the American experience with the drug. Although there are great similarities between American and British societies, differences still exist. Patterns of drug use are dependent on a wide range of economic, social, political and cultural variables. Consequently, comments like that made by the then Home Office minister David Mellor in 1985, stating that 'when the U.S. sneezes Europe catches a cold',[42] should be considered with a great deal of caution. It is worth noting the observations of Jerry Mandel. Discussing this issue, he concludes that 'drug use is not an uncontrolled epidemic, spreading between countries .... No germ crosses national, or subcultural boundaries.' Mandel poses the question, 'If there is a time-lag before "backward cultures" emulate number one cultures, how long is it supposed to take, and what will the copy-cat culture's year-to-year fluctuations look like?' He concludes that 'British drug problems and trends are uniquely their own, as are the U.S.'s.'[43] To believe that the United States is the rather grim model that other nations are destined to follow is a misguided assumption. National drug control policies need to be developed according to specific societal needs. For example, Susanne MacGregor concludes, in 'Could Britain inherit the American nightmare?', that despite the 'hurricane crossing the Atlantic', there could be an alternative practical and pragmatic approach to drug use in the UK. MacGregor argues that a policy somewhere between the liberal Dutch approach and the US war on drugs could be a realistic stance for the UK to adopt. She illustrates, therefore, the unique nature of national drug situations and the specific responses required. Restrictions put in place by the UN consequently may only hinder national efforts to create pragmatic and realistic drug control strategies. The UK currently concurs with the major thrust of the UN strategy, and is therefore comfortable, for the time being at least, with the control framework. Other nations, however, are experiencing more serious legislative restrictions.

The Netherlands is the classic example of a nation that has been attempting to move away from a predominantly prohibitive approach to drug control. Having assessed the drug problem in their country, the Dutch authorities concluded that their policies should focus on the health and safety of the drug user. By adopting a public health-oriented policy, which was based on the demand side of the issue, the Dutch authorities made a break from the established prohibitive doctrine. Within the guidelines laid down by the Minister of Justice in 1976, the 'Dutch government translated the international trend into the less prohibitionist, less restrictive and less punitive criminal justice policy traditionally pursued by the Dutch, in an attempt to reconcile its international obligations with its national commitments and national political options'.[45] Despite American condemnation, for example that of the chairman of the House Select Committee on Narcotics Abuse and Control, Charles Rangel, the Netherlands has sought to alleviate some problems associated with drug use in a pragmatic and undogmatic fashion. In a speech that espoused an approach alternative to that actively pursued by the UN, the Dutch Minister of Justice clearly expressed the Netherlands' humane and realistic stance. At the 1988 UN Conference on Drug Abuse and Illicit Trafficking, the Minister, a member of a conservative government, stated that

> The protection of health and social well being in general and the improvement of the health of those who are already addicted must be our primary

aim. We always bear in mind that the drug abuse problem is basically and principally a matter of health and social being. It is not, in our view, primarily a problem of police and criminal justice . . . . We are fully aware of the necessity to prevent as much as possible a situation in which more harm is caused by criminal proceedings than by the use of the substance itself.[46]

Nevertheless, despite the Dutch establishment's belief that such an approach is the best strategy for their country, international treaty commitments do greatly restrict available policy options. The Dutch attitude has brought the Netherlands into conflict with the dominant international mood, and the authorities there have to be careful not to alienate the international community. The Netherlands' drug control policies work within the laws of the UN and rely on 'prosecutorial discretion and the informal development of more liberal practices to bend the conventions to Dutch traditions'.[47] Dutch adherence to international conventions, principally the 1961 Single Convention, meant that the political desire for cannabis legalization in the early 1970s was forcibly downgraded to an alteration of the law within the confines of the prohibitive regime. International limitations prevent Dutch officials from introducing laws that move further away from the American prohibitive model. The risk of reactionary international condemnation for breaking UN law has proved to be a great factor in stifling further liberalization. Eddy Engelsman, head of the Drugs Branch of the Dutch Ministry of Welfare, Health and Cultural Affairs, noted in 1987 that 'The Netherlands has a lot of international interests, both economically and in several international bodies.' The Netherlands, he continued, consequently did not want to become the 'Libya of Europe'.[48] Although Engelsman commented in 1987 that threats of international sanctions had not been made 'openly', four years later a colleague left no doubts about the Dutch predicament within the international community. Leo Zaal, the Chief Inspector of the Head Office of Amsterdam Police Intelligence, noted in 1991 that 'efforts to liberalize drug policies are constrained by a complex network of international treaties . . . as well as informal but intense pressure from the U.S. Government'.[49] Consequently, all liberal policies adopted in the Netherlands force the government to play a dangerous game of dare in order to remain within the confines of UN international law.

The Netherlands is of course not the only Western country whose freedom to produce national legislation is restricted by the conventions of the UN. Although the Dutch predicament has received a great deal of attention within drug policy circles, movements in other European nations are also blaming international constrictions for the maintenance of rigidly prohibitive national drug control strategies. The re-evaluation, from several

quarters, of European national drug control policies has produced growing criticism of the restrictive function performed by the UN conventions
on drug control. It has become increasingly obvious that moves to tackle
the drug issue from an alternative non-prohibitionist angle have encountered great inertia from the UN control framework. In Europe there has
been a growth in the number of pressure groups and political parties
working for a restructuring of drug control paradigms. Among them is the
European Cities on Drug Policy (ECDP). The EDCP's 1990 Frankfurt
Resolution reiterated the organization's principles towards the realization
of a pragmatic and 'accepting' drug policy that rejected the criminalization
of users. Indeed, moves are under way throughout Europe to develop
realistic drug control strategies. However, as another important reform
movement, the International Antiprohibition League (IAL), points out,

> all this thought, this analysis, these propositions, these pilot experiences are
> confronted by an insurmountable obstacle which, if not removed, will
> prevent any future progress of the antiprohibitionist campaign. This
> obstacle is precisely the UN Conventions in the area. Indeed, no draft law
> and no pilot experience based on legalisation can be attempted as long as the
> international legal framework – the primary cause of prohibition imposed
> by the Conventions – is not left behind.[50]

The UN, therefore, does indeed play an important role in the development
and operation of national drug control strategies. Although the impact
may vary between countries, the restrictive cordons constructed by the
UN conventions ensure that nations can jettison the law of prohibition
only at the risk of alienating influential sections of the international
community.

THE INTERNATIONAL REGIME AS A LEGITIMIZER FOR THE US OVERSEAS WAR ON DRUGS

As we have seen, the United States has effectively used the UN in an effort
to create a prohibitive norm for international drug control and promote its
own moral value system towards drug use in other nations. This it has
achieved by a combination of international treaty obligations and economic coercion. The USA has also entered into bilateral treaties with 35
nations since 1961, and seeks co-operation under these agreements within
the multilateral framework established by the Single Convention. However, direct overseas intervention by US agencies and the US military is
playing an increasingly central role in the American fight against drugs.
American dissatisfaction with what is perceived to be the slow progress of

multilateral control efforts has led successive US administrations to pursue their own campaigns against drugs abroad, while simultaneously pushing for strict international legislation at the UN. Such unilateral actions have no formal authority from the UN. Yet the UNDCP's rhetoric and the growing imagery of a global drug war that surround the international prohibitive regime effectively legitimize the expansion of the US extranational fight against drugs. The concept that US efforts operate within a wider ethical framework designed to rid the world of the 'scourge' of drugs goes some way to validating the existence of US overseas endeavours; in essence it provides them with a moral mandate. In much the same way as President Bush used the UN to legitimate direct action against Saddam Hussein's Iraq in 1990–91, successive US administrations have harnessed the image of the organization as a moral shield for the conduct of aggressive source-oriented policies. This section provides an outline of the growing phenomenon of what can be called US anti-drug interventionism. It examines both the militarization of the fight against drugs in Latin America, particularly the Andean ridge, and the application of economic leverage on source nations around the world. The damaging consequences, multiple motives and ultimate futility of Washington's supply-side-oriented war on drugs will also be highlighted.

The militarization of the war on drugs in Latin America

The American proclivity to locate the source of domestic drug problems abroad has, since the early 1980s, resulted in the escalation of US anti-drug activity in those sovereign nations deemed to be major source or transit countries. It is little surprise that Latin America has been the focus of much US attention, and by 1990 there were more than 30 US government entities involved in the war on drugs in the region alone. These included the DEA, the US Customs, the US Information Agency, the Bureau for International Narcotic Matters (INM), the FBI, the CIA and the Agency for International Development. The creation in 1984 of the so-called Leopards, a US-trained and US-supervised Bolivian paramilitary force to combat coca growing and refining, however, foreshadowed Washington's increasing reliance upon the use of both US and Latin American armed forces in the Andean region. To be sure, US militarization of the war on drugs in the Western Hemisphere burgeoned dramatically in the mid-1980s, Operation Blast Furnace in 1986 and Operation Snowcap in 1987, being the most visible manifestations of this process, as we shall see.

Despite initial opposition from the Department of Defense (DoD), the 1980s saw the increasing involvement of the US military in the American crusade in Latin America. Three successive defence secretaries argued against the use of the military in the US war on drugs, only to be dragged into the fray by the Executive and Congress. Frank Carlucci, Caspar Weinberger and Richard Cheney all claimed that military personnel should not become involved in matters that were beyond the military's jurisdiction and argued that the DoD should avoid involvement in the war on drugs. High-ranking officials within the DoD agreed that interdiction simply would not work. Showing an attitude much like Anslinger's initial response to the growing marijuana problem in the United States during the 1930s, the DoD was reluctant to become embroiled in a battle that appeared impossible to win. Additionally, it was claimed that involvement in law enforcement activities would detract from military readiness. Its job, after all, was to protect the USA from foreign armies, not from drug traffickers. With Cold War concerns in the Western Hemisphere still topping the military agenda, the Pentagon felt it had enough to do monitoring and countering perceived communist aggression in the region. Another worrying implication for the DoD concerned the possibility that, like the anti-drug forces of many Latin American nations, the US military would be exposed to the endemic corruption surrounding the illicit drug trade. Nevertheless, considerable backing for the inclusion of the military in the anti-drug campaign came from across the political spectrum. Growing domestic concern regarding the flow of illegal drugs from Latin America and the crack cocaine epidemic sweeping many American inner cities fuelled support for an increase in resources for military interdiction at the US border and the high seas. Taking the traditional supply-side strategy one step further, bipartisan advocates of militarization also called for the deployment of US forces abroad. Adhering to familiar nativistic tendencies, many felt that the drug problem was 'an insidious form of foreign invasion that warranted nothing less than the full-scale mobilization of the U.S. armed forces'.[51]

President Reagan, provoked by the dramatic growth of the US–Andean cocaine trade, won congressional support for moves to amend the 1878 Posse Comitatus Act, which had historically prohibited army involvement in civilian law enforcement. A 1981 amendment removed a major barrier to the militarization process and authorized the US armed forces to share drug-related intelligence from military sources with civilian officials, lend military equipment to US law enforcement agencies and assist in its operation, and make military facilities available to federal agencies. Working within these parameters, the DoD began to play an expanded, though still reluctant, role in US narcotics control in the Caribbean and Latin America. Between 1982 and 1985 the US military provided support for US and local law enforcement agencies. Operations such as HAT Trick I and II and BAT involved limited numbers of US personnel providing helicopter transportation for insertion teams on seizure and arrest missions. The actions were relatively small scale and achieved only temporary success, disrupting and re-routeing illicit drug flow rather than eradicating it. Nevertheless, they provided a taste of the future of military involvement in the Western Hemisphere.

It was fitting that increasing military involvement in the war on drugs came during the Reagan presidency. His 1981 inaugural address had contained a vow to conquer the 'evil scourge' of drug abuse and Reagan clearly had few qualms about employing US armed forces to achieve that goal. Had Harry Anslinger been alive he would have no doubt approved of a strategy that he had strongly favoured sixty or so years earlier. In 1928 he had suggested the use of the army and the navy to enforce alcohol prohibition. Responding to rising political pressures in the lead-up to the November 1986 midterm elections, Reagan set the stage for a rapid expansion of military participation in interdiction at US borders and, significantly, deployment abroad. In April 1986, he issued a National Security Decision Directive (NSDD) declaring drug trafficking a 'lethal' threat to US national security. Reagan's declaration became arguably the most significant aspect of US policy towards the Andean ridge, preparing the way for further militarization. Owing largely to domestic factors, such as rising consumption, crime and drug-related deaths, Washington policymakers demanded a prompt and effective solution to trafficking. In so issuing the NSDD the President justified military escalation by elevating the drug issue to foreign-policy priority status and portraying those involved in the illicit traffic as direct aggressors against the United States. Despite the lack of long-term success of earlier operations, Reagan ushered in a new phase of militarization and ordered Operation Blast Furnace in Bolivia. The move prompted the Speaker of the House Tip O'Neil, to say, 'I approve of what the president did. We've got to go to the source of the drugs.'[52] Ostensibly a response to President Victor Paz Estenssoro's appeal for US assistance in halting the production, processing and trafficking of cocaine, Blast Furnace was in reality also a product of US economic coercion. While Paz Estenssoro welcomed the operation during a period when drug traffickers threatened to challenge state authority, the President was greatly motivated by Washington's threat to cut US economic aid. Bolivia's failure to carry out what the US felt to be credible eradication and substitution schemes prompted the Reagan administration to employ economic suasion. This policy, as we shall see, has become a central pillar of US unilateralism in Latin America.

Blast Furnace was a four-month mission during which the US military worked closely with the DEA and Bolivian police forces to locate and

destroy cocaine-processing laboratories and airstrips used by the traffickers, arrest traffickers, and confiscate planes, documents and precursor
chemicals necessary for the production of cocaine. The US military contribution comprised six army Black Hawk helicopters, and crews and
logistical support teams numbering 150 personnel. US pilots flew Bolivian
Rural Mobile Patrol Units (UMOPAR) and DEA agents to pre-selected
sites, staying with the aircraft while teams were deployed to destroy
facilities and make arrests. As with earlier operations, the success of Blast
Furnace proved to be only temporary and limited. Twenty-one laboratories were destroyed but Blast Furnace yielded no major arrests,
corrupt Bolivian personnel being blamed for warning traffickers of targets
in advance of the arrival of anti-drug personnel. The decline in cocaine
processing in Bolivia resulted in a brief slump in coca leaf prices, the
growers lacking buyers for their crops. Nevertheless, the operation had no
noticeable impact upon the availability of cocaine in the United States,
with coca leaf prices returning to pre-Blast Furnace levels in November
1986 when US forces withdrew. The departure of US military equipment
and personnel was marked by the return of traffickers who had taken a
temporary break from their highly profitable business by hiding in remote
areas of Bolivia or in Brazil.

While Washington claimed that the operation had been a success, the
limited progress achieved was dramatically overshadowed by the political damage it inflicted on the Paz Estenssoro administration. The presence
of the US military in Bolivia exposed the government to great criticism on
the issue of national sovereignty, mass rural and urban protests reflecting
discontent among the populace. It became clear that Blast Furnace had
been politically counterproductive, arousing the fierce anti-US sentiments
that never lie too far beneath the surface in Latin America.

Having assessed Blast Furnace, US officials, evidently undeterred by its
inherent flaws, argued that what was needed in Latin America was a long-
term operation in which the US military would play a vital but discreet
role. Operation Snowcap was consequently a low-key project aiming to
cut the amount of cocaine entering the USA by half over a three-year
period. Functioning with a far lower public profile than Blast Furnace,
DoD involvement included the leasing of six UH-1 Huey helicopters, US
training for Bolivian air force pilots to fly them, and US Special Forces
training for UMOPAR and DEA field agents. By the end of the three-year
period cocaine seizures had increased dramatically. The situation led the
DEA assistant administrator David Westrate to declare, 'We are finally
making progress in the international war against cocaine .... The traffickers are hunted men.'[53] US policymakers, however, apparently ignored
the fact that while cocaine seizures were up, so too was the production of

the drug. In fact, cocaine production was evidently increasing at a faster rate than seizures. A 1990 congressional report on Snowcap noted that cocaine availability had increased dramatically since 1983, with narcotic interdiction efforts in 1989 being 'infrequent and generally ineffective'. As Clare Hargreaves comments, having spent millions of dollars of US taxpayers' money, Snowcap had seized only 0.5 per cent of Bolivia's estimated cocaine hydrochloride and base production.[54] Like previous operations in Latin America, Snowcap made little appreciable impact upon the illicit drugs trade because it ignored the laws of supply and demand. Although press coverage surrounding seizures and the destruction of processing laboratories provided valuable positive publicity for the US war on drugs in the region, drug traffickers continued to operate by altering their methods, shifting the location of processing sites and opening new smuggling routes. The enduring demand in the United States ensured that profits and motivation remained high. Additionally, as some US economists argue, even if eradication programmes in Andean nations succeeded in producing a long-term reduction in cocaine prices this would have a negligible impact upon the price of the drug in the United States. As a Rand Corporation report shows, this is because most of the profits in the drug trade are added at the final link of the chain. For example, in 1986 a kilo of coca at source was worth $1200. On export from Colombia after processing it was worth $7000, the cocaine's value rocketing to $20,000 on arrival in Miami. Wholesale in Detroit the price doubled, and by the time the drug was sold on the street it was worth $250,000.[55] As this graphically illustrates, the economic realities behind the trade make source-based strategies unlikely to succeed.

Continued support for Snowcap from Washington in the late 1980s nevertheless demonstrated that a change in administration would not bring a change in the US approach to international drug control. Echoing Reagan, Bush reaffirmed his commitment to the US war on drugs by promising in his 1988 inaugural speech that the drug 'scourge will end'. The passage of the 1988 Omnibus Anti-Drug Abuse Act initially looked set to introduce moves towards a more demand-side-oriented strategy. The new legislation, however, did not abandon supply-side operations, favouring instead an increase in federal funding for them while simultaneously focusing resources on demand reduction in the United States. Following Reagan's precedent, Bush made moves to escalate militarization in Latin America. In mid-September 1989 Secretary of Defense Cheney signalled the end of Pentagon resistance to involvement with the anti-drug campaign in the Western Hemisphere. Influenced by the dramatic changes under way in the Soviet Union and the resulting uncertain future for the US military in a post-Cold War world, Cheney declared that 'detecting and countering the production and trafficking of illegal drugs is a high-priority national security mission for the Pentagon'. Congressional support for the 1989 National Defense Authorization Act signified strong backing for Bush's approach. The Act ordered the DoD to become the lead agency in the detection and monitoring of aerial and maritime transit of illegal drugs into the United States and assume responsibility for integrating federal command, control, communications and technical intelligence assets involved in drug interdiction into an effective communications network.[56] Any lingering doubts regarding the intentions of the Bush administration's supply-oriented policies were removed with the highly publicized Andean Strategy announced in September 1989.

According to the National Drug Control Strategy Report that launched the project, the United States planned

> to the greatest extent possible . . . [to] disrupt the transportation and trafficking of drugs within their source countries, since the interdiction of drugs and traffickers en route to the United States is an immeasurably more complicated, expensive and less effective means of reducing the drug supply to this country.[57]

The strategy targeted the cocaine trade in the Andean nations of Colombia, Bolivia and Peru, and despite requests from these nations for economic development aid and trade incentives, the US anti-drug assistance primarily funded military and police activities, providing helicopters, patrol boats, ammunition and radar equipment. More US Special Forces advisers were also sent south to train Andean troops, but they maintained a discreet presence in an attempt to avoid anti-American sentiment and were accordingly forbidden to accompany host nation forces on anti-drug operations.

The late 1980s, then, saw funding for DoD anti-drug operations grow, with the Andean strategy reaffirming an increasing willingness to employ both the US military and local forces in the fight against drugs in Latin America. Nevertheless, while the Strategy produced military assistance pacts with Colombia, Peru and Bolivia, other US actions in the region displayed Washington's continuing propensity for unilateralism. Most dramatic was President Bush's decision in December 1989 to authorize US military intervention in Panama. To many in Central and Latin America, the action represented a return to old-style US imperialism. Indeed, after the operation, ex-President Ronald Reagan seemed to confirm such beliefs. Referring to the periodic US occupation of Panama since 1908, he claimed that 'It's ours; we stole it fair and square.'[58] A pretext for so-called Operation Just Cause was the removal of the accused drug trafficker and money launderer General Manuel Noriega. And although the invasion was triggered by a number of factors, one of which was the illicit drug trade, use of the narcotics issue as justification helped to provide Washington with a moral prerogative for what was under the terms of international law an illegal action. As we shall see, the invasion also highlighted inconsistencies present within the US crusade for drug control in the Western Hemisphere.

Yet as a blatant demonstration of US unilateral intentions in the region, Just Cause did not stand alone. As Bruce Bagely notes, equally revealing though less publicized were Washington's deployment of warships off the Colombian coast without Bogotá's prior permission, its construction of Vietnam-style fire bases for DEA operations in Peru's Upper Huallaga Valley, Bush's drug czar William Bennett's oft-repeated statements that US Special Forces might be sent to Andean countries, and the use of intelligence satellites over Mexican territory without informing the Mexican government.[59]

In response to criticism of US unilateralism, notably the Panama invasion, and the hostility provoked by Washington's refusal to offer more trade and economic components within the Andean strategy, Bush moved to publicly promote his commitment to multilateralism and attended an Andean summit in Cartagena, Colombia, in February 1990. At the summit Presidents Virgilio Barco of Colombia, Jaime Paz Zamora of Bolivia and Alan García of Peru met Bush and argued that solutions to the drug problem in the region were to be found in economic development and crop substitution rather than militarization. Ostensibly at least, Cartagena revealed a change in US attitudes on drug control in the hemisphere. Bush recognized that US demand for illicit drugs was an essential factor in the illicit trade and promised to provide development aid, as well as military and police assistance. It was not long, however, before US unilateral action tarnished the protestations of Cartagena. Only a month after the summit, the US navy seized two Colombian freighters within the country's territorial limit without consultation or approval from Bogotá. The brief improvement in North–South relations was also soured by Washington's failure to realize promises made at Cartagena concerning trade agreements. Bush failed to restore the International Coffee Agreement and applied countervailing duties on Colombian cut flowers exported to the United States. Both trades provided a viable economic alternative to the drug trade. Despite limited moves by the United States to introduce the Enterprise for the Americas trade liberalization initiative in June 1990, it was clear that the military approach remained dominant.

The nations at the core of the Andean strategy remained understandably reluctant to embrace the scheme. Yet, while Colombia, Peru and Bolivia were concerned that Washington's emphasis in the region stayed focused upon militarization, the fear of withdrawal of American aid if they resisted US intervention forced all three countries eventually to agree with US demands to increase military involvement. President Paz Zamora, in spite of nationalist resentment of US interference in domestic affairs that lingered from Blast Furnace, agreed to the US programme. Dire economic circumstances ensured that the government could not risk losing important foreign aid. The Peruvian government was also unenthusiastic about accepting Washington's strategy. The existence of the anti-government Maoist-oriented terrorist group the Sendero Luminoso within Peru posed particular difficulties for Peru's new president, Alberto Fujimori. Seeing Sendero as a major threat to national security, the Peruvian military preferred to concentrate on fighting the terrorist group rather than the drug trade. While Sendero gains revenue from the coca-growing peasantry of the Upper Huallaga Valley (UHV) by providing it with protection from Colombian traffickers, its aims are predominantly revolutionary. Washington's insistence on using the military to destroy drugs ignored the fact that anti-drug actions boosted Sendero support in the UHV and further threatened Peruvian state authority. Fujimori preferred to alleviate his domestic problems by instigating economic measures that would undermine support for Sendero and win the confidence of the Peruvian people. Counter-narcotic operations directed by and involving US forces promised to hamper the realization of the President's goal. Nevertheless, the severe economic crisis that gripped Peru underlined the importance of US financial support, with threats from Washington to pull out aid forcing Fujimori to capitulate finally to US demands in May 1991. Although nationalism led the Colombian government to refuse an increase in direct US military activity within its territory, Bogotá accepted military aid, and it is likely that US personnel continue to play a role in providing intelligence and logistical support for anti-drug operations. Thus the Americanization of the Latin American drug war continues.

Washington's faith in the militarization process also increased with the military resolution of other problematic diplomatic issues. In much the same way as US imperial pretensions were buoyed after rapid victory in the Spanish–American war almost a century earlier, the two short wars fought by the Bush administration increased the interest and belief in the military solution to the US domestic drug crisis. Both the invasion of Panama and Operation Desert Storm were short and in militaristic terms successful campaigns, with the action in the Gulf in particular generating massive domestic support for the US military. As noted earlier, reluctant participation in the United States' overseas war on drugs from the DoD also evaporated as world events between 1988 and 1990 presented the use of military resources for traditionally non-military purposes in a more attractive light. The Pentagon, fearful of post-Cold War budget cuts, began to see the drug war as a way to get its share of the peace dividend. Reflecting this mood in February 1990, President Bush called for increased military resources to deal with 'new threats beyond the traditional East–West antagonism of the last 45 years'. 'Narcogangsters', he continued, 'concern us all, already a threat to our national health and spirit . . . . They must be dealt with by our military in the air, on the land, and on the seas.'[60] Maintaining a focus on the supply-side strategy, Bush's policies thus neatly dovetailed with the international regime that the United States had worked so hard to develop.

The start of the 1990s therefore saw no weakening in Washington's resolve to militarize its war on drugs in the Western Hemisphere. Nevertheless, the complex and multifaceted circumstances surrounding US foreign policy in the region inevitably produced inconsistencies and damaging paradoxes that merit our attention at this point. First, it is worth noting that US support for the increasing use of the military in the drug war has, ironically, undermined Washington's long-term goal to promote democracy in the region. The US policy has inadvertently diminished the status of representative governments by increasing the role and influence of the armed forces in countries with fragile democratic systems. This is alarming in nations where the military has traditionally exercised political control. Forcible persuasion has also essentially de-democratized some already unstable democratic governments. Bolivia provides a good example of this process. Policies pursued by the Paz Zamora government to implement US-imposed conditions regarding domestic anti-drug measures were carried out without consultation with broader sections of Bolivian society. In fact, the US Andean strategy was negotiated and implemented with the knowledge only of a few members of the ruling parties, essentially circumventing the machinery of democratic government. Such a situation appears even more contradictory when we look at statements made by the US Bureau for International Narcotic and Law Enforcement Affairs. The bureau states that 'A fundamental goal of our diplomatic strategy is to make democratic governments recognize that the drug trade threatens their national survival' and 'the future of democratic government itself.'[61] While this is true, questions surround Washington's justification of a policy that also threatens democratic government without making an appreciable impact upon the targeted drug trade. It is misguided to assume that the governments of source countries underestimate and even choose to ignore the negative social, economic and political impact that the illicit drug business has upon the societal fabric of their nations. No government wants to be at the mercy of criminals, but no government appreciates externally imposed conditions that infringe upon sovereignty and further threaten national stability.

Interventionist US policy can, however, afford certain benefits to the governments of some source nations, if not the populace. As Peter Smith observes, 'For reasons of its own, the U.S. has strongly encouraged Latin American governments to enlist in the anti-drug wars. And Latin American leaders respond, also for reasons of their own.'[62] A notable reason is that militarization provides the potential for governments forcibly to quash anti-state discontent. Latin American regimes are being given the military capability to fight opposition groups, with no distinction being made between what are being termed narco-terrorists and other anti-government groups with no integral involvement with the drug trade. Evidence suggests that Bogotá has been using US-supplied military equipment to fight ongoing guerrilla campaigns that started well before the illicit drug trade became an issue. While Colombian anti-government groups such as the Revolutionary Armed Forces of Colombia (FARC), the People's Liberation Army (ELP) and the 19th of April Movement (M-19) may sometimes co-operate with drug traffickers, this does not mean that they can be accurately regarded as a single entity labelled narco-terrorists. American military hardware and training consequently influence internal political matters beyond the intended realm of illegal drug production and trafficking.

Second, despite the DoD's full commitment to the military crusade in Latin America, criticism still exists regarding the futility of the process. As one DEA official remarked, 'the military have spent ten years trying to find one goddam hostage in Lebanon. What makes them think that they can come down [to South America] and solve the dope problem?'[63] The rhetoric of the anti-drug campaign may be replete with the semantics of war, but since the campaign is not a traditional state actor versus state actor conflict, there is no hope of a clear-cut victory. No matter how much pressure the United States exerts upon Latin American governments to terminate the illicit drugs trade, it is the drug syndicates that ultimately control the business. Intergovernmental negotiations can have an impact upon levels of official corruption and encourage administrations to mount campaigns against these organizations. Such action may go some way towards placating those in Washington, but success remains limited and costly.

The journey taken by a proscribed drug like cocaine from the coca fields in the Andes to the streets of American and European cities is lengthy and highly complex. This massive logistical challenge has given rise to the emergence of interconnected webs co-ordinating all levels of the illegal trade from production and processing through to trafficking and distribution. These webs are constructed with the aims of safeguarding the passage of the illicit drugs to the marketplace and ensuring the maintenance of high profit margins. The geographical focus of what are today global networks has traditionally been the Colombian cities of Cali and Medellín. Here the so-called cartels have used extreme violence against any elements seen to threaten their existence and prosperity. Fighting between the groups themselves as well as against the government and revolutionary guerrilla organizations has left many hundreds dead and has greatly destabilized Colombian society. While Washington chooses to exert pressure upon Bogotá, actively encouraging the implementation of anti-drug measures that conform to US standards, it is the Colombian government that is exposed to the full force of the cartels' anger. Since the 1980s, the assassination of numerous Colombian police officers, judges, journalists, one Attorney General, two cabinet ministers and three presidential candidates can be attributed to the actions of the cartels. Reacting to an escalation in the fight against drugs, they have sent an unambiguous signal warning against heightened co-operation between Bogotá and Washington. While concerted government action against the organizations has resulted in a decline of the Medellín cartel, the operation controlled by the Cali group continues defiantly, with figures suggesting that in 1995 it controlled around 75 per cent of Colombia's cocaine exports. The continuing existence of the Cali operation is significant because it highlights how, regardless of efforts to halt the influence of the cartels, drug organizations will always form or evolve to fill any void left in the massively lucrative illegal drug market. The emergence of increasingly powerful syndicates in nations such as Mexico, Bolivia and Peru looks set to cause problems for both their host nations and Washington's overseas 'war' against drugs. The American appetite for militarization nevertheless continues unabated despite, and no doubt in some way fuelled by, the lack of unequivocal victories in militaristic terms.

Indeed, as Donald Mabry points out, the logistics of the DoD's anti-drug interdiction operation alone are so daunting that success is unlikely 'unless the military were allowed to operate under wartime conditions'.[64] Despite its status as a 'lethal threat' to US national security, it is unlikely that the drug issue will ever provoke mobilization of the entire US military machine. Some American analysts still favour the adoption of a low-intensity conflict (LIC) approach to US military involvement in the drug war in Latin America. This would involve the U.S. military planning and executing entire anti-drug operations, with Special Forces carrying out search and destroy missions against processing laboratories and other drug-related targets. The theory behind this tactic is that a unified command structure, in-house intelligence and specialist troops would be more effective and less likely to suffer from information leaks than the current anti-drug operations conducted by host nation forces and only supervised and assisted by US military personnel. While the LIC scenario may make for engrossing reading in Tom Clancy's novel *Clear and Present Danger*,[65] the reality of US counter-insurgency operations in the Western Hemisphere has the potential for alarming consequences. Apart from the nationalistic hostility such action would provoke, the notion of LIC invokes too many memories of the American Vietnam tragedy to be considered as a serious option.

A third point for consideration involves a central theme of this study: the subordination of drug control to other foreign-policy considerations. Drug control in the Western Hemisphere has, as discussed, long been a focus for US international attention. The intricacies of a regional policy based for many years predominantly upon anti-communism have, however, resulted in behaviour incongruous with the ostensible goals of US narcotic diplomacy in Latin America. The overtly moral crusades against drugs in the region provided a façade of legitimacy for anti-communist activity during the Cold War, the dynamics of *Realpolitik* producing familiar yet contradictory US narcotic foreign policy.

A critique of US foreign policy towards Latin America and the Caribbean since the early 1980s reveals numerous cases where drug control has been deferred to perceived security interests. For example, the Prime Minister of the Bahamas, Lyndon Pindling, long accused of complicity with drug traffickers, was tolerated by Washington because the islands were seen to be strategically essential to US security interests. As Bullington notes, Pindling's drug activities were simply 'accepted as one cost of doing business with that government'.[66] A higher-profile example possessing attributes similar to those of the Pindling case began to emerge in 1989. While the United States portrayed its invasion of Panama as a strike against the evil drug-running Noriega, that was only half the story. It is true that Noriega was heavily involved in the drug trade; his activities had been known as far back as the 1970s. It should be recalled, however, that the General had also been employed by various US intelligence agencies, notably the CIA, since at least the early 1970s. Nevertheless, Panama's crucial strategic position in the Western Hemisphere ensured that Washington supported Noriega while he remained receptive to US influence. Indeed, the General's co-operation in Panama during the 1980s was seen to be an essential element in US monitoring of left-wing activities in Latin America. This was especially the case when Noriega provided financial assistance and logistical support for the Contras during President Reagan's campaign against the revolutionary Sandinista government in Nicaragua. The details of the complicity of the US government in the trafficking of illicit drugs during the sordid Contra fiasco fill volumes and therefore cannot be discussed in detail here. Nevertheless, it is worth noting that overwhelming evidence suggests that, in exchange for flying weapons and supplies to the Contras during the period of a congressional ban on such activities, elements in the US government allowed drug dealers to fly narcotics into the USA. General Paul F. Gorman, former head of the US Southern Command, points to the obvious fact that 'if you want to go into the subversion business, collect intelligence, and move arms, you deal with the drug movers'.[67] Indeed, in his Iran–Contra diaries the man most associated with the illegal covert operation, Lt.Col. Oliver North of the National Security Council, made numerous references to his own drug-smuggling and money-laundering adventures. A 12 July 1985 entry, for example, reads '$14 million to finance arms came from drugs'.[68] Returning to Noriega's involvement in the drug trade, we can see that the General actually met the late CIA director William Casey in November 1985, yet his illegal activities received little more than a slap on the wrist. Francis J. McNeil, US ambassador to Costa Rica (1980–3), claims that the United States took a 'see no evil' approach to Noriega while he remained useful.[69] The relationship between the USA and Noriega ended only when he outlived his usefulness to Washington. His anti-US rhetoric and the increasing instability of his regime guaranteed a change in US policy towards Panama, which resulted ultimately in Operation Just Cause.

The United States has also been guilty of using other Latin American host nations in the drug war as bases for monitoring 'unfriendly governments' in the region. In April 1989, for example, the Colombian government accused the DoD of using the ruse of the drug-trafficking fight to install a sophisticated radar system on a Colombian island that it said was intended to monitor activities in Nicaragua. While evidence confirming such politically sensitive matters is scarce, what is known indicates that such an incident is unlikely to be exceptional.

It is clear, then, that although the international crusade against drugs existed long before the threat of communism became the core of American foreign policy, it was routinely used as a shield for ideological skirmishes in Latin America. To be sure, as Nicholas Dorn and Nigel South argue, by the end of the 1980s the war on drugs had effectively become a 'lynchpin of the revival of the Monroe Doctrine'.[70] Washington's preoccupation with the perceived threats posed by communism meant that drug policy in Latin America was consistently treated as secondary to other foreign-policy concerns. The pursuit of such a hidden agenda may, as Bullington notes, explain obvious inconsistencies and erratic enforcement practices in relation to the US war on drugs around the world.[71] The subordination of drug control to anti-communist-inspired foreign-policy concerns in both the Golden Crescent and Golden Triangle, as discussed earlier, supports this contention. An end to the Cold War and a decline in the idea of a centrally controlled and monolithic communist threat in Latin America has not, however, produced a situation where the war on drugs occupies centre stage. In the post-Cold War world, the drug war remains a useful vehicle for wider US strategic goals in Latin America. The fight against drugs is almost certainly being used as a cover to increase US influence in the region and reassert hemispheric hegemony.

US–Mexican narco-diplomatic relations

Thus far the discussion has focused predominantly upon US anti-drug policies towards the Big Three cocaine-producing nations of the Andean ridge: Bolivia, Columbia and Peru. The picture of US action in the Western Hemisphere is of course incomplete without consideration of US–Mexican narco-diplomatic relations. Mexico's geographic proximity to the United States and its reputation as a drug-producing and drug transit nation has meant that the country has long endured a tense relationship with its northern neighbour. Indeed, although extreme Mexican nationalism prevents a replication of the Andean militarization experience, US policy towards Mexico can be accurately characterized as 'cynical, often unilateral, contentious and incident prone'.[72]

As mentioned in Chapter 1, Washington's interest in illicit Mexican drugs dates back to the onset of US concern over its own drug abuse problems at the beginning of the twentieth century. An increase in domestic drug problems during the 1936–40 period, however, added urgency to the relationship, leading Washington to 'encourage' the adoption by Mexico of a narcotic control policy similar to that of the United States. With the exception of the years during the Second World War, the US approach towards its southern neighbour has remained constant inasmuch as its aim has been to prevent illicit Mexican drugs from crossing the border. American authorities have consistently sought to realize this goal through interdiction and crop eradication, often resorting to political and economic coercion to achieve desired results. Indeed, what Richard Craig calls the 'pressure-response' scenario had been well established by the late 1940s.[73] In accordance with such a pattern, US concern regarding the production and trafficking of illicit drugs in Mexico in the late 1960s provoked Operation Intercept. This interdiction action set the tone for US–Mexican narcotic diplomacy for decades to come, and since the unilateral imposition of Intercept in 1969 fluctuating levels of tension have characterized the relationship between the two countries.

Operation Intercept, the three-week closure of an essential crossing at the US–Mexican border, was used by President Nixon to 'persuade' the Mexican government to act against marijuana and heroin production. Nixon had already harnessed growing domestic concern for illegal drug use and, setting a precedent for later US presidents to follow, elevated international drug control to a 'foreign policy level of high priority'. The US–Mexican border was an ideal venue for a display of transnational anti-drug prowess. The choice of action was greatly influenced by Nixon's belief that Mexico, in the President's opinion plagued by intrinsic corruption, required coercion before it would take action against the illicit trade. While the operation increased tensions between the two governments, the massive disruption that Intercept caused to legitimate trade and commerce did succeed in forcing the Mexican authorities to confront the illegal drugs issue. The approach gave the issue of drug control a higher priority on the bilateral agenda, and, encouragingly from the US perspective, led to Operation Co-operation. This in turn evolved into a US-style Mexican war on drugs, *La Campaña Permanente*. In co-operation with Washington, and in accordance with a central tenet of the international prohibitive regime, the Permanent Campaign was a supply-side-oriented programme, focusing predominantly on crop eradication and border control.

Nixon's actions in the Near East also heightened US–Mexican collaboration, albeit with Washington retaining the upper hand. Concerned at the diversion of legally grown opium into illicit channels, Washington, in the spirit of Nixon's energetic foreign policy, worked hard on the other side of the world to reduce illegal trafficking. Following the President's calls in June 1971 to wage a 'total offensive' against the drug trade 'worldwide', the Nixon administration used a mixture of diplomatic pressure and promises of $35 million in aid to persuade the Turkish government to impose a total opium ban after its 1972 harvest. However, in a way that highlights the recurring flaw inherent within supply-oriented strategy, opium control in Turkey merely caused an increase in illegal poppy cultivation in Mexico. Adhering to basic economic principles of supply and demand, illicit opium producers continued to supply the illegal, predominantly US, demand for heroin by operating in Mexico's 'critical triangle' region of Sinaloa, Durango and Chihuahua. The area soon became the prime source of illegal heroin entering the United States and consequently the target of aggressive US narco-diplomacy. With assistance from Washington, Mexico escalated its Permanent Campaign and, using US helicopters and defoliant chemicals, launched Operation Condor. For the Nixon administration, this unprecedented aerial herbicide programme displayed Mexico's increasing resolve for US-style anti-drug programmes. To be sure, although the United States retained the dominant role within the relationship, binational efforts continued to improve. The Permanent Campaign dramatically reduced the quantities of marijuana, opium and heroin reaching the US market. Nevertheless, US consumption remained unaffected and the Mexican supply was rapidly replaced by production in other countries, including the United States itself. With demand a constant factor within the drug equation, displaced production will always find another location. This reality can be labelled the 'balloon' effect, since illicit production will relocate when under pressure in much the same way as the air in a partially inflated balloon moves when squeezed.

Good relations between Mexico and the United States began to deteriorate in the 1980s, however. The United States interpreted the discovery of several tons of marijuana in the state of Chihuahua in 1984 and resurgence in trafficking northwards as signs of a weakening of Mexico's anti-drug efforts. Echoing Nixon, the Reagan administration began speaking openly of corruption as the central reason for the decline in the effectiveness of the Permanent Campaign. While various factors, including the exceptionally good weather in 1984, may explain the increased marijuana production and the associated escalation in trafficking, the reality of growing US domestic demand should not be underestimated. Washington nevertheless was remaining loyal to its supply-oriented strategies when the already strained relations between the nations plummeted in 1985. The kidnapping and murder by Mexican drug traffickers of DEA agent Enrique Camarena Salazar unleashed a new cycle of US–Mexico narco-diplomacy. Departing from the previous atmosphere of laboured collaboration, Washington responded to the Camarena incident by initiating a second Operation Intercept. This was a move that the Mexican authorities regarded as unfair since it felt that adequate effort and resources were still being allocated to the Permanent Campaign. To many Mexicans, Washington's return to unilateral action resembled old-style US imperialism and reignited long-standing anti-American nationalism. Indeed, when asked if the Camarena affair marked the lowest point in US–Mexican relations, President de la Madrid replied that it did not. According to the President, that had been in 1847 when the United States 'seized half our territory'.[74]

Although the first decade of Mexico's Permanent Campaign provided an example of collaboration, albeit on American terms, the second Operation Intercept revealed the underlying nature of United States–Mexico relations. As G. G. Gonzalez notes, the general pattern of bilateral discussion and handling of the problems surrounding illegal production and trafficking has been unbalanced and asymmetrical; the diagnosis and prescriptions, as well as concrete policy measures, have for the most part come from the United States.[75] Washington has retained an alarming tendency towards unilateral decision-making within a supposedly bilateral, co-operative framework. While the United States has favoured co-operation during the peaks of the relationship, it reverts to unilateralism in the troughs. The DEA kidnapping of the Mexican national Dr Humberto Alvárez Machain in 1990 graphically illustrates what Craig has called the 'go-it-alone – and – damn-the-torpedoes mode'[76] employed by US officials in times of crisis. Alvárez, a gynaecologist who reportedly served as physician to several major drug kingpins, had allegedly participated in the torture and murder of Camarena. His indictment by a grand jury in Los Angeles and subsequent abduction by US law enforcement personnel put a strain on US–Mexican relations, raising familiar questions of national sovereignty.

Such a sequential pattern of incident and acrimony,[77] however, may be on the wane. The so-called new 'spirit of Houston', arising from the meeting of President Bush and President-elect Salinas in Texas in November 1988, has demonstrated the will to emphasize the positive aspects of the US–Mexican relationship in order to achieve common goals. As we shall see in the next chapter, an issue like the North American Free Trade Agreement has the potential to create a collaborative environment for discussion, with US concern for trade overriding potential points of conflict within the realm of drug control.

The US certification process

As we have seen, militarization represents a significant component of US drug policy in Latin America, but Washington has also used economic suasion to great effect. The two policies frequently complement one another in much the same way as coercion within the UN encourages sovereign nations to adhere to the norms of the international regime. Epitomizing the US tendency for unilateralism, economic linkage has long been important in the exportation of American-style drug control programmes abroad. Nevertheless, it was not until 1986 that Washington moved to formalize economically coercive policies with the introduction of the so-called certification process. Exploiting the same explosion of US domestic concern for the illegal drug issue that helped initiate militarization in Latin America, policymakers introduced legislation to systematize policy tying American foreign aid to the anti-drug measures adopted by foreign governments. The procedure expands our discussion beyond the Western Hemisphere because although certification has a particular impact upon nations in the region its focus is global in scope.

The 1986 Anti-Drug Abuse Act was designed to strongly encourage source and transshipment nations to follow anti-narcotic programmes that meet with US approval; the statute makes it clear that there is to be a definite relationship between the provision of foreign assistance and positive performance on narcotics control. The legislation demands that, at the beginning of every fiscal year, the President give Congress a list of major drug-producing and trafficking countries that he has certified as eligible to receive US financial assistance, positive votes in multilateral lending institutions, and trade preferences. Congress then undertakes a 45-day review process, during which time it can override the President's certification if it disagrees with executive assessment of each decision. In order to gain certification a nation must be seen to have 'co-operated fully' with US narcotic reduction goals and/or have taken 'adequate steps on its own' in tandem with US goals. Failure to comply with such prerequisites can result in decertification and the cessation, except for humanitarian aid and international narcotic control assistance, of US assistance.

Although the consequences may vary in intensity depending upon Washington's assessment of the level of a nation's commitment towards drug control, the process has a considerable impact upon those countries reliant on US military and economic aid. The stigma of being labelled a drug-producing and trafficking nation can also have serious negative economic repercussions. Colombia's decertification in August 1997 looks likely to have played an important role in unsettling the economy and in turn deterring much-needed financial investment.

Based more on political and moral judgements than on technical assessments, the certification process has become the source of considerable irritation for many governments and societies in the Western Hemisphere, particularly those in Latin America. As Maria Toro has noted, Latin Americans do not understand why supposedly co-operative control efforts should be judged unilaterally by the country that they believe created the entire problem in the first place.[78] Like militarization, the policy also whips up fierce nationalism and anti-American resentment. To Latin Americans, increasing US extraterritorial influence represents almost as important a threat as losing the war against the traffickers and drug barons themselves. It represents the loss of state control. Ironically, one result of this concern is to hinder US control efforts. As the United States strives to encourage nations like Mexico to fight the illegal drug trade, Mexican drug control authorities simultaneously endeavour to maintain autonomy and prevent US law enforcement agencies encroaching upon their jurisdiction. Consequently, while perhaps satisfying a hunger in some US quarters for escalating the war on drugs in the region and providing Congress with an opportunity to demonstrate its anti-drug resolve, certification's punitive approach has done little to improve genuine North–South co-operation. The procedure contains another inherent problem. Threats of economic sanctions, and ultimately varying levels of decertification, can themselves hinder the ability of a government to operate effectively and hamper economic growth. A concomitant de-stabilization of social, economic and political conditions does little to help the fight against illicit drug trafficking and production, however sincerely a source nation may be addressing the issue.

Bearing in mind the frequent deferral of US drug control efforts to other foreign-policy considerations, it should come as no surprise to discover that the process contains a national-interest waiver allowing nations to escape decertification if US 'vital national interests' preclude sanctions. Indeed, despite ferocious anti-drug rhetoric during the late 1980s, both Reagan and Bush were reluctant to decertify nations regarded as crucial to other foreign-policy interests. For example, in 1988 Reagan certified Mexico, Bolivia, Peru, Paraguay and the Bahamas. The President's actions caused the chairman of the House Foreign Affairs Committee Task Force on International Narcotic Control, Larry Smith, to propose a 'resolution of disapproval' and urge his colleagues on the committee to find, as he had, that these nations were doing virtually nothing to stop the flow to the United States. The Bahamas, as discussed earlier, was extremely corrupt during this period, yet was again accorded special treatment owing to its strategically important location during the latter years of the Cold War. Reagan's decertification of Iran, Syria, Afghanistan and Panama also proved to be little more than a symbolic gesture for domestic consumption as the nations were not receiving any US foreign or military aid at the time. The use of the 'vital national interests' clause consequently creates inequities within the certification process for the simple reason that US national interests do not remain static. The application of certification can fluctuate without direct reference to the illicit drug issue at all. It is understandable therefore that the Mexican government felt aggrieved at having been decertified in 1989. Mexican authorities believed that they were taking stronger measures to cut back on production and trafficking than strategi-cally important countries like Turkey and Pakistan which continued to avoid US sanctions.

In essence, then, certification remains a prime example of a damaging coercive unilateral policy that satisfies domestic demands for a tough stance against drugs by urging the imposition of a US approach to drug control on sovereign nations. It is still politically safer, it would appear, to advocate and practise the fight against drugs abroad than treat addicts at home. Yet, within the context of the global regime the policy has become part of the humanitarian global anti-narcotic crusade, in some way dispel-ling any negative aspects of the procedure. Placed within the framework of the international drug control regime, certification, like other US actions, gains legitimacy. When judged against the US-instigated and US-maintained global norm of behaviour, such dubious and ultimately deleterious tactics within the overseas war on drugs are viewed as favourable and constructive methodologies. In reference to certification the Bureau for International Narcotic and Law Enforcement Affairs notes that the process holds source nations 'publicly responsible for their actions before their international peers', ensuring that they meet a minimum acceptable standard of co-operation.[79] Acceptable standards and peer review, however, are judged relative to a US perspective. Additionally, since US legislation creates a link between national and transnational law, making certification dependent on nations meeting the goals and objectives of the 1988 UN Convention as well as the American statute, distinctions between US unilateral action and the UN's multilateral campaign become harder to make. Thus, while exploiting the international norm maintained by the UN, the United States pursues an aggressive campaign beyond the realms of the multilateral framework. Despite claiming, as did William Bennett in 1989, that illicit drugs raise matters concerning American national sovereignty, US unilateral action abroad has consistently encroached upon the sovereign jurisdictions of other nations. Some US actions go under the misnomer of bilateralism, yet as Bullington and Block note, 'although generally described as co-operation, bilateral agreements with American personnel acting in advisory capacities' effectively become 'unilateral demands to be carried out under American supervision'.[80] American behaviour in the wake of the Cartegena conference demonstrated Washington's attitude towards genuine co-operation and partnership. The fact also remains that the United States is attempting to export a prohibitive drug control policy that does not even operate effectively in the USA itself. This has led Mack Tanner to note that

> In what has to be one of the most twisted pieces of logic of any foreign policy ever attempted, American DEA agents are assigned to work in foreign countries in the expectation that these agents will be able to help a foreign country achieve the success that the DEA have failed to achieve at home.[81]

Source nation strategies of interdiction and crop eradication alone seem destined to failure because they ignore the demand side of the problem and do not address the 'balloon' response to eradication programmes. Nevertheless, such an approach now appears to be an integral part of the global prohibition regime. Topping these factors is the reality of the systemic limitations of US international drug control. As noted throughout this section, the drugs issue has been consistently subordinated to *Realpolitik* and concerns for other foreign-policy considerations, most notably the containment and rollback of communism. The paradox in the post-Cold War world is that, despite the status of drug trafficking as a 'lethal threat' to US national security, American international drug policy continues to be relegated to other interests. The 1990s, as we shall see in the final chapter, has seen communism give way to trade.

NOTES

1. *Viewpoint* radio programme, 26 December 1959. A US radio show sponsored by an Episcopal church in which Anslinger was interviewed by Dana Kennedy. Recording held with Anslinger Papers, Penn State University.
2. *The United Nations and Drug Abuse Control* (Vienna: United Nations International Drug Control Programme, 1992), p. 15.
3. Jack Donnelly, 'The United Nations and the global drug control regime', in Peter H. Smith (ed.), *Drug Policy in the Americas* (Boulder: Westview Press, 1992), p. 288.
4. S. D. Stein, *International Diplomacy, State Administration and Narcotics Control: The Origins of a Social Problem* (Aldershot: Gower, 1985), p. 6.
5. *United Nations Convention Against Illicit Traffic in Narcotic Drugs and Psychotropic Substances 1988* (New York: United Nations, 1991. Sales no. E.91.XI.6), p. 2.
6. *Drug Abuse: The United Nations and Drug Abuse Control* (New York: UN International Drug Control Programme, 1992. Sales no. E.92.I.31), p. 7.
7. *Ibid.*, p. 84.
8. Richard Hartnoll, 'The international context', in Susanne MacGregor (ed.), *Drugs and British Society: Responses to a Social Problem in the 1980s* (London: Routledge, 1989), p. 39.
9. 'WHO Cocaine Project', *International Journal of Drug Policy*, 6(2) (1995), 63–4. Anthony Henman, one of the report's authors, also confirmed how the WHO almost disowned it because the views it contained did not conform to the official stance on the drug. Telephone conversations with Anthony Henman, 6 January 1995, 3 August 1995.
10. *Independent*, Monday 24 April 1995, p. 6.
11. *Guardian*, 'US government "in campaign to kill talk of drug legalization"', 17 February 1995, p. 12.
12. WHO Cocaine Project, *International Journal of Drug Policy*, 6(2) (1995), 63–4.
13. *Narcotics Control Digest*, 23(4) (17 February 1993), 1.
14. Anthony Henman, Roger Lewis and Tim Maylon, *Big Deal: The Politics of the Illicit Drugs Business* (London: Pluto, 1985), p. 157.
15. David Boaz, 'The consequences of prohibition', in David Boaz (ed.), *The Crisis in Drug Prohibition* (Washington, DC: Cato Institute, 1991), p. 1.
16. Speech made in the US Senate, 17 February 1931. Reprinted in the USA Constitutional Documents, 'Repeal of the Eighteenth Amendment',

Washington, DC, 1931, quoted in Michael Woodiwiss, *Crime, Crusades and Corruption* (London: Pinter, 1988), p. 27.

17. Manuel Barbarena and Kevin N. Wright, 'International control: a review', *New Frontiers in Drug Policy* (Washington, DC: The Drug Policy Foundation, 1991), pp. 371–2.
18. Richard Hartnoll, 'The international context', p. 40.
19. *Drug Abuse: The United Nations and Drug Abuse Control*, p. 53.
20. *Druglink* (September/December, 1987), p. 6.
21. Theodore R. Vallance, *Prohibition's Second Failure: The Quest for a Rational and Humane Drug Policy* (Westport, CT: Praeger, 1993), p. 21.
22. Richard Hartnoll, 'The international context', p. 40.
23. Philip Bean, *The Social Control of Drugs* (London: Martin Robertson, 1974), cited by Richard Hartnoll, 'The international context', p. 40.
24. Richard Hartnoll, 'The international context', p. 41.
25. 'The Plenipotentiary Conference for the Adoption of a Single Convention on Narcotic Drugs', *Bulletin on Narcotics*, **14**(1) (1962), 43.
26. Brian Inglis, *The Forbidden Game: A Social History of Drugs* (London: Hodder and Stoughton, 1975), p. 199.
27. *UN Conference for the Adoption of a Single Convention on Narcotic Drugs*, Vol. 2, (New York: UN Publications, 1964), pp. 306, 307.
28. *Drug Abuse: The United Nations and Drug Abuse Control*, p. 21.
29. Telephone conversation with Dr Anthony Henman, August 1995.
30. Catholic Institute for International Relations, *Coca, Cocaine and the War on Drugs* (London: the Institute, 1993), p. 14.
31. Mark Heil, 'International drug policy: insight from Cochabamba, Bolivia' in A. S. Trebach and K. B. Zeese (eds), *The Great Issues of Drug Policy* (Washington, DC: The Drug Policy Foundation, 1990), p. 134.
32. *Drug Abuse: The United Nations and Drug Abuse Control*, p. 48 iii.
33. Paul Reuter, 'The obligations of states under the Single Convention on Narcotic Drugs, 1961', *Bulletin on Narcotics*, **20**(4) (October–December 1968), p. 4.
34. Adolf Lande, 'The Single Convention on Narcotic Drugs, 1961'. *International Organization*, **16** (1962), 795.
35. Ethan A. Nadelmann, 'Global prohibition regimes: the evolution of norms in international society', *International Organization*, **44**(4) (1990), 480, 481.
36. Rufus King, *The Drug Hang-Up*: America's Fifty-Year Folly (Springfield, IL: Charles C. Thomas, 1974), p. 97, and David Soloman (ed.), *The Marijuana Papers: An Examination of Marijuana in Society, History, and Literature* (London: Panther, 1969), p. 88.
37. David Soloman, *The Marijuana Papers*, p. 89.
38. J.J.B., 'Anslinger: a legend in his own time', *International Drug Report*, (December 1975), p. 2.
39. Interview with Richard Cowan in Washington, DC, May 1994.
40. *Guardian*, 12 July 1995.
41. Telephone interview with Chief Inspector Ron J. Clarke, Greater Manchester Police, 4 August 1995.
42. Jerry Mandel, 'Pussy cats and lions: British versus US drug problems', in A. S. Trebach and K. B. Zeese (eds), *Great Issues of Drug Policy*, p. 179.

43. *Ibid.*, p. 185.
44. Susanne MacGregor, 'Could Britain inherit the American nightmare?', *British Journal of Addiction*, **86** (1990), 871.
45. C. F. Ruter, 'The basis of Dutch policy', in A. S. Trebach and K. B. Zeese (eds), *The Great Issues of Drug Policy*, p. 193.
46. C. F. Ruter, 'The basis of Dutch policy', p. 191.
47. 'Dutch drug liberalism under pressure', *Druglink*, **2**(5) (1987), 5.
48. *Ibid.*
49. Editorial, 'Netherlands, Switzerland, Germany offer models for "Normalization" of both soft and hard drug use', *Drugs and Drug Abuse Education Newsletter*, **22**, (11–12), 112. Substance Abuse News Service (SUNS), Editorial Resources Incorporated, Washington, DC.
50. *For a Revision of the International Policy on Drugs: Report on the possibilities for amending and/or repealing the United Nations Conventions* (Brussels: International Antiprohibitionist League, Paper I, 1994), p. II.
51. Bruce Bagley, 'Myths of militarization: enlisting armed forces in the war on drugs', in Peter H. Smith (ed.), *Drug Policy in the Americas*, p. 129.
52. Clare Hargreaves, *Snowfields: The War on Cocaine in the Andes*, (London: Zed Books, 1992), p. 154.
53. *Ibid.*, p. 157.
54. *Ibid.*
55. *Ibid.*
56. Bruce M. Bagley, 'Myths of militarization', p. 137.
57. Donald J. Mabry, 'The role of the military', in Raphael F. Perl (ed.), *Drugs and Foreign Policy*, (Boulder: Westview Press, 1994), p. 5.
58. Christina Jacqueline Johns, 'Stealing fair and square: the invasion of Panama', in A. S. Trebach and K. B. Zeese (eds), *Great Issues of Drug Policy*, p. 165.
59. Bruce M. Bagley, 'Myths of militarization', p. 138.
60. Mathea Falco, 'Foreign drugs, foreign wars', *Daedalus*, **121**(3) (Summer 1992), 5.
61. US Department of State, International Narcotics Control Strategy Report, March 1997, Bureau for International Narcotic and Law Enforcement Affairs, Next Steps, p. 2.
62. Peter H. Smith, 'The political economy of drugs: conceptual issues and policy options', in Peter H. Smith (ed.), *Drug Policy in the Americas*, p. 15.
63. Clare Hargreaves, *Snowfields*, p. 162.
64. Donald J. Mabry, 'The role of the Military,' p. 120.
65. Tom Clancy, *Clear and Present Danger*, (London: HarperCollins, 1989).
66. Bruce Bullington, 'All about eve: the many faces of United States drug policy', in Frank Pearce and Michael Woodiwiss (eds), *Global Crime Connections: Dynamics of Control* (London: Macmillan, 1993), p. 68.
67. 'The drug cartel: beating the rap', *Washington Spectator*, 15 August 1989, p. 2.
68. Clarence Lusane, *Pipe Dream Blues: Racism and the War on Drugs* (Boston: South End Press, 1991), p. 122.
69. *Ibid.*

70. Nicholas Dorn and Nigel South, 'After Mr. Bennett and Mr. Bush: US Foreign Policy and the Prospects for Drug Control', in Frank Pearce and Michael Woodiwiss (eds), *Global Crime Connections*, p. 72.
71. See Bruce Bullington, 'All about Eve', p. 33.
72. Richard Craig, 'U.S. narcotics policy towards Mexico: consequences for the bilateral relationship', in Guadalupe Gonzalez and Marta Tienda (eds), *The Drug Connection in U.S.-Mexican Relations* (San Diego: Center for US–Mexican Studies, University of California, 1989), pp. 71–2.
73. *Ibid.*
74. *Ibid.*, p. 85.
75. Guadalupe Gonzalez and Marta Tienda (eds), *Drug Connection in US–Mexican Relations*, p. 2.
76. Richard Craig, 'U.S. narcotics policy towards Mexico', p. 79.
77. *Ibid.*
78. Maria Celia Toro, 'Unilateralism and bilateralism,' in Peter H. Smith (ed.), *Drug Policy in the Americas*, p. 318.
79. US Department of State, International Narcotics Control Strategy Report, March 1997, Bureau for International Narcotic and Law Enforcement Affairs, Executive Summary, p. 5.
80. Bruce Bullington and Alan Block, 'A Trojan horse: anti-communism and the war on drugs', *Contemporary Crisis*, **14**(1) (1990), 40.
81. Mack Tanner, 'International drug suppression follies', in A. S. Trebach and Kevin B. Zeese (eds), *New Frontiers in Drug Policy* (Washington, DC: The Drug Policy Foundation, 1991), p. 345.

EPILOGUE

The scale of the contemporary drug problem guarantees that international control remains a high and apparently increasing priority for both the United States and the UN. Indeed, at the General Assembly Special Session (UNGASS) on Drugs in 1990, Javier Pérez de Cuéllar, then Secretary-General of the UN, demonstrated his level of concern when he stated that 'Drug abuse is a time bomb ticking away in the heart of our civilization' and that the organization 'must now find measures to deal with it before it explodes and destroys us'.[1] Eight years on, at the next UNGASS on Drugs, Under Secretary-General Pino Arlacchi, executive director of the UNDCP, reaffirmed the organization's concern for the issue when he stated that 'Narcotics and organized crime are the major threats to the world in the next century.'[2] Domestically motivated interest in the transnational component of the drug issue also ensured that President Bill Clinton's protestations on the topic have matched the gravity of those made by UN officials. Displaying a characteristically American moral stance, Clinton told world leaders in 1995 that the perils of the Cold War had been buried only to be replaced by the scourge of drugs. Clearly, such public statements led onlookers to believe that both Washington and the UN regarded the illicit drug issue as a priority for the future and were accordingly keen to pursue transnational strategies that would realistically address the problem. It appears, however, that little is changing concerning the adoption of an effective international approach to control. In the Introduction, I suggested that the fluctuating fortunes of the American crusade to internationalize drug prohibition could be interpreted through a thematic triumvirate. This, to recap, consists of the relationship between hegemonic stability and the internationalization of prohibition, US moralism and systemically induced duality within the formulation of US narcotic diplomacy. As an examination of evidence for future trends will show, while these themes remain robust, prospects for a deviation from the US-instigated global drug prohibition regime seem unlikely.

The close of the so-called American century has inevitably provoked debate about continuing US hegemony and the decline of the Pax Americana. Alterations in the global balance of power, and so the US position within the UN, could be expected to affect the dynamics of the international drug control regime. The relationship between a modification of US international influence and the philosophy of the international drug control framework is not a simple one, however.

As noted in the introduction, much of the United States' success at globalizing its drug prohibition policy is attributable to a lack of widespread and forcible opposition. This is not to say that co-operation is indicative of complete agreement. As Friedrich Kratochwill has pointed out, rule following differs significantly from an exercise of empathy.[3] Yet, as we have seen throughout the text, rule following can be heavily encouraged by the influence of a powerful state that stands to gain from regime adherence. Unwillingness on the part of independent nations to challenge a superpower like the United States on issues of drug control and possibly jeopardize relations with Washington in other, particularly economic, areas, has consequently resulted in little significant resistance. Indeed, as the chairman of the Senate Foreign Relations Committee, J. William Fulbright, reflected in 1972, 'having controlled the UN for many years as tightly and as easily as a big-city boss controls his party machine, we had got used to the idea that the UN was a place where we could work our will'.[4] US domination, at both formal and informal levels within the drug control framework of the UN, has ensured that even without unequivocal multinational support, international drug control law has pursued a prohibitive line. The present UN-sanctioned prohibition-based international drug control system can, as has been demonstrated, be seen as the product of ninety years of endeavour by the United States.

Bruun, Pan and Rexed remarked in 1975 that the USA's strength within the UN's drug control sphere is probably indicative of its position in all areas of concern in the UN, in that the nation has always been the largest contributor to the UN budget.[5] Twenty-three years on, the United States theoretically continues to be the organization's major financial benefactor. In practice, however, there is a problem with this interpretation. As of October 1995, Washington's payments to the UN were in arrears by $1.4 billion. The USA, to use the words of President Bill Clinton, has become 'the biggest piker in the UN'.[6] The USA's reluctance to provide fiscal support to the UN as it once did is likely to be both the cause and the result of an alteration in the nation's position within the organization. In 1985, Jeanne Kirkpatrick, then the US permanent representative to the UN, noted that from an American perspective there has been a decline in Washington's influence in the UN since the mid-1960s.[7] This perceived decline can have done little to encourage successive US administrations to continue to plough US dollars into the organization. A subsequent reduction in US contributions, it can be argued, could then have led to a further erosion of American influence within the UN as a whole, including its drug control functions. It is nevertheless doubtful that such a process will affect the prohibitive approach of the UNDCP and the maintenance of the international regime for control. This is the product of several factors.

First, American dominance during the two formative decades after 1945 helped to guarantee that prohibition became central to the organization's international drug control strategy. The United States' pre-eminent role in the formulation and implementation of UN legislation during this period, particularly the 1961 Single Convention, effectively primed the organization's control system for the future. As Judith Goldstein has noted in what has been called her archaeological approach to regime theory, contemporary international regimes largely reflect the views of dominant states at the time of founding.[8] Because US strength initially ensured that the UN's drug control apparatus adopted a prohibitive course, any decline in the nation's influence within the organization as a whole is unlikely to result in a modification of policy. Like a supertanker at cruising speed, the prohibitive regime would take considerable time to alter direction. Additionally, if American international influence and its associated role in the UN were to decline, it is unlikely that transnational norms for the control of drugs would alter greatly because of 'regime persistence'. The phenomenon, discussed by Robert Keohane in *After Hegemony*,[9] allows for the continued functioning of a regime even in the absence of a hegemonic actor. The ostensibly benevolent appeal of the UN drug control programme, and the belief that national adherence to international norms is for the good of humanity, has already gone a long way to give the regime momentum independent of any individual state actor. A sense of obligation seems to induce many states to repeat international agreements, with norms and rules almost exerting a 'compliance pull' of their own. O. R. Young, who talks of 'pure institutionalism', takes up such a concept and maintains that states often comply with global norms simply because the regime exists. Institutions assume a power of their own and socialize their members into compliant behaviour.[10] It possible to argue that the supposedly universal benefits of regime adherence preclude the need for a hegemonic actor corralling nation states into line. In the absence of a hegemon, the regime itself could further develop the ability to encourage conformity. Nevertheless, discussions concerning the demise of the United States as a hegemonic actor may be premature bearing in mind the continuing distribution of power within the organization and, as we shall see, the international community as a whole. Although most observers agree that Washington's relationship with the UN has changed since 1945, diplomats involved with the day-to-day operation of the organization realize that the United States still plays a crucial role. As Abba Eban, former Israeli Foreign Minister and veteran UN diplomat, remarked in 1995, 'Nothing can happen without the Americans. Everything can happen with them.'[11]

Secondly, regardless of Washington's unwillingness to keep up with its payments to the organization as a whole, the United States still attaches a high priority to the UN's drug control functions. The organization's fiftieth anniversary celebration in October 1995 saw Clinton put full US backing behind the UN's work in the field, warning that the USA would punish countries that declined to co-operate.[12] Mr Mehdi M. Ali, chief of the UNDCP's Resources Mobilization and Interagency Co-ordination Service, noted in December 1995 that the United States has indeed been 'reviewing its priorities in all areas of public expenditure, including contributions to the United Nations and its specialized organizations'.[13] However, according to Ali, despite the USA's decision to withhold funds from the organization, American commitment to the UNDCP remains solid. He continued:

> This political stand has been translated in recent years into increased voluntary contributions from the U.S. in support of the Programme's [UNDCP's] worldwide activities. In 1995, the U.S. Government pledged US$5.9 million (as compared to US$2.5 million in 1992) and is among the major contributors to UNDCP.[14]

Since the UNDCP relies upon voluntary contributions for the majority of its resources, increased funding from Washington helps to ensure that the United States continues to hold considerable influence over the organization's drug control policies. It should come as little surprise, then, to discover that, despite declarations concerning an increased focus on the demand side of the illegal drugs problem made at UNGASS in June 1998, the UNDCP has pledged to follow the ongoing prohibitionist agenda, preferring to emphasize the problems associated with source rather than consumer nations. An unprecedented open letter to Secretary-General Kofi Annan calling for a re-evaluation of the present UN drug control strategy thus had little impact upon the outcome of the General Assembly special session in New York. The petition contained 500 signatures, including those of a host of distinguished politicians, doctors and academics from around the world. Participants in the project, who significantly included the former UN Secretary-General Javier Pérez de Cuéllar and the former US Secretary of State George P. Shultz, asserted that the global war on drugs now causes more harm than drug abuse itself. No longer limited by the constraints of office, both men took the opportunity to speak out against the UN's current drug control policies. Nonetheless, while the protest demonstrated the extent of opposition to the war on drugs, it also highlighted the unwillingness of the UNDCP to listen to alternative approaches.

The fact that the letter was dismissed by the US government as merely a rallying cry for drug legalization is indicative of its continuing dedication to the ideal of drug prohibition both at home and abroad. Preferring to see any calls for a 'truly open and honest dialogue' on the issue simply as a euphemism for demands to legalize all drugs, President Clinton's drug czar, the retired army officer General Barry R. McCaffrey, called the protest part of a 'slick misinformation campaign'. McCaffrey's dogmatic approach to the multifaceted drug problem is by no means unique. Views held among American diplomats involved with international control indicate the faith that Washington still has in current policies. Despite the existence of some dissenters, like Mathea Falco, who was the Assistant Secretary of State for International Narcotic Matters (INM) between 1977 and 1981, diplomats today steadfastly adhere to policies based on prohibition. The stigma of being labelled 'soft on drugs' appears to prevent anyone from suggesting the consideration of policies not based on prohibition while holding office. Although Falco's own experiences with INM led him later to comment that 'We continue to pursue a policy that does not and cannot work',[15] US governmental policies remain consistent. This is evident in the stance of Melvyn Levitsky, who in June 1989 was appointed to the position formerly held by Falco. Levitsky's comments appear to confuse fact and fiction, and illustrate the myopia that affects the US government's policies on both national and international drug control. He optimistically states that

> With our national strategy in place and producing results, and with the emergence, for the first time of an international antinarcotics cartel of producer, transit and consumer countries, the prospects for expanded progress are good. Indeed, the pursuit of these initiatives promises to make the next decade one that further reduces the international drug threat.[16]

Since INM represents the United States at the UN and other international drug control organizations, and co-ordinates the relevant international drug control programmes of all US government agencies, it appears inevitable that current US policies towards transnational drug control will remain unaltered.

The Department of State's belief in 1996 that its international successes against the drugs trade 'confirm the general soundness of [our] approach'[17] affirms that the United States pursues an international strategy based on prohibition with the same enthusiasm today as it did in the early decades of the twentieth century. American officials follow the same path as that trodden by Brent, Wright, Porter and Anslinger. A steadfast belief in the moral superiority and practical effectiveness of US prohibitive policies has maintained the momentum of proselytization. This has remained so despite abundant historical and contemporary evidence to show that the policy is ineffectual in dealing with illegal drug use. References to the drug trade as an 'opportunistic disease that breeds only amidst social and moral decay'[18] demonstrate a continuing preoccupation with morality rather than the concrete socio-economic realities that often underpin illicit drug use. The increasingly draconian character of US domestic drug legislation has done nothing to reduce the problems associated with illegal drug use. Such a dramatic failure to address the phenomenon can be attributed to the history of American prohibitive drug policies. The US national strategy of which Levitsky speaks is, as has been discussed, the product of a variety of components. And in order to understand the American crusade against the ingestion of certain psychoactive substances, it is essential to view it through a lens distorted by a complex mix of morality, racism, pseudo-scientific analysis, bureaucratic rivalry and a foreign policy based for many years on a fear of communism. American drug control legislation is the reaction to numerous diverse factors, only one of which was actually drug use. Such circumstances have led Mario Lap of the Netherlands Institute for Alcohol and Drugs to comment that 'the theory of drug prohibition is thin. It is not based on its usefulness. Its basis is to be found in history.'[19] The result has been the creation of an illogical, ill-suited and ineffective policy – a policy which continues to locate the source of the United States' drug problems beyond the boundaries of American society, and lays the blame upon other nations and racial groups. Regardless of this, US international endeavours at both bilateral and multilateral levels have helped to ensure that the approach has been successfully exported to the rest of the world.

American reaction to events in Australia and Switzerland in late 1997 demonstrated the continuing rigidity of both the US prohibitive stance and that of the international drug control regime. In an attempt to reduce societal and individual harm, the Swiss government and the city of Canberra, Australia, have chosen to implement experimental trials for heroin prescription to addicts. Both nations are locked into the international prohibitive regime, having signed the 1961 UN convention, yet by adhering to the clause in the convention concerning 'medical and scientific research ... including clinical trials' they are staying within international law. At odds with the US approach to the issue, such action has provoked a characteristically tough response from Washington. Remarks made by Bob Gelbard, the US Assistant Secretary of State for Narcotics and Law Enforcement, that 'The United States viewed with concern any countries who appear to be or are actively considering liberalisation of drug laws'[20] only hinted at the measures Washington is apparently prepared to take to counter such moves. While US reaction to the developments in both nations was equally scathing, geopolitical realities look set to ensure differing success. The US Congressional Subcommittee on National Security, International Affairs and Criminal Justice has condemned the Swiss Federal Office of Public Health. The chairman of the subcommittee, J. Dennis Hastert (R-IL), commented that 'this is a real national security issue' and that he opposed the 'immoral act of giving away heroin and expanding the risk of even higher drug abuse'. His views were forcibly supported by Bob Barr (R-GA), who said that he had visited Switzerland to see how these heroin 'giveaway' clinics worked, and was 'shocked' that so 'civilized' a nation would be 'flirting with disaster and gambling with the future they pass to their children'.[21] While such comments convey US displeasure with the Swiss policy, they have little tangible impact upon Berne. Switzerland retains its historical independence and resistance to external influence. Provided the Swiss authorities do not break the rules of the 1961 convention, they must suffer only US prohibitionist rhetoric.

Events in Australia provoked similar condemnation, but officials in Canberra appear to be more susceptible to direct US coercion. The Australian Achilles heel is the legal opium-growing industry of Tasmania. This highly profitable enterprise exists and prospers only with approval from the UN's INCB and the United States. Evidence suggests that the USA is applying pressure unilaterally and through the INCB upon Canberra to halt the so-called ACT heroin trials. The loss of the A$80 million a year Tasmanian opium business seems to be a significant inducement encouraging the Australian authorities to follow the prohibitive line dictated by Washington and maintained by the global drug prohibition regime. Time will tell. The irony of the Australian dilemma is that the contemporary domestic heroin problem can be attributed directly to US action at the close of the Vietnam War. According to Alfred McCoy in his *Drug Traffic, Narcotics and Organised Crime in Australia*, the DEA successfully prevented heroin following addicted GIs back to the United States. This action, McCoy continues, in effect compelled the drug syndicates in Southeast Asia to sell heroin originally produced for American addicts in alternative markets. In short, the DEA simply diverted Southeast Asian heroin from the United States into European and Australian markets.[22] This was one case where US action inadvertently influenced the dynamics of the drug problem within the boundaries of other nations. As we have noted, US diplomatic aims have often undermined the goals of Washington's own international drug control efforts. Contemporary US narcotic foreign policy remains precarious in relation to other diplomatic concerns.

Despite statements like those made by Levitsky that 'narcotics control will remain an important foreign policy priority',[23] the US practice of deferring narcotics issues to other foreign-policy concerns remains consistent. It should come as no surprise to hear comments like those made by Dr Lee P. Brown, the Director of the Office of National Drug Control Policy (ONDCP). In November 1994, Dr Brown noted that 'It is well known inside the Federal Government that State traditionally has relegated international narcotics enforcement around the world to a low rung on its priority ladder.'[24] Brown in effect admitted that although one side of the US strategy continues to ensure the existence of prohibitive international policies, the State Department simultaneously subordinates the war on drugs to other diplomatic concerns.

The end of the Cold War has meant that the diplomacy of anti-communism no longer overshadows the goals of US narcotic foreign policy as it once did. Yet international drug control continues to be the casualty of systemically imposed conflicts between the moral idealism behind US narcotic diplomacy and realist concerns for wider national interest. Among the numerous examples of US incongruity of policy since 1909, this aspect of narcotic diplomacy has, ironically, remained consistent. A brief examination of the interrelationship between US international drug policy in the Western Hemisphere and the North American Free Trade Agreement (NAFTA) will validate my earlier contention that Washington's current interest in trade has replaced communism as a central factor in the continuing deferral of the goals of the American crusade.

January 1994 saw NAFTA come into effect, linking the United States, Mexico and Canada in a pact to increase trade and investment. A glance at the media reveals the issue's central position on the foreign-policy agendas of both Mexico and the United States, and it is also becoming clear just how large an impact the agreement is having upon the contours of narco-diplomatic relations between the two countries. Washington's desire to forge beneficial economic relations with Mexico has produced serious inconsistencies in its drug policy towards its southern neighbours. Additionally, in attempting to embrace free-market economic principles, while simultaneously adhering to prohibition and supply-oriented policies, the United States faces awkward practical and ideological dilemmas. Indeed, efforts to square the circle have led the USA to succumb to what could be termed post-Cold War schizophrenia in the formulation of its narcotic foreign policy.

Despite nominal moves towards demand-side strategies, the Clinton administration continues to follow the traditional overseas war on drugs inherited from its predecessors. It is perhaps appropriate therefore that recent drug policy regarding Mexico should also adhere to another well-established tradition: that of subordinating narco-diplomacy to other foreign-policy considerations. In a characteristic display of incongruity, Washington's fundamentally flawed supply-side strategies are themselves being undermined by economically driven foreign-policy concerns. This remains the case although the illicit drug issue is, as noted in the previous chapter, still an important part of US foreign policy in the region. Regardless of this fact, economic priorities determined that the drug issue was effectively side-stepped during the NAFTA negotiations, being placed in a 'too hot to handle' category. US officials took no chances that the drugs spectre might taint the creation of a new hemispheric economic order. Evidence suggests that since 1994 the United States has been making concessions in its war on drugs in Latin America in order to ensure favourable terms of trade. Presumably such action adheres to the clause in the certification legislation referring to national interest. This appears strange, considering the 'lethal' threat drugs are seen to pose to US national security. Indeed, it was abundantly clear that NAFTA and the trade issue were the central concerns of Clinton's October 1997 tour of Latin America. Working hard to improve historically strained relations and promote his dream of a free-trade zone from Alaska to Argentina by 2005,[25] Clinton ensured that the illegal drug trade did not spoil the image of one big happy economic family of nations. At the turn of the century, economic determinism coincided with drug control goals in China. Today there is a considerable collision of interests. It is little surprise therefore that the administration's stance on free trade is forcing incongruous policy decisions.

While the continuing high levels of trafficking and drug-related corruption in Mexico should, within the context of President Reagan's 'lethal threat' scenario discussed in the last chapter, result in decertification, it looks unlikely that President Clinton will fail to certify the United States' important new trading partner in the near future. News in February 1997 that Mexico's top anti-narcotics official was arrested on charges of working for the country's most notorious drug lord did nothing to prevent President Clinton from certifying Mexico for another year as a co-operative partner in the US war on drugs. Similarly, despite continuing charges of drug-related corruption, Mexico again received certification in 1998.

As noted, NAFTA also introduces difficult ideological problems for the US policymakers to deal with. While the free trade pact unleashes market forces – loosening government controls over the flow of goods, services, information and capital – it unintentionally encourages and facilitates not only legal economic activity but illegal activity as well. As Peter Andreas lucidly argues, trade liberalization and economic integration help Mexico's traffickers to penetrate the lucrative US market.[26] More worrying still perhaps, drug lords are starting to launder narco-dollars and move into legitimate enterprises through the purchase of increasingly buoyant NAFTA-related businesses.

While the Clinton administration has worked hard on the problem, it is becoming more difficult to de-link trade and drugs as policy issues. Thus, while a 1994 Gallup poll revealed that curbing the flow of illicit drugs into the United States was the priority of 89 per cent of those interviewed, US customs and drug enforcement personnel openly called NAFTA the 'North American Drug Trade Agreement'.[27] However, such openness is in forcible decline. Within the climate of the drug war it is perhaps appropriate that that the maxim 'careless talk costs lives' should be revived to read 'careless talk costs jobs'. US border agents interviewed by *Newsweek* in 1997 say that they have been warned not to associate NAFTA with narcotics traffic, apparently for fear of political fallout. A former head of the DEA in El Paso, Texas, noted that 'The directors said we were not to say anything negative about the impact of NAFTA.'[28] Nevertheless, the increasing flow of traffic and migrants from Mexico to the United States has meant that the border is becoming harder, perhaps impossible, to police. As a response, US authorities are moving to create a latter-day high-tech Maginot Line in an attempt to protect the United States from illegal migrants and drug trafficking. While it does little to reduce dramatically the northward flow of illicit drugs, the escalation of the interdiction policy at the US–Mexican border is already proving to have disastrous consequences. The tragic fatal shooting of an 18-year-old Texan goat herder by a US Marine under the command of the US Border Patrol in 1997 raises not only questions concerning training procedures, but also wider issues relating to the increasing use of the US military in the drug war on American soil. The US administration nevertheless seems unperturbed. In his 1998 State of the Union address, Clinton asked Congress to join him in a 'ground-breaking effort to hire a thousand new Border Patrol agents and deploy the most sophisticated available new technologies to help close the door on drugs at our borders'.[29] Such behaviour hardly conforms to the principles of economic integration, trust and co-operation as embodied in NAFTA. Among various other concerns, Washington therefore also faces a significant ideological impasse in its approach to hemispheric drug control policy.

One positive outcome of the NAFTA-induced confusion is that Washington's commitment to trade now permits the Mexican government to chart its own drug course without the fear of decertification that has plagued the supposedly co-operative relationship for several years. It is ironic that a degree of Mexican autonomy on the drug issue is an incidental spin-off of economically driven US foreign policy rather than an integral component of a truly collaborative bilateral endeavour. Perhaps a similar situation will occur in other Latin American nations. Despite the rhetoric surrounding the US war on drugs, this could be a reality if the potential economic rewards of open markets are allowed either consciously or inadvertently to becloud the goals of drug control. This, however, seems unlikely while tangible US interests apart from narcotics remain weak in most other nations in the Andean region.

Such duality stands as a central paradox among the many inconsistencies surrounding the American crusade. While the solidity of the US-driven global drug control regime remains firm, testimony to the successful internationalization of prohibition, Washington continues to defer its own narcotic diplomacy to other foreign-policy concerns. And despite growing resistance to current policies, the international framework has constructed a restrictive intellectual *cordon sanitaire* that not only limits national responses to illicit drug control but also validates the increasingly militaristic US overseas war on drugs. The unfamiliar political landscape of the post-Cold War world has thrown drug control to the forefront of American transnational concerns. Yet while Washington continues to hold divergent views on exactly what constitutes national interest, confusion and contradiction look set to characterize the future of US international drug control policy.

NOTES

1. General Assembly Special Session on Drugs (UN Department of Public Information DP1/1061-40342-March 1990-15M), p. 8.
2. BBC Newsonline, 'UN host global drug summit', 8 June 1998.
3. Friedrich Kratochwill V, 'The force of prescriptions', *International Organization*, **38**(4) (1984), 706.
4. Shirley Hazzard, *Countenance of Truth: The United Nations and the Waldheim Case*, p. 32.
5. Kettil Bruun, Lynn Pan and Ingemur Rexed, *The Gentlemen's Club: International Control of Drugs and Alcohol*, p. 147.
6. *Newsweek*, 30 October, 1995, p. 14.
7. Rosemary Righter, *Utopia Lost: The United Nations and World Order*, p. 220.
8. Judith Goldstein, (1986), 'The political economy of trade: institutions of protection', *American Political Science Review*, **80** (1986), 161–84.
9. Robert O. Keohune, *After Hegemony: Discord in the World Political Economy*, pp. 101–2.

10. O. R. Young, *International Cooperation: Building Regimes for Natural Resources and the Environment* (Ithaca, NY: Cornell University Press, 1989) cited by Harald Muller, 'The internationalization of principles, norms and rules by governments: the case of security regimes', in Volker Rittberger (ed.), *Regime Theory and International Relations*, p. 361.
11. James Walsh, 'The UN at 50: who needs it?', *Time International*, 23 October 1995, p. 39.
12. *Guardian*, 23 October 1995, p. 8.
13. Letter from Mehdi M. Ali, Chief, Resources Mobilization and Interagency Coordination Service, UNDCP, Vienna, to author, 7 December 1995.
14. *Ibid.*
15. Steven B. Duke and Albert C. Gross, *America's Longest War*, p. 200.
16. Melvyn Levitsky, 'US foreign policy and international narcotic control: challenges and opportunities in the 1990s and beyond', in Raphael Perl (ed.), *Drugs and Foreign Policy: A Critical Review*, p. 59.
17. *US Department of State, International Narcotics Control Strategy Report*, March 1997, Bureau for International Law Enforcement Affairs, Executive Summary, Policy and Program Overview for 1996, pp. 1, 2.
18. *Ibid.*, p. 4.
19. Mario Lap of the Netherlands Institute for Alcohol and Drugs, Utrecht, speaking at the Liberty Conference, 17 June 1995, Central Hall, London, UK.
20. David Marr and Bernard Lagan, 'The real drug war: why the U.S. won't let Australia reform its drug laws,' *Sydney Morning Herald*, 19 July 1997.
21. US Congress press release, 18 September 1997, 'Swiss experts warn U.S. about dangers of needle exchange', report on US Congressional Subcommittee on National Security, International Affairs and Criminal Justice.
22. Alfred McCoy, *Drug Traffic, Narcotics and Organized Crime in Australia*, cited by David Marr and Bernard Lagan, 'The real drug war'. (See n. 20)
23. Melvyn Levitsky, 'US foreign policy and international narcotic policy', p. 58.
24. *Narcotics Control Digest*, **24**(23) (1994), 1.
25. Michael Hirsh and Martha Brant, 'Playing to the crowd', *Newsweek*, 27 October 1997, p. 18.
26. Peter Andreas, 'U.S.–Mexico: open markets, closed borders', *Foreign Policy*, **103** (1996), 58.
27. *Ibid.*
28. Michael Hirsh and Martha Brant, 'Playing to the crowd', p. 19.
29. President Clinton's State of the Union Address, 27 January 1998, from Official Text, US Information Service, US embassy, London.

BIBLIOGRAPHY

The bibliography is organized into six sections:
A. Manuscript sources
B. Published official documents
C. Newspapers and news bulletins
D. Books
E. Articles
F. Libraries and other sources

A. MANUSCRIPT SOURCES

Official Documents: United Kingdom

Foreign Office Records Group FO371.
Public Record Office, Somerset House, Kew, London

Official Documents: United States

Record Group 56. NA 501. BD NARCOTICS and NA 340.19
National Archives, Washington, DC

Private Collections

Harry J. Anslinger Papers
Pattee Library, Pennsylvania State University, University Park,
Pennsylvania

Harry J. Anslinger Papers
Harry S. Truman Library, Independence, Missouri

Harry J. Anslinger Collection
Drug Enforcement Administration Library, Washington, DC

B. PUBLISHED OFFICIAL DOCUMENTS

United Nations

International Narcotics Drug Control, United Nations Publications, sales no. 65.I.22, 1965

UN Conference for the Adoption of a Single Convention on Narcotic Drugs, Vol. 1, New York: United Nations Publications, 1964

UN Conference for the Adoption of a Single Convention on Narcotic Drugs, Vol. 2, New York: United Nations Publications, 1964

UN Chronicle, Vol. 24, no. 2, May 1987

Declaration of the International Conference on Drug Abuse and Illicit Trafficking and Comprehensive Multidisciplinary Outline on Future Activities in Drug Abuse Control, United Nations, New York, 1988

Basic Facts about the United Nations, United Nations Department of Public Information, New York, 1989

General Assembly Special Session on Drugs, United Nations Department of Public Information, March 1990

United Nations Convention Against Illicit Traffic in Narcotic Drugs and Psychotropic Substances 1988, United Nations, New York, 1991

UN Drug Abuse Control, United Nations Drug Control Programme, United Nations Department of Public Information, November 1992

Official Records of the Economic and Social Council

Summary Records of CND meetings 1947–65. UN classification E/CN.7/SR.

United States

Traffic in Opium and Other Dangerous Drugs, for the year ended 1946, US Treasury Department Bureau of Narcotics, Washington, DC, 1947

House of Representatives, Annual Report for the Year 1984 of the Select Committee on Narcotics Abuse and Control, US Government Printing Office, Washington, DC, 1985

US Department of State, International Narcotics Control Strategy Report, March 1997, Bureau for International Narcotic and Law Enforcement Affairs.
Official Text, US Information Service, US Embassy, London.

United Kingdom

Rolleston Report, Ministry of Health, Departmental Committee on Morphine and Heroin Addiction, London: His Majesty's Stationery Office, 1926

C. NEWSPAPERS AND NEWS BULLETINS

Daily Telegraph, 1995
Guardian, 1993 and 1995
Independent, 1995
New York Times, 1952, 1962, 1975
The Sunday Times, 1995
Sydney Morning Herald, 1997
South China Morning Post, 1953
The Times, 1952, 1953, 1955, 1961

Drug Link, Institute for the Study of Drug Dependence, 1987
Drug Abuse and Drug Abuse Education, Washington, DC, 1991
International Drug Report, Washington, DC, 1975
Newsweek, 1997
Washington Crime News Services' Narcotics Control Digest, 1993 and 1994.

D. BOOKS

Anslinger, Harry J., and W. F. Tompkins, *Traffic in Narcotics,* New York: Funk and Wagnall, 1953.
Anslinger, Harry J., and Will Oursler, *The Murderers: The Story of the Narcotics Gangs,* New York: Farrar, Straus and Cudaahy, 1961.
Anslinger, Harry J., *The Protectors,* New York: Farrar, Straus, 1964.
Antonil, *Mama Coca,* London: Hassel Free Press, 1978.
Baehr, Peter R., and Leon Gordenker, *The United Nations: Reality and Ideal,* New York: Praeger, 1984.
Becker, Howard, *Outsiders: Study in the Sociology of Deviance,* New York: New York Press, 1963.

Boaz, David (ed.), *The Crisis in Drug Prohibition*, Washington, DC: Cato Institute, 1991.

Bonnie, Richard J., and Charles H. Whitebread II, *The Marihuana Conviction: A History of Marihuana Prohibition in the US*, Charlottesville: University Press of Virginia, 1974.

Boyle, Peter G., *American–Soviet Relations: From the Russian Revolution to the Fall of Communism*, London: Routledge, 1993.

Bradsher, Henry S., *Afghanistan and the Soviet Union*, Durham, NC: Duke Press Policy Studies, 1983.

Bruun, Kettil, Lynn Pan and Ingemar Rexed, *The Gentlemen's Club: International Control of Drugs and Alcohol*, Chicago: University of Chicago Press, 1975.

Buell, R. L., *The International Opium Conference*, Boston: World Peace Foundation, 1925.

Candlin, H. Stanton, *Psychochemical Warfare: The Chinese Communist Drug Offensive Against the West*, New York: Arlington House – New Rochelle, 1973.

Carr, Edward Hallett, *The Twenty Year Crisis 1919–1939: An Introduction to the Study of International Relations*, New York: Harper Torchbooks, 1964.

Catholic Institute for International Relations, *Coca, Cocaine and the War on Drugs*, London: the Institute, 1993.

Chattergee, S. K., *Legal Aspects of International Control*, London: Martinus Nijhoff, 1981.

Clancy, Tom, *Clear and Present Danger*, London: HarperCollins, 1989.

Clark, Norman H., *Deliver Us from Evil: An Interpretation of American Prohibition*, New York: Norton, 1976.

Davis, Allen F., and Harold D. Woodman (eds), *Conflict and Consensus in Modern American History*, D. C. Heath, 1992.

Deverall, Richard, *Mao Tse-tung: Stop This Dirty Opium Business!*, Tokyo, 1954.

Dorn, Nicholas, and Nigel South, (eds) *A Land Fit For Heroin?* Drugs Policies, Prevention and Practice, Macmillan Education, 1987.

Duke, Steven B. and Albert C. Gross, *America's Longest War: Rethinking Our Tragic Crusade against Drugs*, New York: G. P. Putnam's Sons, 1993.

Edwards, Griffith, John Strang and Jerome H. Jaffe, *Drugs, Alcohol, and Tobacco: Making the Science and Policy Connections*, Oxford: Oxford Medical Publications, 1993.

Eisenlohr, L.E.S., *International Narcotics Control*, London: George Allen and Unwin, 1934.

Gardner, Lloyd C., *Safe for Democracy*, New York: Oxford University Press, 1984.

George, Susan, *The Debt Boomerang: How the Third World Debt Harms Us All*, London: Pluto Press, 1992.

Gonzalez, Guadalupe and Marta Tienda, (eds), *The Drug Connection in US–Mexican Relations*, San Diego: Center for U.S.-Mexican Studies, University of California, 1989.

Goodrich, Leyland M., *The United Nations*, London: Stevens, 1960.

Gossop, Michael, *Living with Drugs*, Aldershot: Ashgate, 1993.

Gregg, Robert W., *About Face?: The United States and the United Nations*, Boulder: Lynne Rienner Publishers, 1993.

Gregg, Robert W., and Michael Barkun (eds), *The United Nations System and Its Functions: Selected Readings*, New York: Van Nostrand, 1968.

The Guardian and Channel 4, *UN Blues: 50 Years of the United Nations*, (ed.) Apala Chowdhurry and Joanna Griffin. London: The Guardian and PDU in association with Channel 4, 1995.

Haas, Ernst B., *When Knowledge Is Power: Three Models of Change in International Organizations*, Berkeley: University of California Press, 1990.

Hadwen, John and Johan Kaufman, *How UN Decisions Are Made*, Leyden: A. W. Sythoff; New York: Oceana Publications, 1962.

Hamburger, Gerd and Rudolf Shermann, *The Peking Bomb: The Psychochemical War Against America*, Washington: Robert B. Luce Inc., 1975.

Hamowy, Ronald (ed.), *Dealing with Drugs: The Consequences of Government Control*, Lexington: University of Kentucky Press, 1987.

Hargreaves, Clare, *Snowfields: The War on Cocaine in the Andes*, London: Zed Books, 1992.

Hasenclever, Andreas, Peter Mayer and Volker Rittberger, *Theories of International Regimes*, Cambridge: Cambridge University Press, 1997.

Hazzard, Shirley, *Countenance of Truth: The United Nations and the Waldheim Case*, London: Chatto and Windus, 1990.

Helmer, John, *Drugs and Minority Oppression*, New York: Seabury Press, 1975.

Henman, Anthony, Roger Lewis and Tim Maylon, *Big Deal: The Politics of the Illicit Drugs Business*, London: Pluto, 1985.

Himmelstien, Jerome L., *The Strange Career of Marihuana: Politics and Ideology of Drug Control in America*, Westport, CT: Greenwood Press, 1983.

Hoffman, Stanley, *Primacy or World Order: American Foreign Policy since the Cold War*, New York; McGraw-Hill Book Company, 1978.

Hoff-Wilson, Joan, *American Business and Foreign Policy, 1920–1933*, Lexington: University of Kentucky Press, 1971.

Hubbard, Ursula P., 'The cooperation of the United States with the League of Nations, 1931–1936', *International Conciliation*, no. 329, New York: Carnegie Endowment for International Peace, 1937.

Hyde, L. K., *The US and the UN: Promoting the Public Welfare. Examples of American Cooperation 1945–1955*, National Studies on International Organization, prepared for the Carnegie Endowment for International Peace, New York: Manhattan Publishing Co., 1960.

Inciardi, James A. (ed.), *The Handbook of Drug Control in the United States*, Westport, CT: Greenwood Press, 1990.

Inciardi, James A. (ed.), *The Drug Legalization Debate*, London: Sage, 1991.

Inglis, Brian, *The Forbidden Game: A Social History of Drugs*, London: Hodder and Stoughton, 1975.

Kegley, Charles W., Jr., and Eugene R. Wittkopf, *American Foreign Policy: Pattern and Process*, London: Macmillan Education, 1987 (3rd edn).

Kegley, Charles W., Jr., and Eugene R. Wittkopf, *American Foreign Policy: Pattern and Process*, London: Macmillan Education, 1987 (4th edn).

Kennedy, Paul, *The Rise and Fall of the Great Powers: Economic Change and Military Conflict from 1500 to 2000*, London: Fontana, 1988 (4th edn).

Keohane, Robert O., *After Hegemony: Cooperation and Discord in the World Political Economy*, Princeton: Princeton University Press, 1984.

King, Rufus, *The Drug Hang-Up*, Springfield, IL: Charles Thomas, 1974.

Kinney, Jack, Ronald Christensen, Wilfor Welch, Gerald Bush and Arthus Lowenthal, *A Study of International Control of Narcotics and Dangerous Drugs*, Arthur D. Little Inc., submitted to the Bureau of Narcotics and Dangerous Drugs, May 1972.

Kleiman, M., *Against Excess: Drug Policy for Results*, New York: Basic Books, 1992.

Kohn, Marek, *Narcomania*, London: Faber and Faber, 1987.

Lie, Trygve, *In the Cause of Peace: Seven Years with the United Nations*, New York: Macmillan, 1954.

Lowes, Peter D., *The Genesis of International Narcotics Control*, Geneva: Librairie Droz, 1966.

Luard, Evan, *The United Nations: How It Works and What It Does*, New York: St Martin's Press, 1979.

Luard, Evan, *A History of the United Nations*: Vol. 1, *The Years of Western Dominance, 1944–1955*, New York: Macmillan, 1982.

Lusane, Clarence, *Pipe Dream Blues: Racism and the War on Drugs*, Boston: South End Press, 1991.

McCoy, Alfred W., *Drug Traffic, Narcotics and Organized Crime in Australia*, Sidney: Harper Row, 1980.

McCoy, Alfred W., *The Politics of Heroin: CIA Complicity in the Global Drug Trade*, New York: Lawrence Hill, 1991.

MacGregor, Susanne (ed.), *Drugs and British Society: Responses to a Social Problem in the 1980s*, London: Routledge, 1989.

McWilliams, John C., *The Protectors: Harry J. Anslinger and the Federal*

Bureau of Narcotics, 1930–1962, Newark: University of Delaware Press, 1990.

Miller, Richard Lawrence, *The Case for Legalizing Drugs*, Westport, CT: Praeger, 1991.

Musto, David F., *The American Disease: Origins of Narcotic Control*, Oxford: Oxford University Press, 1987.

Nadelmann, Ethan A., *Cops across Borders: The Internationalization of U.S. Criminal Law Enforcement*, University Park: Pennsylvania State University, 1993.

Northedge, Peter S. *The League of Nations: Its Life and Times, 1920–1946*, Leicester: Leicester University Press, 1986.

Pearce, Frank and Michael Woodiwiss (eds), *Global Crime Connections: Dynamics and Control*, London: Macmillan, 1993.

Perl, Raphael F. (ed.), *Drugs and Foreign Policy: A Critical Review*, Boulder: Westview Press, 1994.

Questioning Prohibition: 1994 International Report on Drugs, Brussels: International Antiprohibitionist League, 1994.

Renborg, Bertil A., *International Drug Control: A Study of International Administration by and through the League of Nations*, Washington, DC: Carnegie Endowment for International Peace, 1947.

Righter, Rosemary, *Utopia Lost: The United Nations and World Order*, New York: Twentieth Century Fund Press, 1995.

Rittberger, Volker (ed.), *Regime Theory and International Relations*, Oxford: Oxford University Press, 1995.

Schmeckebier, Lawrence F., *The Bureau of Prohibition: Its History, Activities and Organization*, Washington, DC: Brookings Institute, 1929.

Schur, Edwin M., *Narcotic Addiction in Britain and America: The Impact of Public Policy*, London: Tavistock Publications, 1962.

Scott, J.M., *The White Poppy: The History of Opium*, London: Heinemann, 1969.

Scott, Peter Dale and Jonathan Marshall, *Cocaine Politics: Drugs, Armies and the CIA in Latin America*, Berkeley: University of California Press, 1991.

Simmons, Luis R. S., and Abdul A. Said (eds), *Drugs, Politics and Diplomacy*, Beverly Hills: Sage, 1974.

Smith, Peter H. (ed.), *Drug Policy in the Americas*, Boulder: Westview Press, 1992.

Soloman, David (ed.), *The Marijuana Papers: An Examination of Marijuana in Society, History and Literature*, London: Panther Modern Society, 1969.

Stein, S. D., *International Diplomacy, State Administration and Narcotics Control: The Origins of a Social Problem*, London: Gower, 1985.

Taylor, Arnold H., *American Diplomacy and the Narcotics Traffic 1900–1939*, Durham, NC: Duke University Press, 1969.

Trebach, Arnold S., *The Heroin Solution*, New Haven, CT: Yale University Press, 1982.

Trebach, Arnold S., *The Great Drug War and Radical Proposals That Could Make America Safe Again*, New York: Macmillan, 1987.

Trebach, Arnold S., and Kevin B. Zeese (eds), *The Great Issues of Drug Policy*, Washington, DC: Drug Policy Foundation, 1990.

Trebach, Arnold S., and Kevin B. Zeese (eds), *Drug Prohibition and the Conscience of Nations*, Washington, DC: Drug Policy Foundation, 1990.

Trebach, Arnold S., and Kevin B. Zeese (eds), *New Frontiers in Drug Policy*, Washington, DC: Drug Policy Foundation, 1991.

Tyler, Gus (ed.), *Organised Crime in America: A Book of Readings*, Ann Arbor: University of Michigan Press, 1962.

Vallance, Theodore R., *Prohibition's Second Failure: The Quest for a Rational and Humane Drug Policy*, Westport, CT: Praeger, 1993.

Von Vorys, Karl, *American National Interest: Virtue and Power in Foreign Policy*, Westport, CT: Praeger, 1990.

Walker, William O., III, *Drug Control in the Americas*, Alberquerque: University of New Mexico Press, 1989.

Walker, William O., III, *Opium and Foreign Policy: The Anglo-American Search for Order, 1912–1954*, Chapel Hill: University of North Carolina Press, 1991.

Walker, William O., III, (ed.), *Drug Control Policy: Essays in Historical and Comparative Perspective*, University Park: Pennsylvania State University Press, 1992.

Wayne Morgan, H., *Drugs in America: A Social History, 1800–1980*, Syracuse, NY: Syracuse University Press, 1981.

Weeks, John, and Phil Gunson, *Panama: Made in the USA*, London: Latin American Bureau, 1991.

Weibe, Robert H., *The Search for Order 1877–1920*, New York: Hill and Wang, 1967.

Weil, Andrew, *The Natural Mind: An Investigation of Drugs and Higher Consciousness*, Boston: Houghton Mifflin, 1986.

Whitaker, Ben, *The Global Fix: The Crisis of Drug Addiction*, London: Methuen, 1987.

Wisotsky, Steven, *Breaking the Impasse on the War on Drugs*, Westport, CT: Greenwood Press, 1986.

Wisotsky, Steven, *Beyond the War on Drugs: Overcoming a Failed Public Policy*, New York: Prometheus, 1990.

Woodiwiss, Michael, *Crime, Crusades and Corruption: Prohibitions in the United States 1900–1987*, London: Pinter, 1988.

E. ARTICLES

Andreas, Peter, 'U.S.–Mexico: open markets, closed borders', *Foreign Policy*, **103**, (Summer) (1996), 51–69.

Anslinger, Harry J., 'A proposed codification of the multilateral treaty law on narcotic drugs', *Food Drug Cosmetic Law Journal*, **13**(11) (1958), 692–7.

Block, Alan A., 'European drug traffic and traffickers between the wars: suppression and its consequences', *Journal of Social History*, **23** (1989–90), 315–37.

Bullington, Bruce and Alan Block, 'A Trojan horse: anti-communism and the war on drugs', *Contemporary Crises*, **14**(1) (1990), 46–56.

Bullington, Bruce, 'War and peace: drug policy in the United States and the Netherlands', *Crime, Law and Social Change*, **22**(3) (1994/95), 213–38.

Falco, Mathea, 'Foreign drugs, foreign wars', *Daedalus*, **121** (3) (1992), 1–14.

Falco, Mathea, 'America's drug problem and its policy of denial', *Current History*, **97** (618) (1998), 145–9.

Goldstein, Judith, 'The political economy of trade: institutions of protection', *American Political Science Review*, **80** (1986), 161–84.

Kinder, Douglas Clark, 'Bureaucratic Cold Warrior: Harry J. Anslinger and illicit narcotics traffic', *Pacific Historical Review*, **50** (1981), 169–91.

Kinder, Douglas Clark, and William O. Walker III, 'Stable force in a storm: Harry J. Anslinger and United States narcotic foreign policy, 1930–1962', *Journal of American History*, **71**(4) (1986), 908–27.

Koppes, Clayton, 'The good neighbour policy and the nationalization of Mexican oil: a reinterpretation', *Journal of American History*, **69** (1) (1982), 62–81.

Krasner, Stephen D., 'Structural causes and regime consequences: regimes as intervening variables', *International Organization*, **36** (2) (1982), 185–205.

Kratochwill, Friedrich, 'The force of prescriptions', *International Organization*, **38** (4) (1984), 685–708.

Lande, Adolf, 'The Single Convention on Narcotic Drugs 1961', *International Organization*, **16** (1962), 776–97.

Lap, Mario, and Ernest Drucker, 'Recent changes in the Dutch cannabis trade: the case for regulated domestic production', *International Journal of Drug Policy*, **5**(4) (1994), 249–53.

MacGregor, Susanne, 'Could Britain inherit the American nightmare?', *British Journal of Addiction*, **86** (1990), 863–72.

McWilliams, John C., 'Unsung partner against crime: Harry J. Anslinger and the FBN, 1930–1962', *Pennsylvania Magazine of History and Biography*, **113**(2) (April 1988), 207–36.

McWilliams, John C., 'Covert connections: the FBN, the OSS and the CIA', *Historian*, **53**(4) (1991), 657–78.

May, Herbert L., 'The international control of drugs', *International Conciliation*, **441** (May 1984), 303–80.

Maylon, Tim, 'Full tilt towards a no-win "Vietnam" war on drugs', *New Statesman*, 17 October 1987, pp. 7–10.

Nadelmann, Ethan A., 'Drug prohibition in the United States: costs, consequences and alternatives', *Science*, **245** (1985), 939–47.

Nadelmann, Ethan A., 'Global prohibition regimes: the evolution of norms in international society', *International Organization*, **44**(4) (1990), 479–526.

Reinarman, Craig, 'Glasnost in US drug policy? Clinton constrained', *International Journal of Drug Policy*, **5**(2) (1994), 98–104.

Renborg, Bertil A., 'The Grand Old Men of the League of Nations', *Bulletin on Narcotics*, **16**(4) (1964), 1–11.

Reuter, Paul, 'The obligations of states under the Single Convention on Narcotic Drugs, 1961', *Bulletin on Narcotics*, **20**(4) (1968), 3–7.

Schaller, Michael, 'The federal prohibition of marihuana', *Journal of Social History*, **4** (1970), 208–21.

UN Secretariat, 'The Plenipotentiary Conference for the Adoption of a Single Convention on Narcotic Drugs', *Bulletin on Narcotics*, **14**(1) (1962), 40–3.

UN Secretariat, 'The United States' Views on the Single Convention on Narcotic Drugs', *Bulletin on Narcotics*, **15**(2) (1963), 9–11.

UN Secretariat, 'Twenty years of narcotics control under the United Nations: review of the work of the Commission on Narcotic Drugs from its 1st to its 20th session', *Bulletin on Narcotics*, **18**(1) (1966), 1–60.

Van den Haag, Ernest, 'The busyness of American foreign policy', *Foreign Affairs*, (Fall) (1985), 113–29.

Walker, William O., III, 'Bernath Lecture: Drug control and the issue of culture in American foreign relations', *Diplomatic History*, **12** (1988), 365–82.

Wodak, Alex, 'The world illicit drug crisis: from prohibition to reform', *International Journal of Drug Issues*, **5**(4) (1994), 218–20.

F. LIBRARIES AND OTHER SOURCES

United States

National Organization for the Reform of the Marijuana Laws (NORML)
Washington Drug Policy Foundation, Washington, DC
Library of Congress, Washington, DC
De Paul University Library, Chicago
University of Southern Mississippi (USM) Library, Hattiesburg, Mississippi

United Kingdom

Institute for the Study of Drug Dependence (ISDD), London
London School of Economics Library, London
British Library, London
National Criminal Intelligence Service (NCIS), London
Birmingham City Central Library, Birmingham
Senate House Library, University of London
Home Office Library, Queen Annes Gate, London
University of Wales Library, Cardiff
Personal and Telephone Interviews, Correspondence

In-person and Telephone Interviews, Correspondence

In-person Interviews

Thomas Charles Green (UK Representative, Commission on Narcotic Drugs, United Nations, 1957–64). October 1993
Richard Cowen (National Director, NORML). May 1994
Stephen Kennedy (Senior Strategic Intelligence Analyst, National Criminal Intelligence Service, UK). May 1995

Telephone Interviews

Chief Inspector Ron J. Clarke, Community Affairs Department, Greater Manchester Police. August 1995
Dr Anthony Henman, author and member of the International Anti-prohibition League. January and August 1995
Dr Nicholas Dorn (Institute for the Study of Drug Dependence). August 1995

Correspondence

Bing Spear (Home Office Drugs Branch, 1952–86). August 1993
Thomas Charles Greeen (UK Representative, Commission on Narcotic Drugs, United Nations, 1957–64). September 1993.

INDEX